Bureaucracy in Canada: Control and Reform

This is Volume 43 in the series of studies commissioned as part of the research program of the Royal Commission on the Economic Union and Development Prospects for Canada.

This volume reflects the views of its authors and does not imply endorsement by the Chairman or Commissioners.

Bureaucracy in Canada: Control and Reform

Sharon L. Sutherland
and
G. Bruce Doern

Published by the University of Toronto Press in cooperation with the Royal Commission on the Economic Union and Development Prospects for Canada and the Canadian Government Publishing Centre, Supply and Services Canada

University of Toronto Press
Toronto   Buffalo   London

Grateful acknowledgment is made to the following for permission to reprint previously published and unpublished material: Chief Statistician of Canada; Minister of Supply and Services Canada; Sage Publications.

©Minister of Supply and Services Canada 1985

Printed in Canada
ISBN 0-8020-7288-7
ISSN 0829-2396
Cat. No. Z1-1983/1-41-43E

CANADIAN CATALOGUING IN PUBLICATION DATA

Sutherland, S.L. (Sharon Lynn), 1940–
Bureaucracy in Canada

(*The Collected research studies / Royal Commission on the Economic Union and Development Prospects for Canada,*
ISSN 0829-2396 ; 43)
Includes bibliographical references.
ISBN 0-8020-7288-7

1. Bureaucracy — Canada. 2. Canada — Officials and employees. 3. Civil service reform — Canada. 4. Canada — Politics and government. I. Doern, G. Bruce, 1942– II. Royal Commission on the Economic Union and Development Prospects for Canada. III. Title. IV. Series: The Collected research studies (Royal Commission on the Economic Union and Development Prospects for Canada) ; 43.

JL108.S96 1985   354.7107   C85-099503-5

PUBLISHING COORDINATION: Ampersand Communications Services Inc.
COVER DESIGN: Will Rueter
INTERIOR DESIGN: Brant Cowie/Artplus Limited

CONTENTS

FOREWORD

When the members of the Rowell-Sirois Commission began their collective task in 1937, very little was known about the evolution of the Canadian economy. What was known, moreover, had not been extensively analyzed by the slender cadre of social scientists of the day.

When we set out upon our task nearly 50 years later, we enjoyed a substantial advantage over our predecessors; we had a wealth of information. We inherited the work of scholars at universities across Canada and we had the benefit of the work of experts from private research institutes and publicly sponsored organizations such as the Ontario Economic Council and the Economic Council of Canada. Although there were still important gaps, our problem was not a shortage of information; it was to interrelate and integrate — to synthesize — the results of much of the information we already had.

The mandate of this Commission is unusually broad. It encompasses many of the fundamental policy issues expected to confront the people of Canada and their governments for the next several decades. The nature of the mandate also identified, in advance, the subject matter for much of the research and suggested the scope of enquiry and the need for vigorous efforts to interrelate and integrate the research disciplines. The resulting research program, therefore, is particularly noteworthy in three respects: along with original research studies, it includes survey papers which synthesize work already done in specialized fields; it avoids duplication of work which, in the judgment of the Canadian research community, has already been well done; and, considered as a whole, it is the most thorough examination of the Canadian economic, political and legal systems ever undertaken by an independent agency.

The Commission's research program was carried out under the joint direction of three prominent and highly respected Canadian scholars: Dr. Ivan Bernier (*Law and Constitutional Issues*), Dr. Alan Cairns (*Politics and Institutions of Government*) and Dr. David C. Smith (*Economics*).

Dr. Ivan Bernier is Dean of the Faculty of Law at Laval University. Dr. Alan Cairns is former Head of the Department of Political Science at the University of British Columbia and, prior to joining the Commission, was William Lyon Mackenzie King Visiting Professor of Canadian Studies at Harvard University. Dr. David C. Smith, former Head of the Department of Economics at Queen's University in Kingston, is now Principal of that University. When Dr. Smith assumed his new responsibilities at Queen's in September 1984, he was succeeded by Dr. Kenneth Norrie of the University of Alberta and John Sargent of the federal Department of Finance, who together acted as Co-directors of Research for the concluding phase of the Economics research program.

I am confident that the efforts of the Research Directors, research coordinators and authors whose work appears in this and other volumes, have provided the community of Canadian scholars and policy makers with a series of publications that will continue to be of value for many years to come. And I hope that the value of the research program to Canadian scholarship will be enhanced by the fact that Commission research is being made available to interested readers in both English and French.

I extend my personal thanks, and that of my fellow Commissioners, to the Research Directors and those immediately associated with them in the Commission's research program. I also want to thank the members of the many research advisory groups whose counsel contributed so substantially to this undertaking.

DONALD S. MACDONALD

At its most general level, the Royal Commission's research program has examined how the Canadian political economy can better adapt to change. As a basis of enquiry, this question reflects our belief that the future will always take us partly by surprise. Our political, legal and economic institutions should therefore be flexible enough to accommodate surprises and yet solid enough to ensure that they help us meet our future goals. This theme of an adaptive political economy led us to explore the interdependencies between political, legal and economic systems and drew our research efforts in an interdisciplinary direction.

The sheer magnitude of the research output (more than 280 separate studies in 72 volumes) as well as its disciplinary and ideological diversity have, however, made complete integration impossible and, we have concluded, undesirable. The research output as a whole brings varying perspectives and methodologies to the study of common problems and we therefore urge readers to look beyond their particular field of interest and to explore topics across disciplines.

The three research areas — *Law and Constitutional Issues*, under Ivan Bernier; *Politics and Institutions of Government*, under Alan Cairns; and *Economics*, under David C. Smith (co-directed with Kenneth Norrie and John Sargent for the concluding phase of the research program) — were further divided into 19 sections headed by research coordinators.

The area *Law and Constitutional Issues* has been organized into five major sections headed by the research coordinators identified below.

- Law, Society and the Economy — *Ivan Bernier and Andrée Lajoie*
- The International Legal Environment — *John J. Quinn*
- The Canadian Economic Union — *Mark Krasnick*

- Harmonization of Laws in Canada — *Ronald C.C. Cuming*
- Institutional and Constitutional Arrangements — *Clare F. Beckton and A. Wayne MacKay*

Since law in its numerous manifestations is the most fundamental means of implementing state policy, it was necessary to investigate how and when law could be mobilized most effectively to address the problems raised by the Commission's mandate. Adopting a broad perspective, researchers examined Canada's legal system from the standpoint of how law evolves as a result of social, economic and political changes and how, in turn, law brings about changes in our social, economic and political conduct.

Within *Politics and Institutions of Government*, research has been organized into seven major sections.

- Canada and the International Political Economy — *Denis Stairs and Gilbert Winham*
- State and Society in the Modern Era — *Keith Banting*
- Constitutionalism, Citizenship and Society — *Alan Cairns and Cynthia Williams*
- The Politics of Canadian Federalism — *Richard Simeon*
- Representative Institutions — *Peter Aucoin*
- The Politics of Economic Policy — *G. Bruce Doern*
- Industrial Policy — *André Blais*

This area examines a number of developments which have led Canadians to question their ability to govern themselves wisely and effectively. Many of these developments are not unique to Canada and a number of comparative studies canvass and assess how others have coped with similar problems. Within the context of the Canadian heritage of parliamentary government, federalism, a mixed economy, and a bilingual and multicultural society, the research also explores ways of rearranging the relationships of power and influence among institutions to restore and enhance the fundamental democratic principles of representativeness, responsiveness and accountability.

Economics research was organized into seven major sections.

- Macroeconomics — *John Sargent*
- Federalism and the Economic Union — *Kenneth Norrie*
- Industrial Structure — *Donald G. McFetridge*
- International Trade — *John Whalley*
- Income Distribution and Economic Security — *François Vaillancourt*
- Labour Markets and Labour Relations — *Craig Riddell*
- Economic Ideas and Social Issues — *David Laidler*

Economics research examines the allocation of Canada's human and other resources, the ways in which institutions and policies affect this allocation, and the distribution of the gains from their use. It also considers the nature of economic development, the forces that shape our regional and industrial structure, and our economic interdependence with other countries. The thrust of the research in economics is to increase our comprehension of what determines our economic potential and how instruments of economic policy may move us closer to our future goals.

One section from each of the three research areas — The Canadian Economic Union, The Politics of Canadian Federalism, and Federalism and the Economic Union — have been blended into one unified research effort. Consequently, the volumes on Federalism and the Economic Union as well as the volume on The North are the results of an interdisciplinary research effort.

We owe a special debt to the research coordinators. Not only did they organize, assemble and analyze the many research studies and combine their major findings in overviews, but they also made substantial contributions to the Final Report. We wish to thank them for their performance, often under heavy pressure.

Unfortunately, space does not permit us to thank all members of the Commission staff individually. However, we are particularly grateful to the Chairman, The Hon. Donald S. Macdonald; the Commission's Executive Director, J. Gerald Godsoe; and the Director of Policy, Alan Nymark, all of whom were closely involved with the Research Program and played key roles in the contribution of Research to the Final Report. We wish to express our appreciation to the Commission's Administrative Advisor, Harry Stewart, for his guidance and advice, and to the Director of Publishing, Ed Matheson, who managed the research publication process. A special thanks to Jamie Benidickson, Policy Coordinator and Special Assistant to the Chairman, who played a valuable liaison role between Research and the Chairman and Commissioners. We are also grateful to our office administrator, Donna Stebbing, and to our secretarial staff, Monique Carpentier, Barbara Cowtan, Tina DeLuca, Françoise Guilbault and Marilyn Sheldon.

Finally, a well-deserved thank you to our closest assistants: Jacques J.M. Shore, *Law and Constitutional Issues*; Cynthia Williams and her successor Karen Jackson, *Politics and Institutions of Government*; and I. Lilla Connidis, *Economics*. We appreciate not only their individual contribution to each research area, but also their cooperative contribution to the research program and the Commission.

IVAN BERNIER
ALAN CAIRNS
DAVID C. SMITH

The scope and terms of reference of this study are drawn from the mandate of the present Royal Commission, supplemented by the authors' awareness of gaps in the existing published literature on the Canadian public service bureaucracies as political institutions.

The Commission's mandate included the study of a number of core institutions, among them the Canadian federation, cabinet-parliamentary government and the modern public service, in order to examine several major related themes. These include the adequacy of our basic goal-setting processes, the growth of government and the extent to which basic democratic accountability is preserved, given the development of these core institutions and their close interdependence.

The first purpose of this study, derived from this formidable task, is to present an historical view of the evolution of public service bureaucracies as political institutions over the past three or four decades. While our historical analysis builds on existing literature, in three areas this literature proved inadequate to deal with the concerns of the Commission mandate. Moreover, these were areas essential to forming any prospective view of where future reform agendas might lie. The three are:

- the emergence of a cluster of public service organizations which we refer to as the "control" bureaucracy or, in the context of our historical typology presented in the introduction, simply as Public Service Bureaucracy III;
- the increasing degree to which public service bureaucracy has been treated as the object of public policy in such a way as to strain its capacity to carry out its basic function of implementing policy; and

- the role of political parties as institutions with primary and fundamental responsibilities in the democratic control of the public service.

Thus, the second purpose of this study is to evaluate the modern public service reform agenda in light of these less recognized, undervalued phenomena as well as in the context of the general historical setting.

The contemporary public service reform agenda covers many issues which, in the course of pursuing the first two purposes of the study, we will examine; for example, the power and influence of senior public servants versus the control and accountability of entire public service agencies; the role of merit in a rights-oriented society, collective bargaining in the public service; and the public servant as citizen, including the right to political participation. In addition, we believe that this study contributes toward some greater integration of the study of federal and provincial public services. Our focus is still on the former but we have attempted to bring together some existing material on the provinces and to add to it where feasible. We have updated and expanded the quantitative data on the growth and characteristics of the public service.

The organization of the study reflects its dual purpose. The Introduction presents a basic sketch of the authors' framework used to build an understanding of the historic evolution of public service bureaucracies in Canada. The framework is threefold, involving: the traditional line departments; the quasi-independent, quasi-representative cluster of bodies including regulatory boards, Crown corporations, and educational and health bureaucracies; and the control bureaucracy, a cluster of bodies such as central agencies, ombudsmen, policy advisory bodies, auditors, human rights agencies, and information rights bodies.

For the expert reader, some parts of our analysis will be too detailed, others not detailed enough. We have tried to resolve these inevitable assessments in favour of that larger group of informed lay readers who, in the context of the Commission's mandate, are invited to look at the broader administrative state so as to understand how it has evolved in recent decades.

Chapter 1 elaborates on the framework by examining in detail why each of the three elements or phases of the public service has evolved and now concurrently exists, and how each fits or is partially distorted in relation to basic, underlying constitutional concepts such as federalism, parliamentary government, and representativeness. It presents the basis for the main lines of reform which we highlight in the study.

The next four chapters revisit the three public service bureaucracies in order to view them from different perspectives. Chapter 2 examines the array of controls that exist, most of them, paradoxically, relating to the first bureaucracy, the one that is often characterized as being most out of control. This is followed in Chapter 3 by a basic quantitative mapping of employment in the bureaucracy so that one gains a sense of what has grown, what is in or out of control, and most important, what distinctions must be made, between the growth of officialdom as such and that of government and programs. Chapters 4 and 5 then examine the issues of "bureaucracy as an object of policy," that is, bureaucracy as a social and economic policy laboratory, and the role of political parties, both as public service control institutions and as advocates of bureaucratic reform.

In Chapter 6, we offer several concluding observations on the main themes of the study and on the general directions of the whole reform agenda. We do not offer detailed reforms; rather, we address general lines of reform on the issues set out above.

SHARON L. SUTHERLAND
AND
G. BRUCE DOERN

ACKNOWLEDGMENTS

We wish to thank several people who greatly assisted our work. A special debt is owed to David Justinich who carried out important background research, and to Terry Moore, who coordinated the considerable assistance from Statistics Canada's Public Institutions Division. Statistics Canada and Public Service Commission officials were also extremely helpful. Iain Gow, Ronald Watts and Kenneth Kernaghan provided useful criticisms which helped improve the final product as did Alan Cairns and Peter Aucoin, members of the Commission's research team, and Don Rowat, Vince Wilson and Michael Prince, our colleagues at Carleton University. Eric Tanenbaum of the University of Essex provided important insights. Finally, we thank Margaret Johnson, Bev Riley and Monica Wright for their usual high quality of assistance, and Karen Jackson at the Commission for untold administrative service cheerfully given.

S.S. AND G.B.D.

A Framework for Analysis

When one thinks of all the major institutions of Canadian society and of how they have evolved in the past four decades, it is perhaps the public service, the bureaucracy, that has changed the most. It is no longer sufficient to view the federal or the provincial public service in terms of a broad constitutional role as the implementor of the policies, legislation and orders promulgated through the democratic process, or as the neutral non-partisan advisor to elected politicians. While this classic role remains, the bureaucracy, representing total direct public sector employment, has also become a significant social and economic institution — indeed, the source of employment for about one-fifth of all working Canadians. The bureaucracy writ large has itself increasingly become an object of public policy: the crucible in which some kinds of social experimentation are carried out, either as an example to the private sector and society as a whole or as a substitute for more extensive political action.

The metaphor of the blind men rambling around an elephant, arguing about the correct categories for organizing a description, is an appropriate one when beginning a study of bureaucracy. It becomes apparent immediately that the beast is massive and varied in its parts, but one is stymied as to what to say next, or how to characterize the whole. How, then, to characterize the public service across Canada? If one does not like what bureaucracies have become, what reform goals make sense and what kinds of policies and institutional change are likely to produce the desired results? These are the overriding questions examined in this study. Since we are interested in the overall trends rather than in every ripple and bump along the path to the 1980s, we propose a framework for examining the evolution and current composition and roles of the public service at the federal and provincial levels of government.

First, it is necessary to define what is meant by the word "government." All useful definitions of what constitutes government are multidimensional. The British political scientist Richard Rose, for example, defines government as:

> . . . Organizations established by the constitution or public law, headed by elected officials or having their heads appointed by elected officials, and/or primarily financed by tax revenues or owned by the state.[1]

The use of several attributes to separate governmental from non-governmental institutions, Rose says, serves to emphasize and reflect the diversity of forms taken by modern governmental organizations. His definition focusses upon the constitutional and legal status of public organizations, the fact that there is some political accountability for their direction, and the fact that they rely on public finance.

Our own framework for discussing government bureaucracy accepts Rose's basic definition of what organizations are part of government. But, because we are interested in bureaucracy as a political institution, we posit a framework that emphasizes the accountability link between elected leadership and permanent officials. This framework distinguishes three public service bureaucracies that have evolved: the traditional civil service that is closely controlled by the cabinet; a conglomerate of a great variety of non-departmental forms, all of which are distinguished by indirect accountability links; and a "control" bureaucracy which nominally assists the cabinet and Parliament in surveillance of the first two bureaucracies and which also, very importantly, presumes to exercise significant if not total independence in action.

Before describing the framework, however, it is important to refresh the reader's view of what a bureaucracy is, and how it is a precondition of representative democracy.

Definition of Bureaucracy: Pervasive, Necessary

The concept of bureaucracy is for organizations what the rule of law is for society as a whole: control by rules is substituted for control by individual personalities. The philosopher, historian and sociologist Max Weber judged the development of bureaucracy to be the single most important feature of modern industrial society, in socialist and capitalist states alike. To be organized "bureaucratically" is to be organized by a well-articulated and public set of policies and rules. To quote Weber:

> The development of the modern form of the organization of corporate groups in all fields is nothing less than identical with the development and continued spread of bureaucratic administration. This is true of church and

state, or armies, political parties, economic enterprises, organizations to promote all kinds of causes, private associations, clubs, and many others. . . . Its development, largely under capitalist auspices, has created an urgent need for stable, strict, intensive and calculable administration. It is this need which gives bureaucracy a crucial role in our society as the central element in any kind of large-scale administration.[2]

Bureaucratic organization is therefore essential for a democratic government because it is reliable, and hence capable of being controlled. Weber's word "calculable" suggests that it is possible to anticipate what a bureaucracy will do in a given instance. This is what makes the form desirable. Efficiency, in the sense that a bureaucracy will follow the "best" route for the individual case, is much less significant. (See Chapter 1 for a discussion of efficiency as a contending value.) Indeed, and notoriously, the rule-correct way of doing something is not necessarily the most efficient. In fact, in a trivial sense, rule-breaking will almost always be more efficient in the individual case. That is, once the rules have been set up, a quick analysis of them will often reveal how to do "efficient" end runs. For example, the person who cuts in on an orderly line-up is making use of a bureaucratic mode of organization at the same time as he or she flouts it. Overall, therefore, the main reasons for the pervasiveness of bureaucracy in modern life have little to do with simple efficiency. In the words of the contemporary British sociologist Kenneth Thompson:

> Weber's explanation for its success includes a wider list of operational virtues: precision, speed, unambiguity, knowledge of the files, continuity, discretion, strict subordination, reduction of friction and of material and personal costs. Certain other developments in industrial society also favour the spread of bureaucracy, such as the speed up on communication and transport, the adoption of modern accounting methods, the demand for equal treatment by citizens in a democracy and the growth of mass production and mass administration. Weber was thus offering a general theory of modern culture, rationalization in all spheres.[3]

"Rationalization" is to be understood as applying to the whole organization, to whole classes of actions. This is why bureaucracy is the ideal, indeed the only, form for administration in a representative democracy. Representative democracy, whereby we elect some few individuals from among our numbers to represent our interests and concerns in popular assemblies, is the best we can aspire to. Direct democracy, in which each citizen represents him- or herself, is the familiar ideal, but it is not realizable except for limited purposes in very small settings. The resort to elected representatives is a stage away from the ideal. When administration, or the carrying out of decisions in accordance with law and due process, and the keeping of records, is delegated to salaried officers who are directly appointed and controlled by the elected persons, we are removed still one more stage from popular control. The final step away from direct popular control is the use, for administration, of "personnel who are neither elected nor politically appointive and removable, but rather are chosen on bases of stated criteria . . . and, once appointed, are protected from removal on political grounds."[4]

In an idealized (and likely unrealizable) sense, democracy as popular sovereignty is to be attained if one can build in "control" to substitute for the lost directness. Therefore the more that administration is "bureaucratic," that is, according to rules, laws and due process with the objects set by the elected representatives, the more positive democratic control we have. We can indeed go just slightly further and say that any authority at all which is delegated must be handled "bureaucratically." The elected politician who makes patronage appointments and does not try to control them is substituting the idiosyncratic rule of an officer for his or her own ultimately accountable (through the ballot box) rule. Administrations must be bureaucracies in order to be able to accept direction. In a democracy, any external authority that cuts into the chain of command and diverts the permanent officers from seeking the ends of the elected officers, ideally through a replicable process, is a threat to the democratic control of policy as defined above. In this sense, ad hoc "efficiency," while not unimportant as one political value, is not to be preferred to rule-bound, and therefore accountable, "inefficiencies." Accountability for the proper process is at least as important as efficiency in executing the task.

At the level of the organization, then, a bureaucracy should be fully calculable, in Weber's terms. The complementary idea at the individual level is that a bureaucracy must be staffed by "experts" of process, people with the skill and background to be able to learn, appreciate and apply the rules by which the whole organization runs. The "bureaupaths" in Merton's lexicon[5] are not formerly competent people gone bad from overindulgence in rules; rather, they are incompetent officers who fail to understand the purpose of a particular process, or are not sufficiently professional to be able to carry out a process smoothly. They will confuse and bottle up the traffic until they are isolated and ordered off the roads. In Weber's words, "Bureaucratic authority is specifically rational in character." And, "Bureaucratic authority is specifically rational in the sense of being bound to discursively analysable rules."[6] Officials know what to do and why they are doing it.

The organizational evils of a political or other type of patronage appointment to a regular civil service position can be understood from this perspective. The quality of the whole organization is jeopardized to the extent that the person does not merit the position.

But despite the approval and support that logic, such as that above, gives to bureaucratic structures, almost all of us worry about bureaucracy and control from many perspectives, often in an inherently contradictory way. We worry that bureaucracy is uncontrolled or out of control in its very nature, that it is so complex as to be ineffective by definition. In almost the same breath, we can worry that bureaucracy is too impersonal and too much in control, in the sense that ordinary activities of life such as education, marrying, having children, dying, are bent out of shape by the formal requirements of the state. Such concerns span the continuum of political ideology, from furthest right to left.

It is because of this ambivalence about large-scale bureaucracy that, in discussing our framework, we use the combination of "public service" and "bureaucracy" for each of its three parts. This is done to provide a constant reminder of the basically ambivalent and all-encompassing role that public service bureaucrats play in a democracy. The words "public service" evoke a positive notion of the role, in which the delivery and implementation of services, and the idea of the public official as a servant of democracy, are paramount. The word "bureaucracy," on the other hand, as often as not, carries all the unfortunate connotations we have just discussed: formality, insensitivity and the usurpation of power.

The Three Public Service Bureaucracies: A Framework for Analysis

As with an examination of any major institution, it is insufficient to view the bureaucracy as a monolith. This is not just because we are dealing with both federal and provincial public services; rather, it arises from the need to appreciate what modern Canadian public services have become.

The framework outlined below distinguishes three public service bureaucracies, I, II and III, which in total constitute the public sector. Table 0-1 portrays their basic characteristics. As with any table, the categories are visually portrayed as if they were watertight. Inevitably, there is some leakage across categories and considerable diversity within the categories. The table is perhaps better thought of as a form of a layer cake in which Public Service Bureaucracy II is added onto a basic foundation of Public Service Bureaucracy I, and Public Service Bureaucracy III becomes the top layer. We are interested in both the total and in its cumulative construction.

A range of characteristics is shown in the left hand column. We characterize each of public service bureaucracies I, II and III in relation to: its main structural manifestation; the primary constitutional/normative ideas associated with it; examples of the type of officials that could be considered to be most characteristic of it; its basic size and growth characteristics; its main period of development and ascendance; and its basic links with other institutions such as cabinet-parliamentary government and federalism. While we elaborate on why the three bureaucracies have emerged in Chapter 1, and on the characteristics in greater detail through the study, our first task is to highlight the basic features of each.

TABLE 0-1 Framework for Analysis: The Three Public Services

	Bureaucracy I	Bureaucracy II	Bureaucracy III
Structure	• the line department headed by an elected minister	• non-line forms not headed directly by ministers (e.g., regulatory boards, Crown corporations, educational institutions, hospitals)	• the advisory body, the expanded central agency, numerous small agencies and units, Parliament's control bureaucracy
Predominant Norms and Ideas	• classical: individual ministerial responsibility and collective cabinet responsibility • neutral career public service chosen by merit principle • limited political rights	• replacement themes: representative collective appointed leadership • expertise and professionalism • expansion of work force rights	• no established democratic norms • emphasize efficiency • rights advocacy • rationality • information • pluralism
Types of Officials	• deputy minister • immigration officer • tax collector • soldier	• regulatory analyst • teacher, professor, nurse • hydro official • airline pilot	• human rights commissioner • ombudsman • rentalsman • efficiency evaluator and "policy type" • auditor and program evaluator

	Bureaucracy I	Bureaucracy II	Bureaucracy III
Growth Characteristics (employment data)	• moderate size	• numerically large, especially at provincial level	• numerically small
Period of Main Ascendancy and Development	• gradually since Confederation but especially post-World War I to 1950	• 1950s, 1960s, early 1970s plus some links to World War II	• 1970s and 1980s bureaucracy
Institutional Links vis-à-vis Parliamentary government	Accountability through minister to Parliament	Indirect accountability lines	Expansion of watchdogs and "rights" agencies that report to Parliament directly
Federalism	No explicitly defined link	Executive federalism, and some control through competing expertise	None

Public Service Bureaucracy I:
Traditional Departmental "Civil Service"

The main structural manifestation of Public Service Bureaucracy I is the classic line department of government headed by an elected minister. The line departments of Bureaucracy I perform the most traditional functions of government.

J.E. Hodgetts, in his survey of the evolution of Canadian federal departments of government, remarks that his "recital of an administrative evolution covering nearly a century leaves the impression that the founding fathers were remarkably perceptive in selecting departmental portfolios that could survive the test of time and the accumulating burden of responsibilities. The charts . . . reveal that seven of the original roster of operating departments have survived intact, at least as to title: Agriculture, Finance, Justice, Post Office, Privy Council Office, Public Works, and Secretary of State."[7] He carries on to name another dozen departments whose antecedents in the first governments were clear.

The superficial historical continuity noted by Hodgetts is not unique to Canada. Although scholars will always disagree on whether particular features of the state are appropriate or necessary, all are agreed that worldwide, the need for protection and civil order is basic. The demand for justice, whether or not met, is also universal. To provide these goods, the state has historically monopolized the capacity to exercise force, a capacity that brings with it some numbers of officials. And, so that it is not necessary to continually exert force, all states set up some mechanisms for encouraging consent by the population to orderly rule. These range from elections to consultative exercises and from royalty and symbolic occasions to the use of propaganda.

If one moves forward to Chapter 3, which provides counts of officials under "functions" of government at all levels in Canada, one sees a contemporary classification that can encompass these ancient needs: protection of persons and property, which includes defence, courts, incarceration, policing; foreign affairs; general services, which includes "management," taxation and the apparatus for generating consent; transportation; industrial development; labour and employment; and immigration. The areas that encompass the positive functions of the state are less related to the old and basic coercion than to generating the consent of the largest numbers of those being governed and represent one of the major divisions between the ideological right and the left. Here we see health, education, social services (jointly the welfare state), conservation and environment and some aspects of culture. Other major debating points are, of course, which functions must be provided and managed by government, perhaps in the loosely managed arm's-length public corporations, and which properly belong to the profit-making activities of the private sector.

Regardless of beliefs about whether or not governments ought to perform various functions, however, all are agreed that modernization has brought great complexity. Each of the federal departments has added a multitude of organizational subdivisions, so that the activity that takes place under any of the historical departmental headings is many times more varied than one hundred years ago. Even a quick glance through the annual estimates of expenditure — the definitive description of departmental organization for any given year because it is the Crown's request to Parliament for funds — would convince the reader of the proliferation of demands (albeit within the same broad categories) that modern life makes on the core bureaucracy.

The primary normative ideas associated with Bureaucracy I are: the doctrine of individual ministerial responsibility and collective cabinet responsibility to an elected House of Commons or provincial legislature; the neutral non-partisan public servant chosen on the basis of merit, whose duty it is to advise ministers as objectively and forthrightly as possible and to implement policy in accordance with the law; limited political rights of the public servant as citizen in exchange for security of tenure. The type of official who readily comes to mind in this category ranges from the deputy minister of a department to the immigration officer, the tax collector and the agricultural scientist. Relative to the non-departmental sector, this one is of moderate size and its growth has been more incremental, spanning a period that obviously predates Confederation. The two periods of strongest growth were from World War I to about 1950, and from the 1960s to the mid-1970s, as social programs expanded.

Bureaucracy I's main institutional link is with Parliament through the doctrine of ministerial responsibility for administration. The chain of accountability is therefore our traditional democratic one, from public servant to minister to the House of Commons, to the electorate. Another central doctrine is the power of the purse, that is, the right of the Commons to grant or deny supply or money to the government. The link of the public service to federalism as an institution is not explicit since the Constitution, in the form of the 1867 British North America Act, does not deal with the public service as such. The formal implication, however, is that federal and provincial public services operate in their own domains with accountability being through ministers to parliaments and legislatures within each jurisdiction.

Public Service Bureaucracy II: Non-Departmental Forms

Public Service Bureaucracy II is less clear-cut structurally. It is best described in the negative in that, if anything, it manifests a preference for a variety of non-line departmental forms of organization, labelled by Hodgetts as "structural heretics," and is not headed directly by ministers, but is still capable of being controlled by elected politicians. There is thus a greater preference for agencies, boards, Crown corporations and commissions organized on an arm's-length basis from ministers and often headed by collective decision-making, multi-member executive structures. Included in this array of bodies across the nation are universities and colleges, hospitals and similar institutions of the modern social welfare state, government-owned businesses and regulatory agencies. We also categorize schools here and thus think of the rank and file of teachers as government workers with indirect accountability links to provincial governments, despite the fact that they also answer to their school boards, which will be elected (not appointed) locally. This complexity is rooted in history, as many school boards predated provincial administrations, and is eclipsed (for our purposes) by the fact that provincial governments have the power of the purse and can thereby overrule school boards.

A mix of different ideas and norms governs this category. The idea of "representing" the population and the various interest groups through appointments to the leadership of these agencies is more prevalent but it is often melded with the idea of partial self-government by experts as well. Thus the professionalism of the work force, defined broadly, can exist in a form of tension with representative norms. Perhaps one should say "quasi-representative" because the leadership appointees are not, with the notable exception of school boards, chosen by popular election. A considerable broadening of political and economic rights of the public servant as citizen also defines the work force of this category. In particular, the work force has enjoyed fewer restrictions on its rights to bargain collectively and to strike than the departmental service. Thus, Public Service Bureaucracy II begins to embrace somewhat more explicitly the notion that the public service is an environment separate and apart from "the government." As such, it can be treated as an object of social policy and not just as the implementor of policy. The type of public servant most characteristic of this category ranges from the teacher or professor to the nurse, hydro official, airline pilot or regulatory official. This category has the largest number of employees, especially at the provincial level, and saw quite rapid growth in the 1950s, 1960s and early 1970s. Some of its features are traceable to the expansion of the public service after World War II.

The main institutional links with this category are different. Almost by definition it is one step further removed from Parliament as an institution. Far more often than not the chain of accountability to the public has proceeded even more indirectly, from the chief manager, an official, to independent "representative"/expert board, to minister, to legislative body. Indeed, accountability may even skirt ministers and proceed to legislative bodies, but only in the minimum informational sense. The power of the purse has also become one step further removed in those public service bureaucracies that have had independent sources of revenue (endowments or profits) and/or were influenced by large conditional grants and other transfers of funds from a senior to a more junior level of government. Unlike government departments, they have been able to amass unused appropriations and revenue from year to year, thus avoiding in significant ways Parliament's control of the purse. Vis-à-vis federalism, a virtually extra-constitutional pattern of accountability among the executives of federal and provincial governments has evolved. Thus, there exist two loose accountability systems: an elaborate pattern of co-operative and competitive executive federalism and a secondary system wherein one level of bureaucracy has been partially held to account, albeit behind the scenes, by the other. Some organizations in this arm's-length group have also developed more explicit lines of contact between themselves and private sector clienteles (through normal lobbying relationships and also through statutory hearing requirements and numerous advisory bodies) than are possible in the departmental public service.

Public Service Bureaucracy III:
The New "Control" Bureaucracy

The third category is more ambiguous, in part because it is more recent. Its structure resembles neither the classic line department nor the quasi-independent board and agency. Rather, it consists of units attached to the existing apparatus in the form of advisory bodies, the newer central agencies that have a de facto role in the formulation of broad policy, and other specialized units, often of a watchdog ("audit" and evaluation) and/or "rights advocacy" nature. Though present at both federal and provincial levels, these units are perhaps more obvious at the federal level, since the latter have had an even more diverse range of interests to which these units have become, in part, a way of responding. The control agencies are, in part, a response to a perception that the public sector's weight and penetration of social life were actually out of control. Ironically, this perception was probably created as much by the proliferation of non-line agencies as by growth in the departmental, traditional public services. But because there are by definition more opportunities to scrutinize and criticize the traditional public service than the arm's-length sector, it is the former that has been subjected to still further constraints.

The normative ideas that both accompanied and resulted from the emergence of this category include the general notion that public service bureaucracies should be not just implementors of public policy but should themselves be examples of social experimentation as good employers and good citizens in pursuit of contemporary ideas of equity and fairness. But this category has also come to include units whose existence was the result of pressure from groups who thought that government and bureaucracy was now "the problem." Thus, there emerged numerous professional evaluators and watchdogs and "policy types." Of some importance in the development of this new entourage, or even industry, was the expansion of what one might usefully call "acceptable patronage," that is, in the sense of government as patron. By this we do not mean the old-style patronage, wholly devoid of either merit or proper tendering and contracting practices, but rather a modern form: "patronage with a professional veneer." So it was that significant numbers of mainly professional and well-educated middle-class Canadians, most of whom would not style themselves as bureaucrats, became dependent on the public service even while they were being hired or contracted to bring about its reform.

The public servants of Bureaucracy III ranged from language and human rights commissioners to comprehensive auditors, consultants, policy analysts, legal aid lawyers and advisors of various sorts. While this category is the smallest of the three, it is not insignificant in terms of the costs and benefits incurred in the system to meet its requirements and to defend against its criticisms. The primary period of growth for this category is the 1970s and the early 1980s.

The institutional links between this group of organizations and traditional parliamentary government and federalism are also more subtle, indeed sometimes in doubt. Some of the units in this category — for example, ombudsmen and other rights commissioners — were appointed as direct agents of legislative bodies rather than of the cabinet. This idea of accountability conflicts with the notion of responsibility in the theory of parliamentary government. (This problem is explored in Chapters 1 and 2.) The very existence of other new organizations, however, can also be attributed, in part, to the growing concern of legislators, particularly on the opposition side, that government and bureaucracy had to be better controlled, assessed and evaluated. The expansion of the Office of the Auditor General after the mid-1970s and the appointment of the information and privacy commissioners for access to information are examples. Some may be tempted to label many of these rights and audit bodies as having only advisory powers, but this is not true legally for many of them and, moreover, it belies their actual overall impact. The relationship to federalism did not change appreciably, because both levels of government were establishing their own versions of Public Service Bureaucracy III, in part to emulate and checkmate each other and in part because both were subject to similar social and economic reform pressures in the 1970s and early 1980s.

These, then, are the three public service bureaucracies in profile. What exists in the 1980s is a mélange. Our framework differentiates the three, in order both to elaborate on how the public service bureaucracy has evolved and to indicate how each major phase or form is, in part, a reaction to the past. At the same time, it shows in précis the cumulative set of norms and values expected to be reflected in, or promoted by, the Canadian administrative state as a whole. The three categories also help one to make greater sense of the ideas embodied in the current and likely medium-term reform agenda. Thus the observer should continually ask which specific aspects of public service bureaucracy particular interests wish to reform or retain, so as to be able to examine the ideas and interests that inevitably accompany reform proposals.

Chapter 1

The Public Service Bureaucracies and Major Constitutional Norms

Introduction

This chapter will examine in more detail the three public service bureaucracies, both in terms of their constitutional position among the institutions of our democracy and in terms of why they have evolved to their present state.

In effect, constitutions are blueprints of the major institutions and the networks of relationships that must exist between them in order to realize a certain kind of government. In the case of parliamentary government according to the British model, the internal constitutional principles by which the "goodness" of any one actual government is judged are those of representativeness and responsibility.

The idea of bureaucratic neutrality/instrumentality is thus central to our belief that our political system is driven by popular sovereignty — in other words, that the "amateurs" who are the elected representatives of the people do, in fact, take the main decisions about public policy. Even though we may accept that the bureaucracy is expert in Weber's sense, we also believe that its expertise, and even the power of rationality or logic as a principle for decision making, must be mediated by the political rationality at the head of the system.

Representative government exists when the governors are chosen by the citizens from among themselves according to formal democratic procedures. Responsibility exists when it is possible for electorates to identify and, if necessary, discipline those responsible for policy by removing them from office, again according to formal procedures. With regard to bureaucracy, we normally assume that it is under control, thereby fulfilling a condition for realization of an indirect democracy, if it _it_ seems clear that public policy decisions flow from identifiable actors and structures within the political decision-making structures that, in turn, accept legal and political responsibility. Doubtless this last statement should be qualified: let us say that policy decisions that have an impact in setting basic rules and relationships, or that have a "constituent" effect in building the society, should come from democratically chosen, removable, political actors. In this chapter, we intend to test the usefulness of the framework of public service bureaucracy set out above by examining the rules which govern each of the three aspects against these two basic ideas: representativeness and responsibility.

It is also important to view the network of Canadian governments from outside, ideally from a distant vantage point. Such an analysis might reveal that some problems which appear to be caused by too much bureaucracy or by lack of political control in any one government might, in fact, be features of only one kind of bureaucracy, or even be traced to other parts of the constitutional structure. Since the eleven governments of Canada reflect the division of powers between the national and provincial governments as set out in the BNA Act and subsequent amendments, each government's public sector reflects its jurisdictions, the levels of service that represent political allocations, and some amount of incremental growth.

But the impact of the eleven autonomous governments of the federation on Canadian society is not orchestrated by any one all-seeing centre, and perhaps is too complex to be controllable. Therefore, even though each individual government and its public sector may be, arguably, under control in its own terms, the whole situation has evolved through the interaction of ad hoc strategies of all participating governments rather than through the operation of fully formalized constitutional processes. In this sense, Canada is perhaps stronger on pluralism than on popular sovereignty, because the citizens who go to the polls for both the federal and provincial governments, as members of the two electorates, do not determine the aggregate situation, even though it is the one they live in. They may get more government and more bureaucracy than they anticipated, if jurisdictions are blurred or the federal and provincial governments choose to compete with one another. They may even get much less, if the political actors cannot agree about which government should provide a particular service. The point is that a problem that is ultimately traceable to relations between autonomous governments cannot be rectified by individual governments tinkering with any of the three public service bureaucracies, even if too much or the wrong kind of bureaucracy is the symptom that is apparent.

Considering the role of bureaucracy inside any one Canadian government is therefore very different from considering "bureaucracy" and "government" in the aggregate. While focussing in the present chapter on the constitutional constraints on the three public service bureaucracies inside each of the autonomous governments of the federal system, with the national government as the main recipient of our attention, we do wish to point to the aggregate, or federal, nature of the country when it touches our evaluation of whether the constitutional rules as they stand are still adequate for understanding and trying to control the public service bureaucracies. The plan of the chapter is as follows. We first sketch an idealization of the control system inherent in the British parliamentary institutions as adapted for Canada. We then discuss other elements of the Canadian constitutional settlement, and suggest how they have affected the control system, in other words, how they have influenced the capacity of Canadian politicians to control and direct the permanent machinery of the state. Most of the chapter is therefore about cabinet government and its relationship to the traditional departmental or line bureaucracy in the national system. Then follow discussions of the evolution of public service bureaucracies II and III, in which they are evaluated for their conformity to the ideas of representativeness and responsibility. The chapter ends with an assessment of the problems that currently affect the evolution of the public service bureaucracy in Canada.

Public Service Bureaucracy I

Idealized Controls of Cabinet Government

The primary model followed by the Fathers of Confederation, in reaction to the American revolution, was the English constitution. But the English constitution on its own territory is unitary, flexible and parliamentary, whereas the new Canadian state had to be, as a condition of existence, a federation. Therefore, it is more accurate to say that the Fathers attempted to replicate the main relationships that existed between the institutions of parliamentary government in unitary Britain within each one of the constituent, "watertight" governments of the union.

CHIEF ROLES

The chief roles of the Westminster system are those of the executive, the legislature and the judiciary. It has been said that political history in Britain consists of the differentiation of these three roles: the separation of the judiciary from the others, but the linking of the executive and the legislature. In purely formal terms, the executive is the Crown alone. Historically, the Crown has come to bear a certain relationship to the two houses of parliament; in the British model the popularly elected Commons and the aristocratic element, the Lords, represent a way of achieving popular government that has been grafted onto a monarchy. In essence the Crown was subordinated to Parliament, and eventually to the House of Commons, through the legislature's power to grant or deny funds. The eventual mature relationship is succinctly but still subtly prefigured by the "most significant clause" of the *Grand Remonstrance* to the Monarch of 1641: "That his Majesty be humbly petitioned by both Houses to employ such counsellors, ambassadors, and other Ministers, in managing his business at home and abroad as the Parliament may have cause to confide in, without which we cannot give his Majesty such supplies for support of his own estate, nor such assistance to the Protestant party beyond the sea, as is desired."[1] The eventual reciprocity of the relationship between the executive and the legislature is already clear here. Its precondition is that, in order to survive, "his Majesty" could no longer operate as he pleased, but had to be guided by advisors that the Parliament could support.

The formal system does not explicitly provide a rationale for a civil service, that is, a bureaucracy. The main purpose for moving to democratic government was to establish who should have authority to give orders to implement policy, and who therefore should assume the responsibility and the entailed political and legal accountability, the monarch or his ministers. As we all know, the ministers were the eventual winners of the right to wield executive power. The right is, however, conditional on the confidence of the House of Commons; in other words, the ministers and their policies must be those that the House will "confide in," and in return the House grants supply for ongoing support and to implement policy. Each is the prisoner of the other. The rules that govern the civil service, therefore, are a secondary product of the interactions between ministers and the membership of the House of Commons. Ministers are responsible to the House for decisions taken and administration done in their name. The "control" of the bureaucracy emerges from the creative tension of the reciprocal controls between the cabinet and the House of Commons.

HOUSE-CABINET CONTROLS

The controls of the House on the cabinet are the subject of much scholarship,[2] but their essence can be distilled quickly. They have largely to do with the House's requirement for detailed, formal, prospective and retrospective accountability for spending, but a very incomplete ad hoc prospective and retrospective accountability for policy and administration. With regard to spending, while it is true that the cabinet can extract the resources that it wishes by virtue of its control of a majority in the legislature, its proposals must first be laid out in a detailed structure or budget (the Estimates). The House formally agrees. The House, or its agent, then monitors the still more detailed records of expenditure to be sure that actual expenditures match votes, and that probity is consistent throughout. The basis of financial control is therefore as simple as formal, detailed disclosure and its audit. Ideally, the role of the civil service is simple, much like that of the servant who is sent to market and returns with the exact produce and the receipts.

The political defensibility for policy and for non-financial administration, however, is maintained in a much more ad hoc fashion. The House is again the forum, and the networks of relationships between the MPs and their constituents are the traditional sources of information. Problems caused by actions taken in the government's name, whether mistaken or deliberate, are raised in the House[3] for the information and correction of the government. The incompleteness of coverage of potential issues and abuses makes the task manageable for Parliament. The virtual randomness of scanning serves as a deterrent and threat that forces the civil service to discipline itself. "Control" can mean as little as publicizing an issue, and so forcing a minister to look inside his or her department, or as much as dismissal of the government.

Powers of dismissal are exercised in three ways: the House can refuse supply when Estimates are put before it; it can defeat legislation which is crucial to the government, either financial legislation or issues important to policy; and it can pass a direct vote of no confidence. These powers of dismissal remain with the House even though the relatively modern device of party brings great order and predictability to the support that cabinet can generally count on.

CABINET-HOUSE CONTROLS

The controls by cabinet over the House are no less important. The executive retains the right to initiate money bills and thereby control the profligacy of the Commons' tendency to vote expenditures on behalf of its constituents. It means that there is one source of command for the civil service. Spending, and hence taxing, is thereby, ideally, to a plan, and can be made tolerably predictable for the ordinary citizen. The fact that the prime minister, the head of the cabinet, can dissolve the House means that the House membership can be disciplined into stable majorities. Likewise, the cabinet's device of collective responsibility/solidarity serves to reinforce the discipline of the House. The cabinet can shield ministers as it chooses by making an issue a matter of confidence in the government as a whole and, therefore, of dissolution. If the cabinet did not decide when to invoke solidarity, and therefore when to assume the collective political responsibility for whatever error a minister might have made, the House could pick off ministers one after another. One can argue that, ideally, the notion of individual ministerial responsibility in the moral and legal sense serves as a focus for redress of injuries caused by acts of the government. Collective responsibility is better understood as a device for political survival. The various groups that have intense interests in issues taken one by one are by that device forced to abide by the strategies adopted by the alliances that make up parties, the stable majorities we alluded to above.

In brief, the spending that is delegated to the bureaucracy is verifiable by both cabinet and the House by virtue of the completeness and detail of the budget and public accounts. The justifications for policy and advice to ministers and other administrative planning are, in theory, seen by ministers in advance and are certainly available to ministers retrospectively. They are available to the House, however, only at the cabinet's discretion. Retrospective accountability is in effect rationed by the cabinet, and can be almost completely denied, as in wartime.

The essence of the system's set of controls is the setting up of situations of mutual jeopardy. First, the executive and legislature are linked, or have a shared fate, through the device of the cabinet. This makes the executive responsive and responsible, and the legislature capable of disciplined action. Secondly, the political executive and its departmental officials are linked in the idea of the permanent executive, which combines the decision-making authority and the implementing arm. The relationship between them is certainly one of mutual jeopardy, although not so strong as an automatically shared fate. The "good" civil servant is neither seen nor heard. The one who is made fully visible has failed. The device of the permanent executive precludes the dilemmas that come to the fore in systems that are premised on the separability of politics and administration.

The main principles of cabinet government are, in summary:

- ministers who are members of the cabinet are fully legally responsible as individuals for business done in the name of the Crown;
- there is a mutual dependence between cabinet and the majority party in Parliament;
- there exists a collective political responsibility, or solidarity, of the cabinet's members (the corollary of party discipline); and
- the prime minister has the power to appoint and dismiss ministers, to appoint and dismiss deputy ministers, to structure the institutions of government and, except in unusual circumstances, to dissolve the government and Parliament.

PERMANENT CIVIL SERVICE: MERIT

We can turn now to the traditional civil service. The dominant principles of its operation in the modern period are, first, permanence of tenure for those who constitute it, so long as they satisfy the criteria for "good behaviour" (with the exception of deputy ministers, who are removable "at pleasure") and, related to this, the abstention of civil servants from active party politics.[4]

Having a permanent civil service and intending to constitute it on the principle of merit are very naturally related. Merit is a virtual necessity for establishing a permanent civil service and, indeed, is the only realistic substitute for a principle of staffing by the ministers themselves on partisan lines; combined with non-partisanship, it is the condition upon which patronage could be safely relinquished.

"The distribution of patronage was the most important single function of government," according to Sir Wilfrid Laurier's biographer, but the result was very poor administrative performance.[5] The elaboration of the idea of merit is that competition should be open to all qualified individuals and the decision to appoint should be based solely on an individual's suitability for the job. In Britain, the idea of hiring because of merit became the norm during the 1870s, although large-scale patronage was not eliminated until the 1890s. In Canada, progress was somewhat slower, with a new federal Civil Service Act that called for competitive entrance examinations to a large number of positions being passed in 1908. In 1918, the entire national civil service was placed under the Civil Service Commission. The years after World War II, roughly 1945 to 1952, saw some reversals to the system, as returning veterans were given preference over any other candidates if they could merely meet the minimum qualifications for a post. Each of the provinces went through a similar evolution.[6] The joint ideas of merit and political neutrality, in turn, formed a basis for the further development of the civil service as a mature work force. Staff associations developed, and unions were allowed by legislation in 1966. Hence, there has been a steady development toward allowing civil servants what might be called "maximum personhood" compatible with the work.

The idea of merit in hiring and promotion is complemented by that of probity in procurement. Rules for proper tendering for government contracts were elaborated in reforms through the 1860s. In terms of financial probity of public servants in the handling of public money, audits were conducted, by the House of Commons at first, then for the House by an official, by the 1860s. The importance of these reforms is easy to underestimate today, partly because we are accustomed to their operation, and partly because modern electronic methods for financial accounting and auditing have made them far easier for the practitioner. Still, it was a significant phase in removing some direct economic power from ministers, a way of interfering with their power to dispense favours. Overall, it might be said that the goal is to structure the civil service so that the idea of ministerial responsibility has maximum credibility: the minister is distanced from situations of gain that could throw doubt on his disinterest, and the civil servants are distanced from situations that would give them a "class interest" in certain lines of policy which they could then covertly attempt to implement.

Secondary Controls

It is important in talking of the idealized controls of the British model of cabinet government to recognize a second level of controls beyond the tight feedback model of relationship between executive, legislature and the civil service that we have just described. We can name some of the main elements without discussing them in detail. Most important, the judiciary, being separated from direct political and economic power, is the earliest and broadest control on both the political[7] and permanent executives.

Also, the electoral and the mass party systems ideally reinforce the roles that operate in the core system through assisting in the creation of a strong executive based on a stable majority in a two-party House of Commons. Concretely, this effect has been secured in Britain through an electoral system that exaggerates the size of a win for a party with the largest number of popular votes and, at the same time, tends to suffocate third parties. Also ideally, the partisan system should run along invisible cleavages: the United Kingdom has suffered relatively few threats of territorial secession because parties have usually, though not exclusively, been formed on economic ideas and interests as opposed to places.

Besides these traditionally cited controls, there operates what Douglas Yates calls "big loose" control.[8] In effective "big loose" control, each institution and actor partakes of a single, agreed set of received ideas about how the whole should work, has a territorial stake in the whole and therefore watches every other actor and institution for territorial and philosophical deviation from an acceptable norm. A common culture is a precondition for good "big loose" control, as are energetic media that are politically partisan, didactic and varied. Only if journalists work from some declared and defensible point of view can they impose order and coherence on information, and only if they understand their own system of government can they assist in controlling the core institutions.

Intrinsic Problems: Complexity and Secrecy

We have presented an idealized version of cabinet/parliamentary government to illustrate a "best case" of the controls exerted upon the traditional civil service by the political element of government. We do not wish, however, to suggest that there are no inherent problems. Indeed, we see two serious, intrinsic kinds of problems that we would like to raise at this point, before we proceed to discuss further difficulties of control brought about by the peculiarities of the Canadian adaptation of the basic forms. The first concerns the degree of influence of the senior bureaucracy in the making of public policy, and the difficulty in setting limits for its legitimacy. The second has to do with problems related to secrecy and security.

It is evident that bureaucrats have a considerable legitimate capacity to initiate policy.[9] The political system expects and encourages them to do so when it berates them on those occasions when they have failed to plan, to adequately estimate costs and effects, and when legislators leave wide discretionary powers in their hands or assign such powers to separate boards and agencies. But "legitimate territory" is not well mapped.

The reality of decision making in a complex cabinet/bureaucratic structure is that policies are not always clear, frequently conflict with each other, and must be constantly reinterpreted as they are applied to single cases or projects. It is often unclear whether policy is to be found only in the statute that governs a program or department, the cabinet's latest directive, a minister's speech made over the weekend or a combination of all of these. Analysts and advisors at and below the deputy minister level are constantly meeting in departmental, interdepartmental and federal-provincial settings to determine what ministers want or what "my" minister's preference is. As cabinet documents and memoranda are drafted, advisors attempt to add the right nuance of meaning to particular features of a proposal. Data and estimates may be challenged or questioned. Interdepartmental concerns are raised. Questions of timing and cost are identified. All of this is done with advisors engaged in constant discussions "up the line" to the minister through his or her deputy minister, and across departmental lines through other ministers, departmental officials, political aides and central agency officials. In addition, there is also contact with outside interests and with provincial governments.

It should not be surprising, then, that virtually every minister, privately and sometimes publicly, discloses his or her anecdotes about the great idea that was sabotaged by the senior bureaucracy or by the prime minister's henchmen. In each of these it is difficult, if not impossible, to sort out why a given ministerial initiative or pet project may have been changed or stalemated. Was there a difference in values and priorities whereby a deputy was able, by a process of wearing down his minister, to impose a decision on him? Was the deputy, on the contrary, merely playing his proper constitutional role in warning the minister of the pitfalls of the proposal or the possible contradictions between it and the law? Was the proposal in reality killed, not by the sponsoring minister's own bureaucracy, but by other ministers (and their bureaucracies) whose concerns and priorities were different?

In Britain, the late Richard Crossman wrote with great perception of his service as a minister. More recently and closer to home, Flora MacDonald has provided a brief account of her nine-month ministerial experience as secretary of state for external affairs.[10] Her article describes the many ways in which bureaucrats prepare "entrapment devices" for ministers (for example, delayed recommendations, multiple deputy ministerial committees, bogus "options"). It describes her problems in establishing alternative advisory networks of academics and of her personal political staff. MacDonald is careful to say that the problem does not arise from the overt partisanship of senior public servants, but rather that public servants regard themselves as being above the partisan battle. She quotes approvingly from other experienced politicians such as Anthony Wedgwood Benn and Henry Kissinger on this score. But nowhere in MacDonald's account is there a specific example of a policy blocked or an initiative frustrated.

The impression one is left with is that there is a problem, but that it is generic to the politics/administration interface and, therefore, too woolly to be pinned down empirically and solved by some permanent principle. If the problem of supposed preponderance of civil service power is generic to the politics/administration interface, one can only suggest that the system of cabinet government presents no more of a handicap to the politician than do other concrete political systems.

We also suspect that some necessarily unknown but never negligible element of "secret government" is inherent to the form of cabinet/parliamentary government. The relation that the British sociologist K.G. Robertson sees is that "Where administration is clearly subordinate to elected representatives, then information becomes an important element in the political struggle for office and therefore something which governments will seek to control."[11] In Britain, there are very strong secrecy laws to protect state secrets and cabinet's deliberations, and successive governments tend to keep them enforced. As of 1984, there was no freedom of information or access legislation in Britain. There certainly is no tradition of protected whistle-blowing as there is in the United States, although there, because of the separation of powers, the dynamics are quite different. In Britain, civil servants who provide the press with privileged information, however innocuous or well known as an open secret, may be prosecuted to the full extent of the law. In the Canadian federal system, there is a typically uneasy compromise between American and British norms. We have a new access law, but with very broad exemptions for whatever information cabinet might see as touching national security, national unity or its partisan concerns and therefore its solidarity. We also have strong secrets legislation that is, however, never so swiftly and trenchantly applied as in Britain (see Chapter 2).

Once more, we suspect that the problem is generic to government, and more characteristic of cabinet government, where the executive power is so strongly centralized. Indeed, the power to determine the degree of secretiveness is one aspect of the concentration of power in the executive (an enabling factor for which is the close relationship between the executive and the civil service) that is a distinguishing feature of cabinet government. In turn, it creates the risk that cabinet will define more, rather than less, as "secret," a risk that is less compatible with modern norms than it was with paternalistic norms. We live in a rights-conscious, information-seeking culture that is cynical about the motives of those who exercise power. On the other hand, a proponent of the cabinet government form might well ask why we elect representatives to govern us if we are convinced that they are not worthy of trust.

The Canadian Adaptation: Indigenous Problems

We have just described the traditional set of norms of cabinet/parliamentary government that work to minimize the substantive role of permanent officials and to maximize both the substantive role and the legal and political accountability of politicians for the operations of the core parts of government. We also identified two important generic problems with the form. Precisely because cabinet government is designed to make ministers visible and apparently responsible, it drops a curtain between the observer and the policy-related activity of the permanent officials. It can depend heavily on secrecy to control the political agenda and to keep demands for political accountability to manageable levels, and necessarily puts the cabinet in control of the flow of information about its own actions.

Specifically Canadian problems with the form also exist. The first is the simple fact of federalism — the requirement to give the "racially diverse" societies of 1867 control over local matters as a precondition of union. This is an extremely well-trodden subject in Canadian scholarship; hence, it is explored below primarily as it affects the character of the relationships between the executive, the legislature and the permanent officials. The second main source of deviation is our proximity in a number of senses to the United States. The BNA Act of 1867 was arguably English in the spirit of having an unwritten, flexible constitution in that it wrote down as little as possible. Rather, it established representative democracies working on parliamentary principles for the national and provincial governments, and set out a division of powers in sections 91 and 92.[12] Still, the idea of a flexible constitution is really the same as parliamentary supremacy: Parliament, and not a constitutional code that is over and above its power, creates laws for all aspects of collective life, and to do this it must be pre-eminent and unchallenged. The parliament that is intended here, it must be added, is not a legislature alone but rather the core entity forged by the collective determination of the sovereign, the House of Lords and the House of Commons. The heart of the idea is that one polity will constitute the ongoing source of authoritative action for the society.[13]

The BNA Act therefore substituted constitutional government for parliamentary government, a qualitative change from the British model rather than one merely of degree of emphasis. The present situation in Canada is thus the result of a continuing adaptation and elaboration of our own constitutional government. The new Constitution Act of 1982, and the incorporated Charter of Rights and Freedoms, have increased the range of issues on which the courts can test legislation for constitutionality, and have also elaborated the machinery for amendments and the distinctions between ordinary and constitutional laws.

The main implication this has for the operation of cabinet/parliamentary government in Canada is at the very least a decentralization of power from cabinet. The aggregated situation, post-Charter, becomes more and more pluralistic in the sense of allowing contending sources of authority to challenge in the courts the legality of government action against standards other than the division of powers between the federal and provincial governments. If the courts were to routinely arbitrate disputes between one part of a government and another, as in the complaint brought in late 1984 to the Federal Court by the auditor general of Canada against the cabinet, anything like traditional cabinet prerogatives would cease to exist. The standard to which the court will refer in the case is the auditor general's 1977 act. If the court's opinion favours the Office of the Auditor General, the cabinet will surely have to immediately re-open the act to amend it to conform with its own interpretation, or risk establishing a principle that divisions of power inside its government are not arbitrated by cabinet.

FEDERALISM: THE CABINET AND TERRITORIAL LEGITIMATION

Sometimes, too little federalism also brings about difficulties for the national government. In our system, the national institutions are not fully constituted on consistent and direct federal principles as they are in the United States.[14] Hence, the Canadian Senate's members are appointed by the national government on a formula to be indirectly representative of the provinces and regions, instead of being elected by provincial electorates or appointed by provincial legislatures or even executives. Lieutenant-governors of the provinces represent the Crown in provincial areas of sovereignty, and are not ruled by the national government's Governor General. Supreme Court judges are appointed by the federal government, using formulae that respect (in part at least) the racial diversity of the society for which the court will interpret law. The legitimacy of the federal domination of such appointments is seen as dubious by some observers.

The result for the operation of cabinet/parliamentary government in the national institutions is that the main burden of territorial legitimation is borne by the national cabinet itself. Again, the subject of the federalized cabinet in Canada has been exhaustively discussed: our prime ministers must build their ministries on territorial principles as well as talent. We wish primarily to point out the great burden that this puts on the party system in Canada. If the majority party is based disproportionately, or even exclusively, on some regions of the country, the prime minister will not be able to put together a government that has territorial legitimacy. In effect, the use of the federal cabinet for territorial legitimation considerably elaborates the requirements that the party system must meet to fulfil its role in the core control network of cabinet government at the federal level. The basic requirement of the party system in a unitary government is that there should be a party of government and a party of opposition, the "ins" and the "outs." In the Canadian federal system, the "ins" must have a certain territorial distribution which is not assured by the rules of the electoral system. The role of party in Canada is obviously important to an understanding of our central institutions, but it tends to be ignored in relation to the bureaucracy itself. This is why we have devoted a separate chapter to the subject.

In addition, the federal cabinet's bearing the main burden of territorial legitimation has important consequences for the operation of bureaucracies in this country. These can be referenced by the phrases executive federalism and collective administration.

Executive Federalism

The term is familiar from the writings of Donald Smiley, who used it to refer to the permanent co-ordinating machinery between governments.[15] This is a level of "public service" that has no formal constitutional justification, and no formal and direct accountability links to politicians and electorates. Its defining characteristic is a focus on negotiations between the executives (and their officials) of the various governments. Secretariats can outlast the elected politicians of all jurisdictions and gather their own autonomous history. A kind of political power thus accrues to officials, not necessarily from personal ambitions but because there is a gap in the political settlement. Another example of an innovative use of public servants was in the Trudeau government's use of officials as "domestic diplomats": federal appointees located in the provinces but set apart from the regional aspects of the federal government's bureaucratic structure. These individuals reported directly to the federal cabinet, but had considerable discretion in the field.[16]

Collective Administration and Program Bending

Because ministers carry their territorial identity into cabinet, the notion of collective ministerial responsibility has been elaborated in Canada with reference to general administration. That is, if our understanding of the idealized form of cabinet government is appropriate, collective responsibility is classically a defensive political principle having no legal component, whereas individual ministerial responsibility is the legal administrative principle. But a norm developed early that policy with regional implications should be vetted by that region's minister, even if the substance of the policy was not under his departmental aegis. From here it was a fairly easy step to the idea that ministers were collectively responsible, in some residual sense, for what was left over once each had assumed his or her unique responsibility for the activities undertaken legally in their individual names. As well, some of our most vital cabinet functions are individually federalized. In unitary Britain, the bureaucratic activities that help to co-ordinate the departments are executed for one minister, usually the prime minister, or the chancellor of the exchequer. In the Canadian national government, because of the principle of a federalized cabinet, the head of the treasury is not one person, but a board. The secretariat that services the Treasury Board is therefore thought by some commentators to have a responsibility to a collectivity of ministers.[17] More recently, the idea of a collective ministerial responsibility for positive administration has been manifested in an expansion in size, powers and numbers of "central agencies." These agencies have tried to offer processes of synoptic rationality to support political "collective responsibility" for the quality of management as something distinct from the substance of policy.[18] This is, one can suggest, the politics/administration dichotomy in a new dress, and a topic that will be discussed further below.

The idea of collective responsibility of cabinet for the quality of general administration was part of the justification for the 1979–84 experiment with ministries of state (Social Development, and Economic and Regional Development): these agencies actively "harmonized" proposals coming forward to cabinet from departmental bureaucracies. Although these ministries reported to the senior minister in the cabinet committee for the respective policy area, their source of legitimation was the idea of the collectivity of ministers. Although the principles that they invoked were rational, they were not without political effect. Herbert Laframboise coined the term "program bending" for the general results of this and earlier efforts to expand central agencies and analytical capacity.[19] Under the ministry of state system, a minister had no guarantee that he or she would routinely control the content or the timing of a proposal to cabinet for action in his or her department, let alone its disposition.[20] The then prime minister, John Turner, disbanded these ministries in the summer of 1984. His action is regarded as the result of pressure from ministers who had found the idea of collective responsibility too pervasive, in that it militated against the exercise of individual initiative. In effect, it seemed to turn a minister of state into a real minister in the classical sense, and made some of the other ministers who were nominally at the helm of the departments appear to be junior in position.

THE AMERICAN INFLUENCE

It was stated above that the second main source of deviation in Canada, now including the provincial governments, from the model of the parliamentary institutions of the English constitution was the influence of the United States. This influence is brought to bear in two related and mutually reinforcing ways. First, the power of the U.S. constitution provides an alternative model for a constitutional settlement. Federalism in Canada had to be elaborated, and the U.S. constitution provided an example. Secondly, Canadian culture and Canadian political life is being swamped by the mass culture of the United States. Culture and communications are continental.

Cultural Influence

We need mention only one or two examples where our institutions have been assimilated. First, and more central for our purposes, Canadian civil services have consistently looked toward the United States for advice on how they should be organized and articulated. The principles of organization and classification of personnel in the federal civil service do not resemble those extant in Britain, but have instead been strongly influenced by U.S. management theory. The provincial civil services, particularly those of the larger provinces, have experienced similar U.S.-style management exercises that emphasize the potential of management control on objective efficiency grounds. The stability of the administrative grade of the British mandarinate has no counterpart in any Canadian administration[21] (even while new political regimes do not usually feel free to completely politicize top ranks); hence, a common culture for senior officials is built up with difficulty in Canadian bureaucracies, and is open to constant challenge.

Secondly, our political parties have assimilated to some extent the U.S. conception of what a political party is and can do. American parties are brokerage parties, each keeping a multitude of interests together under the one-party umbrella. This solution has in effect been forced on Canadian federal parties by their need to bring all regions of the country under their banner, even though the objective interests of the regions will be antithetical at times. The two main parties have records, in the sense that a minimal pattern can be discerned in their practices in power, but have only occasionally worked out distinctive pre-election programs, because of the danger that saying anything will offend someone. Canadian electorates tend increasingly to be faced with a choice between styles of leadership rather than choices between desired ends and means for achieving them. Provincial parties tend also to assimilate to this style of election, focussing on the party leader. Provincial campaigns will sometimes emphasize only current struggles with the federal government. In this sense, Canadian elections bear some resemblance to the staggered elections for seats in the U.S. legislature, the difference being, of course, that we have no truly "confederal" institution like the U.S. Senate to struggle with the harvests of opinion.

The overflow of U.S. culture and political ideas has two main impacts on the operation of Yates' "big loose" control wherein institutions police one another. First, it influences us to partially misunderstand the roles of our own institutions. Secondly, it influences us to misunderstand the impact on our system of the ideal of efficiency. According to Yates and other writers, efficiency in the U.S. ideological framework is the main contending idea to that of pluralism.

With reference to the first problem, terms and roles derived from the U.S. congressional system influence Canadians' grasp of the parliamentary skeleton under our own federal system. Our notions of what is legitimate and what is not are greatly conditioned by norms originating in the United States: we often see our House of Commons as a blighted Congress, for example, and tend to approve of any fragmentation of power as "pluralism," whether or not it is devolved to elected individuals. We tend also to immediate disapproval of secrecy or centralization of power, preferring pure bargaining. Our own press fails us badly in this regard.[22]

The Efficiency Idea

Like the Americans, we are enthusiastic adherents to the idea of administrative efficiency. To be efficient is, after all, to do the thing right. The idea begins with the common-sensical desire to take basic administrative decisions on some defensible grounds that are not "political" grounds involving narrow interest and gain. The emphasis on efficiency then works its way up the hierarchy of decision, and results in an attempt by administrators to extend the area in which decisions can be taken on non-political (so defined) grounds by extending the use of scientific/rationalist techniques for analysis. Within the confines of the U.S. system, which is pluralistic in the extreme and where outcomes for decisions of importance can be arrived at by pure bargaining, the efficiency model is an important source of redress. It is a force that works to centralize at least some power and consolidate it on rational criteria, rather than allowing unchallenged sway of shifting political alliances. It represents a search for stability. The efficiency idea (and the capacity for sustained analysis that it implies) is thus an important tool in the hands of the presidency; it is a force for centralization of authority and, indeed, a motion toward an assumption of responsibility by the administration for having forged a coalition on the basis of rational persuasion, itself based on evidence gathered in the administration.[23]

On the other hand, in a parliamentary system, stability and predictability (ideally) already exist because power is concentrated in the cabinet. The efficiency idea in this context amounts to a demand to open the top of the political/administrative system in the name of another value — pure, demonstrable efficiency. Because pure efficiency is difficult to demonstrate in specialized areas, in the parliamentary system it translates quite frequently into a demand that power be shared with "experts." It is to some extent an alternative model of who should hold power. It implies that experts, the deserving on rational grounds, should be part of all decision making. Political power based on an electorate is thus de-legitimated to some extent. Indeed, compromises based on political power can be made to appear illegitimate whenever it can be plausibly argued that there exist rational principles than can potentially untie a supposed Gordian knot. In the Canadian system, far from working effectively as the tool of the central political institutions, the ideas of efficiency and rational expertise can easily be used by management experts to take power from central political roles. The location of the line between administrative matters and political/policy matters is therefore of some importance.

Enthusiasts tend to claim far too much for any new technique that purports to enlarge rationality: to insist that it will do the thing right in areas where political judgment should rule on priorities. In summary, while the efficiency idea comes from the periphery in both systems (i.e., it is not fundamental), its effect in each is roughly opposite. And while Americans can quickly see the politically centralizing role of the efficiency idea in their own administrative context, it is much more difficult for Canadians to recognize that a major effect of the idea in Canada is to remove legitimacy from the realm of politics as the pursuit of values by elected politicians. In other words, in Canada, efficiency concerns can lead to a plethora of non-elected experts who possess doubtful standards for judgment. This is not to say that all or even most claims to expertise are false, merely that there is a large grey area where such claims are not fully justified. The danger of the large grey area is that potentially it favours covert bureaucratic politics over politics proper.

We can now summarize our ideas about the role of the traditional civil service in the context of the Constitution, and the extent to which the ideal controls of the system can operate effectively to restrain the exercise of pure bureaucratic power. We have said that even in the key network of reciprocal controls between executive and legislature, the idea of political responsibility/accountability has given way, at least in some respects, to the needs for territorial representation and therefore legitimacy. The basic rules are complicated, and are thus more difficult to understand and to apply. We have also said that much of the complexity, and hence loosening of controls over some aspects of bureaucratic power in our system (here, we refer to the national situation), is due to the federal nature of our political system. This presents a dilemma which could be treated in three basic ways:

- fully federalize all our major national institutions;[24]
- add some additional controls to the operations of the civil service, to make up for the lack of tight central controls of the ideal legislature-executive relationship; and
- explore some novel ways of providing the bureaucracy with more political leadership, thus bringing it more closely under control of the elected element of our Constitution.

Public Service Bureaucracy II

This category, as we saw earlier, contains a greater variety of entities than Public Service Bureaucracy I.[25] Each government provides diverse financial and legal regimes for the organizations that it has chosen, at one time or another, to situate at the fringe of the core, departmental presence. The powers of boards, the conditions of employment of the chief officer, the number of functions under one aegis, the degree of government ownership, and the relation to other organizations of government can all vary widely from any one body to another, within governments and between governments.

"Non-departmental public service" is a very shadowy description of the vigorous presences that have been fundamental to the Canadian identity; the great surface and air transportation and communication industries, Canadian National Railways and Air Canada are two ready examples. Electricity-generating operations, the Hydros of Ontario and Quebec, are other familiar examples.

But the Crown corporations, the entities with corporate form that are wholly or partly owned and controlled by a government, are only one important type. There are many other "families" of entities, a few of which are sketched below in a description that emphasizes the major function of a body. The examples that are given are in the nature of ideal types, for most of the real organizations are mixed types, performing several functions, and hence do not fall neatly into any one category.

After the corporate forms, a second major category is made up of bodies that have powers and obligations of a judicial kind, or which themselves operate on a judicial model to regulate access of competing actors to some scarce natural resource or natural monopoly. Examples here are regulatory commissions such as the Canadian Radio-television and Telecommunications Commission and the National Energy Board, and administrative and appeal tribunals such as the Tariff Board and the Tax Review Board. The administrative and appeal tribunals make judgments about individual cases within the framework of a statute of a legislature, holding hearings that are modelled on the judicial process.

A third major group performs advisory functions to the government and, indeed, to the public at large. Examples are the Economic Council of Canada and the Law Reform Commissions of the federal and provincial governments.

Still another group exists to undertake research of one kind or another, and to issue grants to organizations or individuals to undertake original research. Prominent examples are the Canada Council for the arts, the Medical Research Council, and the newer Social Sciences and Humanities Research Council and the Natural Sciences and Engineering Research Council.

Marketing boards form a class by themselves: they work in areas where both the federal and provincial governments have some jurisdiction and are therefore usually highly specialized enterprises which buy and sell basic produce such as eggs, or establish quotas for orderly marketing.

A final category is that of social welfare institutions, the universities and other places of education, and hospitals, as well as the research and granting bodies mentioned above. The organizations of this varied category, some with very old and complex structures for administration, are of enormous importance to the quality of national life. They are constitutionally in the provincial jurisdiction, although in many respects they have become instruments of federal policy, expressed through spending transfers. Because of the potential for disagreement about where some of these organizations properly belong vis-à-vis their links to one or another government, or the extent to which they enjoy independent status, we have tried to keep the counts of their work forces separate so far as possible in our quantitative presentations in Chapter 3. For purposes of the forthcoming discussion, however, we classify them as a part of the non-departmental sector of government, because their administration is not directly of departmental form, and as belonging to the provincial government rather than as self-governing or responsible primarily to locally constituted authorities, because the provincial government holds the trump card of the power of the purse and can therefore authoritatively state policy parameters.

As a consequence of the variety of non-governmental bodies, and their constant creation and demise (with births greatly outnumbering deaths in some categories), it is difficult to come up with a firm count. In the federal government, for one example, the Financial Administration Act produces one list in its schedules, the Public Accounts another, and the Auditor General's Report has at times contested both of these.[26] Most commentators would probably agree that, in total, there are about twice as many provincial as federal bodies; that neither financial worth nor counts of organizations or employees can adequately describe the scope or significance of non-departmental forms; that the picture becomes really complex when one attempts to account for bodies that are jointly or partly owned by government or which are subsidiaries or subsidiaries of subsidiaries; that the majority of bodies were created between 1960 and 1980; and that most of the really well-known government-owned bodies were created between 1940 and 1960.

This is not to imply that the scope and importance of government's non-departmental activity is in any fundamental sense mysterious or unknowable. Recent years have witnessed an outpouring of government publications, scholarly analyses[27] and popular comment on most of the main areas of government activity that take place outside the traditional departmental boundaries. In this study, we use employment data for government enterprises as defined by Statistics Canada to compare the "size" in number of workers in the non-departmental public sector to that of general government (see Chapter 3). Statistics Canada's Financial Management System (FMS) has been developing classifications and a statistical framework over the last 50 years to produce consistent and comparable statistics on government activity in Canada. To the FMS, government agencies are subordinate bodies created or acquired by governments and owned by them, ownership being defined as the possession of 50 percent or more of the voting shares (or the equivalent) of any agency.[28] Obviously, however, employment measured on this universe is only one of many possible perspectives.

The considerable structural untidiness of the non-departmental segment of the public service reflects the fact that its bodies have grown up in response to a variety of forces, rather than being constructed according to formulae to meet routine kinds of needs, or to deliberately and neatly evade controls of a clearly specified nature. Some bodies, such as schools, predate the formal institutions of the federal and provincial governments. The peculiarities of the Canadian political economy, of its vast lands but small market, stretched like a horizontal image of Chile along the U.S. border, has meant that for some purposes there would be a state vehicle or there would be nothing.[29] Or nothing Canadian at least, for it was assumed that if neither indigenous business nor government acted, an American presence would shortly fill the vacuum. Hence government intervention during the nation-building decades to rescue private sector railway development from bankruptcy and failure, and to set up public enterprises such as the Canadian Broadcasting Corporation, established in the early 1930s, to supply radio of national origin to Canadians. By the 1940s, there was a base of more than a dozen federal public businesses. Then, in the seven years of World War II, more than 30 federal Crown corporations were created to supply and distribute virtually everything, from tools, machinery and munitions, to timber, housing and food. The nature of the goods or service involved would affect the form in each case, as would the character of the time and the milieu in which it was established. After the war, many such corporations were wound up or returned to the private sector, but the net effect was an increase in numbers, and variety in their form and function, and in their cultural/political acceptability to governments and the electorate alike.

Motives for Structural Heretics

Perhaps one of the more illuminating windows on the group of "structural heretics," to use J.E. Hodgetts' phrase, is the question of what the government's motives might have been in deciding, for any given task, to use a non-departmental body instead of one embedded in the traditional departmental structure.[30] Why would a government, having decided that some function or program was necessary, not make use of the panoply of departments and expertise already at its bidding? The motives were varied, the main ones being: 1) to separate the function from "politics," defined as interference by elected politicians; 2) to enhance the play of special interest politics by fragmenting policy spheres and locating decision making in separate arenas, where private interests believe they have more control; 3) to separate the decision-making function from "bureaucracy" in the sense of rigid red tape; and, perhaps related, 4) to find a novel form that would promote co-operation or joint ventures with both other governments and private enterprise.

Given that the defining characteristic — both the jewel in the crown and the sacred cow — of parliamentary government is ministerial responsibility, one may ask why it could seem appropriate to move an entity to arm's length from political control. The answer appears to lie in an assumption that the day-to-day administration in some areas can be performed routinely without much need for political attention; administrative problems can readily be solved by referring to clear policies already specified by the usual political fora. It has been noted that the first recorded non-departmental entity under the British constitution goes back to the reign of Queen Elizabeth I, when she placed certain functions out of the reach of her ministers.[31] Activities deemed to be best managed at arm's length tend to be those fraught with potential conflicts of interest and therefore with political traps, and/or those thought to be best administered by experts.

Obviously, contemporary management of the great corporations falls into both categories. Economic regulation was probably thought to belong under the first during the early years of Confederation, given the potential (and the actual) opportunities for enriching friends and impoverishing enemies, though now management requires expertise as well as disinterest. Later, some forms of regulation took on quasi-judicial characteristics which also argued for quasi-independence and "court-like" procedures. There are also examples where structures evolved from a combined fear of excesses in the use of power and recognition of the fundamental importance of a given function:

. . . the federal government very soon after Confederation chose to vest the day-to-day functions of law enforcement and the prevention of crime with a de-politicized police force operating within a non-departmental structure. That structure serves to separate the police force (namely the Royal Canadian Mounted Police) from political direction with respect to operations and the results of day-to-day police operations are assessed and acted upon by an independent judiciary. The commissioner of the RCMP, rather than a minister of the Crown, is vested by Parliament with "the control and management of the force, and all matters connected therewith," subject to direction on policy from a minister. Similarly, under the National Defence Act the Chief of the Defence Staff is responsible for "the control and administration of the Canadian Forces" subject to the regulations under the Act and under the direction of the Minister of National Defence.[32]

Universities are at even greater distance from the interference of prevailing political orthodoxies. The form of university self-government that exists today in Britain and Canada has roots in the autonomous corporate institutions of the 12th and 13th centuries which were deliberately structured to maximize academic freedom. In contrast, and exclusive of school boards, the governing apparatus for primary and secondary education is an integral part of the state bureaucracy. Related forms of cultural autonomy were also thought necessary for bodies such as the CBC and the Canada Council.

Another reason for establishing an arm's-length body is that private interests simply want decision making located in a quasi-separate arena of power so as to enhance their own control over outcomes: whatever the current arena may be, it is thought that a newer, more controllable one is needed.

The third main reason for distancing a body from the core of government — the desire to keep it free from the influence of "bureaucracy" — is the one most frequently enthusiastically endorsed in anti-bureaucratic times. Administrative constraints in the departmental structure may prevent potential bureaucratic abuses but, it is argued, they also limit the creativity and initiative of staff. An entity stymied by government-wide red tape cannot be managed according to the best practices and principles of the private sector. In the case of universities, bureaucratic due process norms are interwoven with expert and scholarly criteria to allow for the kinds of recruitment, probation and promotion that are thought necessary to recognize and reward the occasional comets of brilliance and to conduct research and teach at the highest levels. With regard to business-type corporations, the usual salary restraints of civil services have long been seen as untenable if government is to recruit the best of private sector talent to run its commercial enterprises. C.D. Howe expressed an opinion still current today when he said in 1951: "No one would suggest that the Polymer Corporation, a $50 million project with a turnover of $40 or $50 million a year, would be operated by a man with a civil service salary."[33]

The fourth reason for setting up a non-departmental body is a desire for more flexibility and freedom from close political and bureaucratic controls in order to engage in less formal partnerships with other main players. Many times the desired partner will be another government. A non-departmental entity can be a way to sidestep the strains and tensions of federalism. Being distanced from politics, it can more readily adopt a pragmatic course of managing, as opposed to "solving," intractable problems, conflicting interests and intergovernmental competitiveness. Initially, such co-operation between governments was limited to the marketing-board kind of arrangement. But the sheer convenience of the form has led to increased use.

Because modern life is an ongoing education in the inadequacies of a set of categories devised at the end of the 19th century, this fragmented, superficially apolitical kind of organizational "federalism" continues to take over in areas that had not been anticipated. In some cases, however, the partnership will be a more innovative, co-operative venture with a private firm, a way of giving some capital or a tax break to finance an activity of which the government approves, but which is less fundamental and more risky than the traditional enterprises. The federal government's support for Dome Petroleum in the 1970s through super-depletion allowances to promote offshore exploration is an example. This last category is sometimes called "chosen instruments," and is strongly disapproved of by those observers who consider it to be unwarranted and unhealthy interference in the normal market activities of the private sector.

Ministerial Responsibility

Does the concept of ministerial responsibility survive the compromises that are made when a task is located outside the traditional departmental structure? One can say only that in many ways it does not; there are still some controls.

As one might expect, the relationship between non-departmental bodies and their designated ministers is not standardized. One entity may be subject to almost the same range of controls by a minister as is a department, while another may be almost free of ministerial involvement. At a minimum, the minister is the conduit for exchanges of information between the entity and the House, such activity necessitating at least an annual report. A minister is also responsible for championing its budget in cabinet and piloting its Estimates through the House if it obtains revenues from the Consolidated Revenue Fund. But even in the most controlled cases, the sense in which the minister is accepted to be responsible for any element of administration or its results is very much less than in the case of a regular department of government. Certainly a minister would not expect to resign because of problems with his or her non-departmental responsibilities, or to be judged by a prime minister as having failed to be a strong minister because of events in the non-departmental area, with the exceptions of education and health. Equally, it is less likely that direct questions of lack of confidence in a government would come up with regard to non-departmental bodies. In this sense, therefore, the non-departmental sector of government is not accountable in terms of traditional norms of full political responsibility. To complicate matters further, the government (most often the governor-in-council) has in some cases the legal power to issue a binding directive which must be obeyed by management, and must also be reported to Parliament. Some observers see in this a considerable element of power without responsibility, because it is cabinet as a whole that is nominally responsible, rather than the designated minister.[34]

The precise degree of de facto, if not legal, responsibility is often nicely calculated by studying the modes and conditions of appointment of the chief officers and board members of non-departmental bodies. Whether the chief executive officer is appointed by the board of directors or by the governor-in-council will often indicate the degree of independence to be exhibited, as will the terms of appointment. These latter also indicate the extent of resistance that determined management can offer to political interference from government. While deputy ministers of government departments, and sometimes even assistant deputy ministers, are appointed "at pleasure," so that they can be moved and removed with a minimum of inconvenience, the top management in non-departmental bodies will most often be appointed "during good behaviour" for a fixed term, removable only "for cause" and, in extreme cases, only removable by joint address of the House of Commons and the Senate. One can also study the terms under which a dependent body receives its budget, and the numbers and kinds of "partitions" in the budget, the most basic being between operating and capital budgets. It must be noted that the appointment mode for the non-departmental body's leadership bears no necessary relation to the status of its employees, whether or not they fall under the provisions of the various civil service acts or the federal government's Public Service Employment Act.

Parliamentary Influence

The relationships between Parliament and non-departmental bodies are also varied. There are only two firm rules, as noted: that ministers need not answer for internal management and that Parliament is entitled to an annual report. It may also receive other reports that a minister has requested, for example, an auditor's report. On the other hand, there is nothing to stop a member of Parliament from criticizing any aspect of policy or performance of a non-departmental body in any debate in which the subject is even tangentially relevant. MPs can seek information and ask questions, but with no guarantee of answers, for ministers are not obligated to answer for anything which is not in their official knowledge.

Full debates are staged when new legislation is introduced to establish a non-departmental body. Here lies the source of bitterness among opposition MPs at the Trudeau government's tendency to use the order-in-council as an instrument to establish public bodies, and also to allow bodies to form their own subsidiaries; since this government strategy evaded discussion in the House. But in general, non-departmental bodies are exempt only from "the Parliamentary process of nagging"[35] by virtue of the fact that ministers need not answer questions about them.

Most non-departmental bodies may be called before a committee of Parliament or of the provincial legislatures to account for themselves. The most frequent forums in the federal House of Commons are the standing committee on miscellaneous estimates, where organizations that are financially dependent on government revenue will be called to discuss almost anything in nominal defence of a budget, and the public accounts committee, which has increasingly in recent years involved itself in the affairs of the Crown corporations. In the federal House, parliamentarians have, at least since 1921, demanded a dedicated standing committee on non-departmental bodies, their primary interest being entities that are potential commercial disasters,[36] such as Canadair. But to date, their demands have had no result, although the new Conservative government may conceivably occupy some of its backbench strength in this way.

Some provinces, notably British Columbia, do have parliamentary committees designated to track the affairs of non-departmental bodies. The classic arguments against involvement by parliamentarians in internal management, and full disclosure to Parliament by the non-departmental bodies through ministers are, of course, that the usefulness of the form would be lost. Many questions legislators ask are about matters other than the financial affairs of the bodies, and if they were to be answered, the governing legislation would have to be changed to give ministers more power. Disclosure of the affairs of commercially competitive bodies might well disadvantage them, again being counter to the original intention, which was to free them from the hobbles of a bureaucrat's lot. Further, the bodies, like regular departments, would require additional resources to deal with parliamentary inquiries (often frivolous in nature), which would blunt their purpose and add to their costs. Finally, they would take more of the House's time, at the expense of the departmental structure proper.

Committees of the past, which predate the federal House of Commons' current structure of standing subject committees, have on occasion had terms of reference that gave them a better opportunity to examine non-departmental bodies. They seldom distinguished themselves, being more interested in partisan politics than their terms of reference. In particular, a committee of the federal House on broadcasting has served as a model of the kind of involvement by Parliament in the affairs of cultural agencies that should be avoided. It turned "into something that came very close to a witch hunt."[37]

Neither the federal auditor general nor his provincial counterparts have had carte blanche to conduct either narrow financial audit or broader-scope studies for legislatures across the full range of non-departmental bodies. Commercial enterprises have normally been excluded from these audits, on the grounds that financial audits of the type conducted in the private sector are both cheaper and more suitable. Recent federal legislation narrowed the range of exemptions from examination by the federal auditor general, but does not seem to have endorsed an across-the-board application of the new broadscope "comprehensive audit," which includes financial audit as only one small part of a multi-faceted review and is extremely costly. Indeed, the question of whether a legislative auditor should conduct a comprehensive audit on non-departmental bodies boils down to whether the government should allow a back door to Parliament for partisan criticism of the internal management of arm's-length bodies.

Overall, therefore, it would appear that Parliament's control or influence over the non-departmental bodies has been sacrificed to a somewhat greater extent than has government's. To understand the extent of any loss, one probably has to make a case-by-case evaluation of whether the theory that policy can be separated from day-to-day operations administered by experts has stood up to the test of time. It is well to remember that the closing of uneconomic branch lines on railways was once regarded as an administrative matter, with no overriding social implications, as were pit closings in British mines. The loss of the opportunity for parliamentary ventilation, and thus politicization, and the loss of parliamentary influence over socially important areas is an evasion of responsible government.

The Substitution of Representation and Expertise for Responsibility

The non-departmental form does have virtues that partly offset its defects. As the discussion of public service bureaucracy in the framework has illustrated, there is more to the control ethos than the formal dictates of responsible government. A significant difference between public service bureaucracies II and III is that the former has deliberately tried to redress the loss of responsibility by strengthening another element of democracy. The substituted "good" is not as coherent as the ideas of parliamentary government, but it embraces certain notions of representation. This representation is not elected. Still, a general preference for collective boards and commissions, as distinct from unitary appointed leadership, is clearly a form of representation, in that power is more widely shared. Thus, the assorted regulatory boards, boards of directors of Crown corporations and, at the provincial level, boards of education, university and hospital boards, do represent a broader range of interests than might be consulted otherwise. In the case of local school boards, direct election is used, adding to the legitimacy of the representation. School boards are a special case. Being elected, they have such convincing democratic legitimacy that they can enter open contests of will with the elected provincial government leadership, even though that leadership enjoys both electoral legitimacy and the power of the purse in the matter of education.

Significantly, however, this form of representation was not initially intended to reduce the influence of bureaucrats, but as often as not was a way to skirt elected ministers and thereby to control their influence. In other words, representation was intended to amplify the original motive, which was to locate a function outside the departmental structure. Thus, particularly in key areas of regulation, the intent (framed within the bounds of a statute) was to devise political arenas in which the "politics" of ministers could be avoided. Hence independent, or at least arguably disinterested, regulatory realms were created in broadcasting, transportation, energy and competition policy, to name a few. It is a moot point as to why these particular areas should be independent whereas other, perhaps equally deserving, ones are not. The choices do not necessarily reflect management science, but rather differences in political power. Thus the power of producer groups is amplified by the use of such bodies, while that of consumers or environmentalists generally is not.

The question of meaningful control becomes even more complicated when one looks at the large commercial Crown corporations that have revenue of their own, and thereby do not have to apply to Parliament for budget. Debate has raged that this realm of bureaucracy is out of control as well. Does the government of Ontario control its bureaucrats in Ontario Hydro, or does Hydro affect the government? How does one know?

Similarly, but in an even more complex set of equations of representativeness, bureaucracy and democracy, one can cite provincial governments' dilemmas in controlling the health and education bureaucrats. There is, of course, no problem with the headquarters official in the line department. But there are confounding problems with the teacher in the classroom who does not teach students how to read or how to act morally in modern life, the university department that somehow cannot produce new vital programs when society clearly needs trained people in this field or that, and the doctor who minimizes his or her own risks by using tests and hospital facilities too often and sends health care costs upward. How are these professionals to be held to account for implementing chosen public service policies, and at the same time be given the necessary freedom to apply their professional expertise? A reconciliation may not often be possible. For example, under conditions of extreme restraint it may not be possible to provide care to medically (professionally) acceptable standards. Politicians find themselves arguing that alternative medical models are more appropriate than the one chosen by their professionals. That is, they are forced to challenge the expertise of their own experts.

In the non-departmental sector, then, expertise and the power of knowledge groups are real forces in the control equation, even if there is not always sufficient financial backing to allow them to implement their chosen model within the imposed political framework. Expertise is, of course, central to all three bureaucracies in the framework, but in this sector it is probably strongest, because it is the most autonomous and concentrated. This is so not only in the social welfare professional bureaucracies but also in the key regulatory realms.

Therefore, we would argue, the world of Public Service Bureaucracy II runs on a version of pluralism in which limited representation partly substitutes for a purer form of representative democracy. Moreover, ministers have a rough and ready way of exerting worst case control: what has been given can be revoked, and what is not clearly revoked can be threatened.

Finally, and not least important, the fragmentation and competition internal to Public Service Bureaucracy II, which is inherent in its model of pluralism, means that there is no one centre of opposition to duly elected authority. There is no focal point from which non-elected officials contest with cabinet for the power to make significant public policy decisions for the whole nation. Some agencies and professions may well regularly "go for broke" in seeking to gain their own interests, but they take little interest in enunciating a vision of the whole society, which is the task of the political actors.

Not least because of the extreme fragmentation of power in Public Service Bureaucracy II, we do not see this realm of activity as the area of government that is most significantly out of control, and therefore most in need of redress. Rather, we argue that the very complexity of the area almost necessarily evokes a perception that it is uncontrolled, in large part because of the enormous effort that is required of the observer to come even partly to terms with it. This perception has encouraged public actors to push for the creation and enlargement of the third sector of the bureaucracy that we described as the "control bureaucracy," on the grounds that only dedicated full-time bodies could develop the expertise and provide the energy for a coming to terms with the control problems posed for politicians. In choosing to delegate such a wide range of problems to a bureaucracy, decision makers set up a dynamic whereby the power and growth of the newest control bodies were directly dependent upon the extent to which their work discredited the older bodies. It is this newest sector, ironically intended to police the others, that is itself most lacking in controls. We would judge that while the jury is still out on parts of the non-departmental sector, for the most part it scores well on its balance of partly distanced responsibility, representativeness of some essential interests, and its use of norms from the business and professional areas. We would also maintain that Public Service Bureaucracy I is over-controlled by internal rules and guidelines.

Public Service Bureaucracy III

In the framework to this study, we sketched a Public Service Bureaucracy III that we have also referred to as "the control bureaucracy" and "Parliament's bureaucracy." There is no single reason for our national legislature's heavy dependence on numerous control bureaucracies to do the job that was once its own, for the trend, if trend it is, is much further advanced in the federal arena than in the provinces. We see the causes as falling into three main categories: 1) continent-wide social/political themes; 2) trends in the national Parliament; and 3) narrower-scale, small-p political factors.

The late 1960s and early 1970s witnessed a continent-wide advocacy of "participation" that, although intense and linked to ideals of "democracy" in many cases, did not refer to specifically electoral legitimation and, in effect, bypassed and downplayed traditional political institutions. This was followed shortly by an emphasis on individual rights in a multitude of settings. One can see the landmarks of the rights ethos in Canada in the various provincial and federal bills of rights, the provincial ombudsman movements, protection of personal privacy, the implementation of criminal legal aid in all provinces, and the eventual entrenchment of individual rights in the federal charter. Thus, what can be called the sanctity of the individual was being emphasized anew at just the time that the institutions of parliamentary democracy were in a period of fairly clear decline.

By the turn of the decade into the 1970s, the federal House had been "modernized," or fragmented, into a committee structure. The simple fact that most business of substantial, as opposed to rhetorical, importance was to be handled in standing committees dramatically decreased the significance and impressiveness of the traditional Committee of the Whole, where the House meets as one entity, and which still holds the formal power. This downgrading of the importance of events on the floor of the House of Commons naturally decreased the power of the opposition to affect the national political agenda. This took place in the midst of one of our recurrent national infatuations with the potential of rational business-type "systems" for complete (and therefore equitable) and efficient restructuring of the administrative machinery.[38] Parliament's traditional ad hoc enforcement of retrospective accountability[39] was diagnosed as inadequate for the task of maintaining quality across the whole spectrum of complex modern administration (therefore preventing damage to the rights of individuals). For so onerous and "expert" a task, something much more systematic and thorough was needed. Finally, the more narrowly political situation favoured the creation of institutions that handled grievances outside of a partisan context.

The political vulnerability of the Liberal government in the late 1960s and early 1970s made it seem convenient to allow the Office of the Auditor General to capture the stewardship of responsibility for the soundness of all management systems, thereby moving much debate from the floor of the House to the public accounts committee.[40] Further, the Public Service Commission existed as a prototype that had handled its semi-autonomy with discretion and professionalism. Hence, the trends of federal and provincial attentiveness to individual citizen rights, the political interests of the government and the sense that Parliament was inadequate to the task all coalesced to favour the substitution of bureaucratic systems for Parliament's imperfections.

We can now investigate this aspect of the public service from the standpoint of the vital norms of parliamentary government: responsibility and representativeness. The agencies of Public Service Bureaucracy III can be seen as falling into three main types:

- "Parliamentary organizations" that are agents or servants of Parliament, and for whom the schemes of ministerial responsibility and accountability do not apply in any normal or clear sense. The most visible at the provincial level are the ombudsmen. The important bodies at the federal level include the auditor general, the Public Service Commission, the commissioner of official languages, the Canadian Human Rights Commission, and the privacy and information commissioner.[41]
- Central agencies that are set into the regular bureaucracy and are themselves responsible for both policy formulation and administration to a minister, but which are justified on managerial rather than constitutional conceptions of collective responsibility of the whole group of ministers.
- A group of bodies that can be seen as transitional between Public Service Bureaucracy II and the newer, more clearly focussed control bureaucracy. These are organizations that exist to monitor both the executive and the bureaucracy in specific domains and policy fields, and which are candidates for attachment to Parliament as elements of the bureaucracy of control. In the following section, we will treat these three main groups in reverse order of importance.

Executive-Based Monitoring and Advisory Bodies

This element of Public Service Bureaucracy III includes a mélange of bodies, each headed by a board that reports to the cabinet or individual ministers for a wide variety of advisory, monitory and regulatory purposes. Early examples of this genre were the Economic Council, the Science Council and the Law Reform Commission. A more recent example is the Advisory Council on the Status of Women. These advisory bodies give some of the interests that are affected by policies in major areas a chance to influence policy proposals in a more formal, structured way. In part they were considered to be policy counterweights to the regular bureaucracy. There are, of course, smaller advisory bodies seeded throughout the departmental and agency structure.

Playing more of a direct monitoring and regulating role are bodies such as the Public Service Staff Relations Board (PSSRB) and the Pay Research Bureau. The PSSRB falls under the Privy Council Office for budgetary purposes, and the minister designated as responsible is the president of the Privy Council. It exercises regulatory powers relating to the granting of collective bargaining rights, processing and resolution of grievances, designation of employees essential to maintain a level of service supporting the public safety (see Chapter 2), declaration of lawfulness of strikes and establishment of conciliation boards. The members of the board itself are order-in-council appointments, while staff are appointed under the normal provisions of the Public Service Employment Act. All order-in-council appointments are during good behaviour, and are for periods of seven or ten years.

Another such body, the Pay Research Bureau, acts in a staff capacity to the Public Service Commission and the Treasury Board secretariat by developing recommendations for salary revisions. It reports to the Treasury Board, the agency that makes the final pay recommendation, and not to the Public Service Commission, which must not be confused with "the employer."

Central Control Agencies

Our Canadian political culture at the federal level encourages a proliferation of central supervisory control agencies that exist to back up the peculiarly Canadian notion of the positive collective responsibility of cabinet for the overall quality of management. This is reinforced by a love for reorganization and, as noted earlier, a strong attachment to the pre-eminent American principles of efficiency and pluralism. Central executive control agencies are set above the normal heads of the permanent executive. They play a watchdog role over the bureaucracy on behalf of the government for the efficiency and effectiveness of bureaucratic process as opposed to the substance of policy. There have also been experiments with staff support agencies to the executive for fairly aggressive policy harmonization across departments and even policy sectors, and for implementation of newer management techniques such as comprehensive strategic planning. The more traditional central agencies of the Privy Council Office, the Treasury Board secretariat and the Department of Finance, and their equivalents at the provincial level of government, look after resource allocation — i.e., the implementation of cabinet's priority-setting exercises — and enforce service-wide standards and guidelines.

Perhaps the most intriguing federal central control agency is the Office of the Comptroller General. It institutionalizes, side by side with Treasury Board secretariat's concerns for allocation, a commitment to the full range of new and old management practices. It exemplifies perfectly the importance of the notion of rational efficiency in Canadian political culture: the government's commitment to in-depth evaluation for effectiveness of all its expenditure programs. Established in 1978, the Office of the Comptroller General still had a small staff in 1983.[42] Its real influence, however, is to be seen in the effects and costs of its policies that are transferred to the departmental civil service. It is a clear example of "program bending," because the ministerial department bureaucracy is diverted from its direct duty to implement policy for which the minister can take clear responsibility; instead, the department bureaucracy has a less clear responsibility to follow the "objective" procedural dictates of a control agency that is itself justified in terms of cabinet's collective responsibility. (The provinces have, on occasion, adopted similar agencies, but have tended to house them in the Treasury Department to minimize the tendency to multiply demands on the departments from the centre.)

Again in the federal government, the ministries of state for Social Development and for Economic and Regional Development, dismantled in May 1984 by the then prime minister, John Turner, were another version of an elaborated central agency structure. They were set up to serve as secretariats to the cabinet subcommittees of the new "envelope" budgetting approach of the policy and expenditure management system, and can be regarded in part as a development of the role of Privy Council Office. In this sense, so long as the envelope system is in place, the abolition of the ministries mainly places "the action" (the power of central bureaucrats to influence substantial policy outcomes by their influence over the agendas of the cabinet and its subcommittees) back into Privy Council Office and Treasury Board.

In another sense, however, the creation of the ministries and their later disbanding was of constitutional significance. The ministry system had, for the first time, established and publicly legitimized permanent, formal weekly meetings of the committees of officials that mirrored the membership of ministers in the cabinet committees. The constitutional significance of the formal acceptance of the role of bureaucrats in the active harmonization of interdepartmental and inter-envelope policy was an acceptance of bureaucrats "playing on the field," to use a former clerk of the Privy Council's phrase.[43] One can speculate that the mirror committees and the ministry system as a whole was an explicit step away from traditional notions of political responsibility for administration toward a system like that of Sweden where administration and politics are structurally separate. In any event, with the disbanding of the ministries the federal system pulled back from such extreme constitutional innovation.

The Watchdog Bureaucracy for "Parliament"

For this group of agencies, again most advanced in the federal government, an attachment to a "parliament" which is ambiguously defined deliberately, is thought both to distance them from the executive and give them an independent source of power and probity. The most significant bodies at the federal level are the Office of the Auditor General, the Office of the Commissioner of Official Languages, and the Public Service Commission. Others that are less clearly ideal types, but nonetheless of considerable importance, are the Canadian Human Rights Commission and the privacy and information commissioners.[44] The PSC's amended legislation dates from 1966 to 1967, Official Languages' from 1968, and the Auditor General Act was amended in 1977. The Human Rights Commission (including the privacy commissioner) was set up in 1977, and the Office of the Information Commissions was added in 1983. We can now discuss these bodies as cases of the organizational type. Our purpose is to explore whether the watchdog bureaucracy is an appropriate instrument of responsible and representative government.

THE PUBLIC SERVICE COMMISSION

Although the constitutional accountability relationships of the Public Service Commission are slightly complicated, its basic internal regime is not. The commission is listed under the secretary of state in the Estimates, the secretary of state is its minister, and its staff are appointed under the terms of the Public Service Employment Act. The three commissioners are order-in-council appointments, with renewable ten-year terms.

It is generally accepted that the Public Service Commission is Parliament's watchdog, — as distinct from the government's oversight agency — for overseeing merit appointments to the public service. In the sense that the commission and its powers were established by legislation rather than by order-in-council, this is undoubtedly true.[45] In Britain, by contrast, the Civil Service Commission and later the department were established by order-in-council, British civil servants are not hired under an act, and the executive simply forbade itself to practise patronage, through an order-in-council. The Canadian commissioners also enjoy protection in their terms of office.[46] These gestures toward "independent" status for the PSC have their costs, however:

> One important consequence . . . is that it has confused the status of the Public Service Commission. On the one hand Parliament views the Commission in a very special sense as its own agency — an agency that has emerged as the result of "the self-denying ordinance" by which Members of Parliament gave over their patronage to an independent body which could handle appointments and promotions in an objective, non-partisan fashion. Thus, for example, we find John Diefenbaker, then Prime Minister, telling the Civil Service Association in 1958 that: " . . . the Commission is not an arm of the government to which Ministers can give direction. It derives its power and basic instructions from Parliament." But the problem is that Parliament has also devolved other managerial powers onto the Governor in Council, powers which in practice are exercised by the Treasury Board. In effect, the sharing out of these management powers has placed the Public Service Commission in an awkward position in which the implementation of decisions which it has the unquestioned legal right to take can be effectively countermanded or modified by the Treasury Board exercising its equally legitimate power to regulate public expenditures.[47]

It can be readily deduced that the contemporary idea that government should sponsor a truly independent and indeed countervailing watchdog bureaucracy had not been clearly formulated when the new legislation for the Public Service Commission was passed in 1966–67. The fact that the executive functions of Treasury Board are delegated to an "independent" body makes it clear that the cabinet that planned the new legislation was working with the classical notion of the linked executive and legislature. Therefore, to have made the Public Service Commission an agent of the House of Commons, when interpreted in the light of party discipline, pays only lip service to independence without giving up basic control. What cabinet parliament writes, it can also strike out. Should cabinet wish to reaffirm its control, it can always redesign the relationships of central and quasi-central agencies. In addition, the form of ministerial responsibility is retained in the provision that the Public Service Commission reports to Parliament through the secretary of state.

Still, an ambiguity exists which, under other leadership, could have been used much more ambitiously. The commission has not allowed itself to be caught up in the Parliament's watchdog rhetoric; rather, it has conducted itself with discretion, saving its energy for those battles that it sees involving the idea of an expert, permanent and neutral public service based on the merit principle. An example of such an issue in the early 1980s is that of the limits on public servants' participation in partisan political activity. The practice of heading the commission with a triumvirate whose members are often career civil servants may have real merit in that it makes for a deliberate style of leadership, imbued in non-partisan norms.

THE OFFICE OF THE AUDITOR GENERAL

The Office of the Auditor General (OAG) is the case at the opposite pole. No minister, not even the prime minister, is designated as responsible. The Auditor General Act specifies that the auditor general is an officer of the House of Commons, appointed by the governor-in-council by a commission under the Great Seal of Canada to hold office during good behaviour for a ten-year term, but not beyond age 65. It is not clear what is meant in the legislation by "House of Commons." If one accepts that the House is legitimately dominated by the executive, it should mean very little. What is clear is that no tasks are to be performed as regular duties for the executive. The office's personnel regime is also uniquely independent (see Chapter 4).

In contrast to the commission's three-person leadership, the Office of the Auditor General is led by one individual. The last few incumbents have not been career civil servants, but have been hired from careers in management consulting and accountancy. The auditor general is the prime minister's appointment, following consultation with the business world, and his subsequent independence is guaranteed by making him removable only on joint address of the House of Commons and the Senate. It is conceivable that under conditions of a minority government, he might not be removable by the government. Unlike the public service commissioners, who report to the House through a minister, the auditor general reports directly to the House of Commons on the financial statements of the government and, under his new legislation, on how well funds have been managed to meet the goals of their expenditure. Hence the Office of the Auditor General is the only significant public service organization (in terms both of size and breadth of authority) whose appointed leadership is beyond even the most minimal forms of normal democratic accountability.

Again unlike the Public Service Commission, the Office of the Auditor General has a House of Commons committee that is dedicated to pursue the substantial issues raised by its work. The committee that reviews the Office of the Auditor General's work is, of course, the public accounts committee, for which the audit of the government's performance is nominally conducted. But the auditor general does not take direction from the committee, which is chaired by a member of the opposition, nor is the office held accountable in any way by this committee for the extreme stances it adopts in pursuit of an expanded mandate, nor for the quality of product it provides in return for its budget. It defines its own mandate according to its own imperatives. The sole apparent accountability link between the auditor general and the electorate is that parliamentary forms are followed to obtain its budget: the office's Estimates are tabled by the minister of finance and reviewed by the Commons' standing committee on miscellaneous estimates. However, since 1973, the office has grown much more rapidly than general government without restraint by this budgetary review process.[48]

Under the new Act of 1977 the Office of the Auditor General has performed its role in a much more expansionary, entrepreneurial way than the Public Service Commission. By the middle of 1984 it was demanding access to cabinet's confidential papers across the board, and had summoned the government before the Federal Court to gain access to some policy and strategy papers of a Crown corporation for which it is not the auditor. Its demands and censures clearly move quite directly into policy.[49] The office's request for unidentified papers was not made through or even endorsed by the public accounts committee or the House of Commons. Indeed, in no case has the OAG ever been denied any part of a primary financial record. The office seems to see itself as the guardian of a very broad public interest that transcends any one government or parliament. The press, who are mistaken in thinking that the OAG will be able to freely share formerly secret information with the media, are the firm supporters of the auditor general's use of his prerogatives to try to drive a wedge between the cabinet and its public service, and in the office's pointed criticism that the decisions of government and Parliament are undoubtedly taken on imperfect or inadequate advice.[50]

The new OAG is, in essence, an entrenched, autonomously-led force at the heart of both policy and management in the federal public sector. Only to the extent that one believes in the possibility of a clear separation of policy from management and administrative forms, in the American style, can one believe that the executive can retain its authority and autonomy of action in the face of such an onslaught against the capacity (and legitimacy) of politicians to manage the public service or to make rational and fair policy. For while the OAG has no share in ongoing executive decision making, having the capacity only to report on the record after the action has been taken, the new scope of its activity (the inclusion of a review of policy advice and of the revenue budget in its self-ascribed mandate) creates an environment where the parameters for action of a cabinet may be seriously limited. And should the auditor general gain routine access to cabinet confidences that he need not fully share with the public accounts committee, he will have the capacity to act virtually as a full cabinet player on chosen issues, without electoral accountability or responsibility. Further, should he win the right to report on government performance as his studies of departments are completed, he will be in addition the master of timing, an important aspect of politics.

Some of the provinces appear to be following in the same path of enlarging the powers of legislative auditors beyond reviewing financial records and systems. Their provincial legislative officers have been granted much more moderate versions of a "value for money" mandate that takes audit into qualitatively new areas.[51] But in no case have the provincial auditors claimed the right to scrutinize the policy advice to ministers: they see their responsibility to be centred on reviewing the implementation of decisions and not on cabinet's process of decision making. They audit administration.

THE OFFICE OF THE COMMISSIONER OF OFFICIAL LANGUAGES

This is another, quite different experiment in organizational forms. Its accountability is somewhere between that of the Public Service Commission and the Office of the Auditor General. The office was established in 1970 to implement the Official Languages Act of 1968–69. The prime minister is designated as responsible, and the office is classified as a department for personnel and management purposes. Its reports go directly to the Speaker of the Senate and the Speaker of the House for tabling in those two bodies. Its Estimates are reviewed by the standing committee on miscellaneous estimates. The commissioner is appointed for a seven-year term on good behaviour, and is eligible for reappointment for a further seven years.

The act is a fundamental piece of legislation, establishing that English and French are the official languages of Canada for all purposes of Parliament and of the Government of Canada. The office's responsibilities in implementing the act are:

- to serve as a protector of language rights of individuals, a kind of ombudsman;
- to serve as an auditor to ensure that all federal agencies are applying the act properly; and
- to serve as a voice on language reform issues, working to increase public awareness and support for the spirit and provisions of the act.[52]

Since 1980, the office has had a dedicated parliamentary forum to review its work, the joint committee on languages policy and programs, which appears to be able to cope with its energy. The commissioners have frankly been advocates for their legislation, entrepreneurial in capturing parliamentary and public attention for the office. The 1981 annual report stated that "Regular and careful scrutiny by Parliament is much more than preventive medicine or an occasional shot in the arm; it is the living proof of a legislature that *cares* how its lofty principles work out in practice."[53]

Three years later, it was apparent that the commissioner still appreciated the parliamentary forum:

> . . . it is quite impossible to overstate the role that a parliamentary committee can play, and indeed has played, in this area of language. Its investigations, its questioning of Ministers and public servants, its reports, the simple fact that a committee of both Houses has the specific responsibility, and now on a permanent basis, as a standing committee, of looking at matters of language policy, language programs, and in general the conduct by the government of this most important area of public policy — is to my mind something that cannot be duplicated by any other agency inside or outside the government family.[54]

But even though the office has been an advocate for its own rights, powers and centrality in the nexus of government concerns, to the extent that the chairman of the joint committee has felt it necessary to point out that it is not a captive of the office,[55] the commissioners seem to have had a sense of subtlety and perhaps even some restraint in applying the act. In the words of the 1981 annual report, "Like the proverbial good gardener, the federal government will have to respect nature's laws; but it will also need to know where to support, cut, push and bend so that nature follows art."[56] This is not to say, however, that the office has walked softly to avoid offending the government. Rather, one is tempted to conclude that Parliament has been much more successful in using the commission as an instrument of its own will. This is perhaps because the commission's work is less obscure than the comprehensive audit, and therefore more engaging of the interest of members of the parliamentary committee, or even perhaps because the narrower scope of the commission's responsibilities is more manageable in the context of the hectic parliamentary timetable.

CANADIAN HUMAN RIGHTS COMMISSION

Both the Canadian Human Rights Commission and the offices of the information and privacy commissioners of Canada report to Parliament through the Department of Justice. Accordingly, they are not quite as prominently independent as the Office of Official Languages or the Office of the Auditor General. The commission exists to implement the Canadian Human Rights Act of 1976–77. Its duties are to receive and investigate complaints of discrimination in areas under federal jurisdiction, including the public service, to work for resolution or settlements in specific instances, and to combat discriminatory practices through public education and research. It is led by three full-time and five part-time commissioners who are appointed by the governor-in-council for seven-year renewable terms during good behaviour.

The commission's Estimates are reviewed by the justice and legal affairs committee of Parliament, which has taken some interest in the reporting and accountability relationship of the body to itself and to government, and in the freedom of operation of the commission. In response to one questioner, Commissioner Gordon Fairweather summarized its position:

> . . . We are asked all the time to make interventions, and we try to do this in some sort of selective way, not in a partisan way. But I often remind people who ask us to intervene that we are not an alternative government. You will be reassured to know that, but you would be surprised at the number of times I have to say it. . . .[57]

Earlier, Fairweather had expressed the commission's determination to assert its jurisdiction, "and not let it be whittled away by public servants who are not comfortable having us around." Perhaps he spoke for all the control bureaucrats when he declared, "Parliament meant us to be nuisances."[58]

INFORMATION AND PRIVACY COMMISSIONERS

The offices of the information and privacy commissioners of Canada are the newest of the federal parliamentary watchdogs. Both are appointed with tenure during behaviour, can be removed only by Parliament, and both report to Parliament through the minister of justice. The Estimates are received by the standing committee on justice and legal affairs. The broad role of the information commissioner is to ensure that federal government organizations comply with the provisions of the Access to Information Act of 1982–83 for release of material that is not deemed confidential. This includes investigating complaints, making recommendations and appearing on behalf of complainants in applications before the Federal Court. The privacy commissioner, whose functions were formerly discharged under the Canadian Human Rights Act (from 1977 to 1983), has the duties to investigate, report and make recommendations to ministers based on complaints by individuals about non-compliance with the Privacy Act, and also to review material held by government and to appear before the Federal Court on behalf of individuals.

Summary

These organizations show the range of conduct possible under the loose "parliamentary" aegis. The Public Service Commission is controlled by a strong sense of probity and self-restraint, while the Office of the Auditor General's adventurousness now presents a constitutional dilemma of the "who will bell the cat" genre. Somewhere between these extremes are the other bodies.

With the parliamentary control bureaucracy, the Canadian system has moved for the first time to organizations whose accountability for policy as well as for management is in some sense independent of the control of an elected officer or even of Parliament as an elected forum. That is, departments are controlled by ministers: they report to ministers and they take direction from ministers for policy, and from ministers, through deputy ministers, for management. Most Crown corporations and agencies take direction from ministers for policy, although they may be deliberately distanced from cabinet on management: a chief executive officer manages the entity, sometimes with the advice of a board. With the parliamentary control agencies, however, we see cabinet almost washing its hands of both individual and collective policy responsibility: it has given the organization an act, and attached it to "Parliament" — the details can work themselves out. Yet Parliament has few sustained mechanisms through which it monitors its own watchdogs and the issues they raise. Some of its own bodies, justified as extensions of Parliament, can be left to float, the outcome of the lack of political control or even interest being left to the contingencies of the leadership of the various bodies.

One may well ask, how are these accidents of bureaucratic autonomy possible under the aegis of our model of responsible government? There are at least three important questions to address:

1. What is "Parliament" or the "House of Commons" in relation to the "government" and the doctrine of ministerial responsibility?
2. What is "Parliament" or the "House of Commons" in terms of its capacity to fight for the concerns of such agencies?
3. What is "Parliament" or the "House of Commons" in terms of its capacity to oversee and direct the actions of such agencies?

With regard to the first question, we suggest that in the government's mind, or at least in the mind of the lawyers who drafted the legislation, "Parliament" is in effect the government, because it controls the majority of seats in the House of Commons. Therefore, in theory, the control/responsibility is maintained but, as we have suggested, the reality is much more dubious.

For the second question, it seems clear that the capacity of the House of Commons to champion the overall concerns of such agencies is still present, even though it may not itself be able to do the work. In essence, the work taken over by agencies is the traditional role of Parliament: an extraction of retrospective accountability from the executive on what might be called the "disaster bring forward" system. The control agencies become a systematic research arm of Parliament, bringing a more complete listing of grievances forward for its attention. It can then, most probably in question period, concentrate on abuses that it deems the worst, or on those that hold most promise in a partisan sense. It is traditional open government along parliamentary lines, made somewhat more systematic by, in a sense, giving the whole House of Commons a series of secretariats.

For the third question, however, we suggest that Parliament provide leadership and oversight to these bodies, and therefore cann. be accountable for many policies they may pursue. The government in its manager's clothes becomes the cabinet, but Parliament as something apart from the party of management, i.e., the government, has no direct way of providing leadership to a bureaucracy. Members of Parliament do not have the sustained organizational capacity to supervise permanent structures, for all the same reasons that MPs could not themselves acquit the tasks performed by the control bureaucracies. It seems clear that two distinguishable issues have become intermingled. That is, establishing bureaucracies to catch management errors and abuses that MPs might miss in their traditional impressionistic scanning is one thing. Pretending that these organizations can work directly for some common interest of all backbench MPs is another thing entirely. It is still worse when they are themselves allowed to define what that common, higher interest might be. The abstract idea that the actions of the control bureaucracies can be justified as "democratic" simply because they owe a vague loyalty to Parliament as an entity above both government and opposition will not hold water. It seems to be the same kind of loose and wishful thinking that tried to justify the expanded policy contribution of the new central agencies on the grounds of the collective responsibility of cabinet. Ministerial responsibility may be largely of symbolic value, but responsibility shared widely and informally lacks even that virtue.

This worry about the autonomy of some control agencies does not apply with equal force to the entire array of units encompassed by Public Service Bureaucracy III. The policy advisory councils (and even some of Parliament's bodies) generally do not do much more than publish and persuade. They could just as easily report to Parliament, provided there was a specific forum to scrutinize their work. Yet some agencies, at least, trade on Parliament's legitimacy only, in varying degrees, to escape its scrutiny. In toto, Parliament's control of its own bureaucracy deserves special rather than weakened scrutiny, since the implicit political theory that guides its day-to-day performance is the most dubious, while the questions that it investigates are often of great importance.

Chapter 2

Organizational Controls and Roles

When people contemplate bureaucracy they often yield to Aladdin's ambivalence when he realized the power of the spirit in his lamp: he needed the genie, but did the genie need him? The purpose of this chapter is to walk through that spectre so as to explore inside public service bureaucracy. Thus we now go beyond the broad constitutional norms examined in Chapter 1. To what extent is the Weberian characterization of bureaucracy, as set out in our framework, an accurate portrayal? Do the internal organizational controls limit the role that it plays in society to that of faithful servant of the political executive's wishes? We must closely examine the detailed array of controls in order to show how they work. It is all too easy for some commentators to assert that the bureaucracy is out of control without much understanding of the realities of the basic system.

Behind every level of controls there is a controller: for example, the penultimate division of powers between Treasury Board and the Public Service Commission must be decided somewhere. Part of that "somewhere" is indicated by the phrase that occurs in most legislation dealing with departments, that the governor-in-council may choose to allocate a variety of other responsibilities to the minister. It is the cabinet, and really the prime minister acting within his prerogative, which designs the relationships that will obtain between organizations.

The phrase giving the governor-in-council discretion for defining new tasks and allocating them also signals the fact that legislation is not usually necessary when the elected government decides to restructure or take other kinds of action. Reorganizations of considerable scope can be executed by orders-in-council issued under the authority of a "general and liberally worded statute,"[1] the Rearrangement and Transfer of

Duties Act. As noted in Chapter 1, the ministries of state for Social Development and Economic and Regional Development were abolished under this authority by the cabinet of John Turner in June 1984. A large part of the massive changes implemented in the late 1960s on the recommendation of the Glassco Commission were likewise accomplished by order-in-council. The governor-in-council has other freedoms, of course, connected with making appointments to many parts of the public sector. This power allows cabinet to exempt any position or part of the public service from the requirements of the Public Service Employment Act, to appoint heads of boards and agencies, and to make diplomatic and judicial appointments (deputy-ministerial appointments are the prime minister's).

Such latitude does not mean that the executive has the authority to do anything that it may wish. What it does must be legal. It must be broadly constitutional, if only in the sense that it can get it by the system of loose control of opposition and the press. More important, if money is required, the executive must submit its proposals to Parliament. The cabinet must always return to Parliament for funds, and these funds must be closely and formally justified under specific programs and votes. Given these caveats, the executive can reorganize to complement the special talents or shortcomings of a particular cabinet, can pull together an organization to implement a new policy, and can delegate to officials, either singly or in organizations. This sketch is generally true of provincial civil services as well. As a result, one can expect to see considerable variation in the detail of their organization around the generic structure of parliamentary institutions on the Westminister model.

As in Chapter 1, the federal public service is our main model. While we do provide illustrative material dealing with the provinces from time to time, we cannot offer an encyclopedic coverage of all the organizations and interrelationships of our eleven autonomous governments. The plan of the chapter is to discuss the basic organizational controls of each of the bureaucracies that we designated I, II and III. We see to what extent each is amenable to direction by the elected central leadership provided by cabinet. The second main part of the chapter discusses controls that are auxiliary to the main legally defined organizational roles and formal organizational hierarchies. Among these are laws, regulations and customs that guide the behaviour of individuals.

Organizational Controls and Public Service Bureaucracy I

It is essential that the personnel regime for departments and departmental agencies be transparent: that is, open, accountable, logical, defensible. The covering term "merit" sums up much of this. In its early days, merit had largely to do with obstacles to hiring on the basis of objective qualifications: political partisanship, race, class, religion, personal family and social connections. (Gender is a recent addition.) The areas which the traditional merit system governs are few but fundamental: appointments, position classification, establishment of minimum examination requirements and class specifications, and promotions.[2] The specific content of any one of these terms evolves as professions evolve and as the political culture changes.

The individual who applies for a position in the traditional civil service, in principle opens his or her life and qualifications to the most stringent and intrusive kinds of assessment and security checking, even if such is not always performed. The system itself must ensure that each appointment is awarded to the candidate having the most merit from among those who made application. What follows is a skeleton description of the personnel regime governing the hiring and employment conditions of the employees of Public Service Bureaucracy I. Exceptions to merit are discussed in a later section on order-in-council appointments.

The contemporary legal framework of the federal government's personnel regime is provided by the Public Service Employment Act (PSEA),[3] the Public Service Staff (PSSRA) of 1966–67 and the Financial Administration Act (FAA), for which significant amendments regarding personnel management were made at the same time, the Official Languages Act, and the Human Rights Act. Of this legislation, the amendments to the FAA were perhaps the most important. We will discuss them first, because they removed some ambiguities in the status of the old Civil Service Commission by relieving it of some duties and powers that gave it an appearance of a managerial authority, and confused its status with Treasury Board.

Financial Administration Act

The Treasury Board was made a separate department of government in 1966; before then, its functions had been carried out by the Department of Finance. The new department was to be responsible for expenditure management, personnel management and the development of practices to improve management throughout the public service. The Financial Administration Act of 1966–67 spelled out Treasury Board's responsibilities regarding personnel management. The act says that the Treasury Board may act "for the Queen's Privy Council for Canada on all matters relating to . . . the organization of the public service or any portion thereof, and the determination and control of establishments therein. . . ." Specifically, Treasury Board is empowered to:

- determine the manpower requirements of the public service;
- determine requirements for training and development;
- develop classifications for positions and employees;

- determine and regulate the pay, hours of work and leave entitlements;
- provide work-force adjustment procedures;
- provide for special rewards for high performance;
- set general standards for discipline;
- provide standards for work environments, health and safety of employees;
- set and regulate travel expenses; and
- provide for conditions of employment for effective personnel management in the public service.[4]

Some of its functions — those not central to its identity as the employer and thus the sole government-side representative in collective bargaining — the Treasury Board delegates to the Public Service Commission, or shares with it. The shared responsibilities are:

- human resource planning;
- programs for special groups: women, indigenous peoples, the handicapped and francophones;
- management of the management category;
- administration of the priorities clearance system to support reorganizations and retrenchment.

The responsibilities that Treasury Board delegates to the Public Service Commission include:

- staff training and development, certification of trainees;
- language training and testing for the bilingual bonus;
- special development programs, including the career assignment program that attempts to identify and develop managers;
- interchanges between government, universities, the private sector, and other levels of government, as well as international exchanges;
- audit of classification, training, pay and benefits, health and safety, staff relations, official languages activities and personal services contracts.

Many of Treasury Board's powers can likewise be delegated to the deputy head of a department or to the chief executive officer of any part of the public service.

It is easy to miss the importance of the service-wide plan of classification of employees into occupational groups. Treasury Board, of course, retains control of this, and from this plan, the public service takes much of its character. This is less elitist than the British civil service: there are no perpendicular divisions between the "officer" class and the other functional groups as in Britain, where one makes one's career in the caste of entry.[5] The current occupational categories of the Canadian public service consist of "job families," each of which is broken down into groups and then into still more specific occupations. In brief, the basic categories are management, scientific and professional, administrative and foreign service, technical, administrative support, and operational. (See Chapter 3 for the numbers of employees in various occupations and groups.) Individual careers can and do cut across categories (with the exception of the foreign service jobs), as well as ascend the hierarchy in any one group as the individual adds formal qualifications and gains in competence. In this regard, the Canadian public service is an open structure.

Public Service Employment Act (PSEA)

The PSEA established and defined the jurisdiction of the Public Service Commission, diminished from what the Civil Service Commission had enjoyed before the emergence of Treasury Board as a separate entity. (Notably missing after 1967 are the traditional responsibilities of job classification, setting of rates of pay and determination of conditions of employment.) The act confirms the independence of the commission as an agent of Parliament, and gives it a number of specific powers. It has exclusive responsibility to:
- make appointments to positions on the basis of merit (which the commission must define);
- set conditions for competitions for jobs, develop and administer examinations;
- hear appeals against particular appointments;
- establish priority lists for employees laid off because of lack of work or reorganization, or who have been replaced while on a leave;
- fire employees for incapacity or incompetence on a deputy's recommendation;
- police the provisions of the act touching on political partisanship of civil servants.

The act also specifies a number of areas where appointments are exempt from the PSC's authority: diplomatic appointments, ministers' staffs, and any appointment made with the approval of the governor-in-council. Such appointments are normally co-ordinated by the Privy Council Office. The PSC can also delegate its functions, excepting those relating to appeals, to the deputy head of a department.

As the commission's powers have been consolidated in this core, its coverage of the federal public sector has been broadened: that is, a larger proportion of employees come under the provisions of the PSEA than had been covered by the old Civil Service Act. Bird, Bucovetsky and Foot discuss this change:

> In 1975 . . . 87 per cent of federal civilian employees were "civil servants" with all that that is usually taken to imply about job security, pensions, and so on, compared with only 58 per cent in 1961. At the provincial level too —

which remains much the more important in terms of total employees — the proportion of government employees included in the civil service appears to have grown in recent years. Since it is these figures which tend to receive most publicity in the media, this phenomenon may have strengthened the apparent general public perception of the growth of public sector employment as a whole.[6]

Bringing a larger proportion of all government employees under the act also implies, however, a more uniform coverage of the merit principle with the reciprocal decrease in patronage, and the submission of the employee to a fairly rigid code of conduct.

Under its act, the commission also has the authority to make regulations as it considers necessary to carry out the intent of the act. Until the advent of the Federal Court in 1970, it also interpreted its own act and regulations. Since then, cases can be brought before the Federal Court and the commission's decisions challenged unless the act empowers the commission to use its discretion in that area. This means, more specifically, that the decisions of the commission's appeal boards can be challenged and overturned.

Public Service Staff Relations Act

The Public Service Staff Relations Act establishes a legal framework for staff associations and the Public Service Staff Relations Board. J.E.Hodgetts points out that it contains two important points for the legal structure of the public service.[7] First, the act presents a clear definition of the employer, "Her Majesty in right of Canada as represented by the Treasury Board for a long list of departments and agencies in Part I of Schedule A," or by the agencies themselves considered as employers, these being listed in Part II. The second important point is actually an omission:

> . . . the Civil Service Commission finds no place in this measure, ample testimony to the desire to relieve it of its ambiguous dual role as a part of the management arm or as in any sense a representative of the employer. Rather than interpose the Civil Service Commission between employer and employee — which might have been possible in view of its judicial, politically neutralized status — a new Public Service Staff Relations Board and a separate Arbitration Board were created.[8]

In addition to these two important points, the PSEA sets out the conditions for "separate employer status." For an organization that is to have such status, the chief executive officer of the organization replaces the Treasury Board in all its personnel and administrative responsibilities. A separate employer has the exclusive authority to establish classification levels and to select, appoint and discipline employees without reference to Treasury Board or the PSC.

Other Service-wide Legislation

There are two additional pieces of legislation that have created the statutory framework for the management of human resources in the labour force. First is the Official Languages Act of 1968 that establishes English and French as the official languages of Canada and sets out criteria to ensure their use in the operations of the federal government. (A similar act has been in force in New Brunswick since 1969.) Three organizations are involved in the administration of this statute. First, the Office of the Commissioner of Official Languages is responsible for monitoring compliance with the spirit and intent of the act across Canada. Next, the Treasury Board secretariat is responsible for developing policy, guidelines, and controlling language training activities. Finally, the Public Service Commission has been delegated by Treasury Board to organize and conduct language training and examination activities.

The second piece of legislation is the Canadian Human Rights Act of 1976. Its coverage is much broader than just the traditional public service, covering all organizations under federal jurisdiction as well as such institutions as banks and agencies engaged in interprovincial transportation and communications. The legislation is intended to ensure equal pay for work of equal value, and to prohibit discrimination in employment and is applied by the Canadian Human Rights Commission. Discrimination exists if the judgment can be shown to have been based on race, national or ethnic origin, colour, religion, age, gender, marital status, physical handicap, or conviction for an offence for which a pardon has been granted.

Departmental Powers and Responsibilities

The organizational structure of the government of Canada was outlined in the Introduction. Only the major parts of this structure are based in legislation. Even here, in the acts for specific departments and agencies, it is the minister who has most powers and responsibilities, not the entities themselves.

While the FAA assigns the responsibility for financial probity to the minister rather than to the deputy,[9] it is the deputy minister who accepts the responsibilities delegated from the commission and from the Treasury Board for appointing personnel and for the classification of jobs. Because the organizational structure is largely the effect of such classifications and available person-years (a person-year being the employment of one person for one full year or the equivalent), this means that, subject to the final approval of Treasury Board, the deputy minister can organize a department as he or she may wish. The PSC delegates staffing functions for the vast majority of positions to most departments, up to the first ranks of management. The appointment of the person is to a particular position with the exception, since 1981, of management levels. Appointments of officers to the management category and above are to levels of work rather than to particular jobs. Thus, while PSC makes the appointments of executives to an appropriate level, deputy heads have since 1981 enjoyed the flexibility of deploying managers between positions, without appeal, providing only that there is no change in the individual's level.

No matter how much authority delegated to it, however, a department must view its needs through the perspective of the prescribed occupational categories and the groups within them. It must also stay within its person-year budget and management complement allocation. Surges of work and work of a unique kind are handled through two significant safety valves: term appointments and personal service contracts. Predictably, when government shows extreme restraint in hiring of regular, "indeterminate" employees, the work so displaced shows up sooner or later in the proportionally increased use of both of these employment modes.

Central Management: Overlaps and Gaps

The clarifications wrought in the legislative package of 1966–67 do not mean, unfortunately, that the situation has been relieved of all ambiguity and confusion. Since then, as noted, two new "surveillance mechanisms," to use the language of the PSC's 1983 annual report, have been established — the Official Languages Act and the Canadian Human Rights Act. Despite an attempt to avoid duplication of functions — for example, the PSC oversees language training and the examination of linguistic status mandated by the terms of the official languages legislation — the PSC was moved to complain in the 1983 report that ". . . several parties may be called upon to deal with the same problem, depending on the interpretation of a specific case"[10] and to doubt that its own ombudsman role is still necessary. In the same report, it asks for a new legislative framework. In the spring of 1985, in an attempt to address some of these jurisdictional confusions, the PSC delegated its investigative powers for discrimination complaints to the Canadian Human Rights Commission.

There are still more weighty concerns, however, that centre on the government and/or Parliament. The Lambert Commission report,[11] probably the most thorough recent discussion on this subject, proposed that the PSC be relieved of its operational responsibility (staffing). This would go to an enhanced Treasury Board, the "Board of Management," which would then have complete management responsibility for people as well as other resources. (Such a model now exists in Quebec, and, at the time of writing, was proposed for New Brunswick.) The motive behind the reform is to address the seeming contradiction between the PSC's activities in staffing and its duties to ensure merit: it apparently scrutinizes itself. Other proposals would make an enhanced PSC the heart of a "department" of the public service with its own minister, which would result in a different relationship to the House of Commons. The PSC would no longer be, ambiguously, a "servant of Parliament," but would report to the House through a minister who would speak and answer for its work. The motive here is to enhance the role of personnel management in government, so that the human resources can be deployed more effectively across the service, and to provide a clearer central focus for the people who work in government.[12]

These latter concerns refuse to be silenced by marginal adjustments to the current regime. Many of the criticisms arise from a view that the present divided responsibilities encourage a proliferation of negative controls at the expense of a positive personnel policy. To take just one example, there is no co-ordinated view of what constitutes a desirable career pattern for individuals on their way to senior ranks in the federal public service. There is thus no vehicle to provide systematically for vital broadening experiences for the senior management complement, considered as a resource in its own right. A frankly elitist system like Britain's can concentrate on developing talent in a manner that cannot even be contemplated by the Canadian national system. For the people in it, the Canadian public service is experienced as a free market in which one entrepreneurially and competitively seeks stable and interesting work and advancement through a bewildering array of organizations and rules.

Order-in-Council Appointments

Order- or governor-in-council appointments are those made by cabinet, for which one can often read the prime minister. Although there are several kinds, all are indiscriminately termed "patronage" appointments by the press because they are made outside the range of the competitive appointments and appeals processes of the PSC. Merit in the competitive PSC sense is not verifiable, but this does not mean that all qualification for the positions has been disregarded. Most governor-in-council appointments will have taken into consideration expertise and qualifications, on which the senior personnel secretariat in the Privy Council Office is usually consulted. A smaller number of such appointments seem to go to partisan politicians or party activists simply as reward for service.

Governor-in-council appointments fall into the categories of appointments in the public service structure, leadership for boards and advisory bodies, ministers' exempt staff, diplomatic appointments, and judicial appointments. The Privy Council Office maintains a listing of about 110 deputy minister positions and about 350 others. There are also about 1,500 part-time positions, some of which are unpaid. Counts for the provinces are harder to obtain, but estimates of the Ontario patronage network, for example, indicate that it is large.[13]

The first category is of most significance for our immediate purposes. The governor-in-council has the power to designate any position in the normal establishment as one to be filled by order-in-council. There are two "good" reasons for this provision. First, "political" appointments to key places in the bureaucracy are a form of bureaucratic control. The American civil service system tries to control the bureaucracy from within: while there are many career bureaucrats, there are also large numbers of politically appointed bureaucrats who leave when each administration changes, and even some specialized "in-and-outers," policy advisors who move between academic or business jobs and government. Governor-in-council appointments are the Canadian vehicle for improving the bureaucracy's responsiveness to political agendas, albeit on a smaller scale than in the United States, but perhaps on a grander scale than in Britain.[14] Deputy ministers of departments are perhaps the most important order-in-council appointments. In these jobs, that link the minister with the department, expertise is essential, as is bureaucratic probity, but small-p political sensitivity is also a critical capacity.

The second good reason for having order-in-council appointments is that their judicious use, perhaps somewhat paradoxically, actually limits the politicization of the public service by restricting political appointments to specific jobs and terms. If the government believes that, for example, a position in a communications division of a department should be filled by a politically sensitive partisan appointment, it legally designates that job as an order-in-council position, and places its own man or woman in it. It gets what it wants directly, without being tempted to covertly influence the PSC's appointment process. The process is visible. It is also temporary, in that the appointee does not have the same rights and protections as a regular public servant; in effect, he or she is in a separate and extremely vulnerable career. Patronage is thereby isolated in the political milieu, supposedly keeping the public service pure.

A minister's exempt staff has been made up of an executive assistant (as of October 1984 this was augmented to a "senior advisor" position) and a few other employees who are chosen and appointed by the minister, outside the ambit of the Public Service Commission. It is believed that the kind of political sensitivity required in the minister's office will not be forthcoming from regular public servants. This belief is a cultural spillover from the United States. In Britain, ministers' staffs, including the private office staff of the prime minister, are mainly secondments from the regular civil service. Such postings are coveted, and are important developmental assignments for officers of the administrative, or mandarin, class. Career officials become sensitized to the political implications of the various instruments of policy, and in turn assist the minister to see his or her opportunities and policies in the context of the actual, ongoing administrative machine. In Britain it is thought that a separate political staff would implicitly contradict a basic premise of the system — that the role of all civil servants is to extend the capacity of the political executive. As such, it is thought to be important that the minister's private office should be well-connected into the civil service proper.

In Canada, even though ministers' staffs are political appointments, there is remarkably little "reverse leakage" from the political staffs into the regular public service. The PSC's rules governing entry of political staffs to the public service are quite strict: executive assistants, for example, get first call on a similar job in the public service only if the PSC finds them qualified and if they have worked for one minister for three full years of unbroken service.

Diplomatic appointments, judicial appointments and board memberships are the most desirable higher level jobs that can be awarded to the party faithful, albeit in widely varying proportions. They tend, generally, to be less important to the quality and tenor of the management of the federal public service than senior order-in-council positions because they are not part of the main structure. However, this is not to say that they are unimportant in the milieus to which they are appointed.

Overuse of the diplomatic service for rewards for partisan politicians is demoralizing for the career foreign service because it can mean that significant postings are clumsily handled by non-professionals for years. It also removes incentives from the career structure of the service: the excellence of Canada's foreign service can be attributed to its capacity to recruit high-calibre entrants and train them well, a capacity that cannot long be maintained if entrants perceive that there is no room for them to advance beyond middle levels.[15]

The political appointments process in the judicial area is more complicated still, coming in two forms from the Department of Justice and the cabinet. The Department of Justice has considerable low-profile "respectable patronage" in its hands in choosing the lawyers who will represent the Crown in litigation. In 1984–85, for example, the federal Department of Justice forecast $3.9 million worth of contracts for legal work, being perhaps the largest single client of the Canadian legal profession. In early 1985, Liberal-affiliated lawyers were being replaced by lawyers who were active members of the Conservative party.[16] The cabinet, of course, appoints judges throughout the judicial system, in provincial and federal courts alike. This can and does result in the appointment of former members of Parliament who have not practised the law for decades. The Canadian Bar Association dislikes cabinet's absolute autonomy in the mode of appointment, perhaps in part because it offsets its own regulating of the profession, but mainly because it does not always make for high-quality law. This in turn throws the legal system into disrespect. Overall there is a growing constituency for the idea that judges should be appointed solely on the basis of merit.[17] The passing of the Charter of Rights enhanced the role of the judiciary in Canada; hence, it is important that our judges be steeped in the long study and practice of the law.

Organizational Controls and Public Service Bureaucracy II

In the public enterprise sector, where government plays the role of owner/financier and facilitator, each minister is responsible directly to Parliament only for policy in an overall sense. The chief executive officer of every enterprise is responsible for management and the full control of the enterprise to fulfil policy demands, and reports to the minister. The appointed officer rather than the minister takes direct responsibility for overseeing a personnel regime that is appropriate to the needs of the organization. The chief officer will follow certain norms but they will be primarily of general cultural, legal and professional origin, rather than stemming from the logic of parliamentary democracy. Here, emphasis is more on the result than on the means employed, which is generally not possible in the departmental sector.

It will surprise no one that there are few regularities in the relationships of these non-departmental bodies to the central financial and personnel agencies of the government. Many of the non-commercial entities are staffed under the provisions of the Public Service Employment Act, but none of the large commercial corporations appear in the PSC's staffing activities. Other non-commercial bodies are designated as in the public service by the Public Service Staff Relations Act, but appointments to them are not made under the Public Service Employment Act. The commercial bodies have the most autonomy in finance and staffing and also in union matters. Even so, in many cases the general pattern set in the classified public service serves as a rough guide for the classification and salary scales of non-management employees. Many will have their own pension schemes, some are fully unionized, while some (for example, the Bank of Canada) are not fully organized into staff associations. Dismissals are perhaps easier to effect in the commercial-type bodies that do not fall under the PSEA, a reflection that the processes of management are not subject to the same safeguards and strictures as in the departmental public service.

Organizational Controls and Public Service Bureaucracy III

For the organizations in Parliament's watchdog bureaucracy, it is thought that the government should provide a legal framework, operating funds and a personnel regime, act as official "employer" (except for the staff of the Office of the Auditor General) and otherwise keep its hands off. The auditor general has been granted recognition as a "separate employer" under the provisions of the Public Service Staff Relations Act. The OAG is the only one of the watchdog bureaucracies to enjoy this status.[18] All the others have Treasury Board as the employer.

Separate employer status is a flag of convenience which gives the OAG much more flexibility than a normal public service manager for classification of positions and salary levels and for negotiation of collective agreements with office unions. This gives the office the best of both worlds: ready equivalences and therefore transferability of personnel between the OAG and the public service proper, but also the potential of higher salaries to assist in recruitment of officers from both the public service and the private sector. It also means that the OAG is not obligated to submit its personnel establishment to the scrutiny of the Public Service Commission (although it is subject to scrutiny of the Official Languages Commission). It should be noted also that the OAG is in control of its own personal services contracts, a factor that gives it great financial power in the professions that it uses: accounting and management consulting. Indeed, in its domination of "respectable patronage" for those professions, it resembles the Department of Justice in its control of the legal profession. With its expanded mandate, as of 1984, for financial audit in the Crown sector, the power and financial domination over the professions is more impressive than ever.

Related Control Dimensions: Bureaucracy for the Bureaucrats

The citizen who is trying to win some good or service from the public service tends to perceive the people who work in it as having volition: they either want to do something for you or, more often, they want not to do it. Weber, on the other hand, described bureaucrats as functioning under the direction of "discursively analysable rules." Ideally then, it is the rules that are for or against the citizen's request. In a bureaucracy of robots — workers without a personal agenda, likes or dislikes — the rules of conduct that came under a description of the job would be sufficient. In a bureaucracy of real people, a variety of other controls are brought into play. We can divide these into two main categories: formal rules with legal penalties and sanctions related to employment conditions, and the informal norms of the various public service cultures.

Persons who work for a government have accepted a number of serious formal restraints upon their behaviour. The main restraints fall under the headings of secrecy and security, political action, broad conflict of interest issues, and probity. Employees not working at management jobs have the right to belong to associations and unions, and the right of redress if wronged through the appointments or promotions processes. Managers do not have the right to join associations, and their rights to appeal are limited in some cases. Everyone has the right to be spared discriminatory treatment and to be free from harassment. There are several kinds of sanctions: through the workplace, where disciplinary action can be a reprimand, a suspension, a financial penalty, dismissal, or revocation of appointment; through the regular justice system, where sanctions can be civil or criminal; or through the actions of a collective bargaining association, where the sanctions are part of the legislation and regulations.

Secrecy and Security

If an individual is being hired for a position that involves handling of classified materials, he or she will, as a condition of service, voluntarily undergo a security check by the Royal Canadian Mounted Police. The police report is submitted to the departmental security officer, who reviews it and adds any information provided by the individual, then passes it to the deputy minister for decision. The person who is denied a job may or may not be told that it was for a security-related "blemish" on his or her record. That can depend, obviously, on security concerns.

On beginning work, successful applicants swear (or affirm) to refrain from disclosing whatever may be learned as a result of their work. New job holders will be informed of the provisions of the Official Secrets Act. Not so draconian as the British act, the Canadian act nonetheless provides for serious penalties.[19]

Nor is the matter of security completely closed once the individual is hired and handling classified materials. The departmental security officer, given any reasonable basis for suspicion, can order another investigation at any time. Individuals whose loyalty or reliability is doubtful, whether through their own fault or because of family or friendship connections, can be disciplined, relocated, or dismissed. In cases that are not satisfactorily resolved, the evidence is reviewed by the departmental security officer and the deputy minister, the interdepartmental security panel, and ultimately the minister.

The most recent declassified cabinet directive on security dates from 1963.[20] This was declassified in 1978. Safeguards for the individual are few. The directive provides that the individual should be informed of the suspicions raised, "to the fullest degree responsible under the circumstances," and that the security panel should keep track of numbers of clearances refused, and the reasons, to review its own record.

Code of Conduct

Each department or agency will have its own variations to a code of conduct. However, a few elements are constant. Central among these are the topics of political behaviour and conflict of interest.

Partisanship

The basic provisions for political partisanship are laid out in the Public Service Employment Act. It provides that no public servant shall "engage in work for, on behalf of, or against a candidate for election as a member of the House of Commons, a member of the legislature of a province, or a member of the Council of the Yukon Territory or the Northwest Territories, or engage in work for, on behalf of, or against a political party; or . . . be a candidate for election. . . ." The severity of the formal ban is mitigated to some extent by a provision that a leave of absence can be granted by the commissioners so that an employee can run for election. Further, a sanction under the PSEA is initiated only on the basis of a complaint made by the aggrieved party, i.e., a candidate for election. (However, other cases, such as that of the public servant who campaigned openly against metrication while working for the federal government, are dealt with under normal disciplinary procedures.)

The restrictions on partisanship were under attack during the summer of 1984. The commissioners, anticipating the September federal election, published an interpretation of the PSEA's provisions in a staff organ.[21] The piece takes the approach that any activity not listed in the PSEA as a positive right should be undertaken only after extremely cautious review as to whether it would raise suspicions about the individual's ability to perform his or her work without bias. The rights are:

* to vote;
* to make financial contributions to political parties;
* to stand for nomination and run in a federal, provincial or territorial election, subject to prior approval by the Public Service Commission, which has been provided with full information on the case by the employee's supervisor;
* to attend meetings of a political party. (The right to attend meetings, however, does not extend to the right to open expression of all viewpoints or preferences. In other words, "Go, but don't wear a button.")

More specifically, the guidelines caution public servants to refrain from making partisan political statements, from campaign activity, or from holding party office.

The new guidelines generated a heated reply from Michael Cassidy, a candidate for the New Democratic Party in the federal Ottawa Centre riding. Besides doubting that the public service commissioners were properly implementing their act, Cassidy charged that the guidelines violate public servants' rights under the Charter to freedom of speech and association. He urged that the government revise the legislation to bar only the most senior public servants from political activity. He has continually emphasized the criticism that the PSC/PSEA anti-activity stance involves a penalty for those who want to donate labour to the party of their choice, while those who want to donate money are completely free to do so. In effect, these two provisions amount to a class bias, meaning that poorer people are unable to promote a partisan choice. Overall, the existing set of restrictions is badly thought out and arbitrary, in his view. Cassidy, who apparently had some difficulty in drawing volunteers for his campaign because of the guidelines, also expressed his intention to bring the commission before the Federal Court on the issue.[22]

The commission's official attitude continued to reflect the stance taken in the guidelines: a hard line against expressions of partisanship. There are signs, however, that the commissioners would welcome a public debate and a legislative revisiting of the PSEA. Jennifer McQueen, in a recent speech, reviewed the provisions for mediating expressions of partisanship in several provinces, in the other parliamentary democracies, and in the United States. The thoroughness of her preparation indicates that the PSC is ready, should the new government choose to review the area.[23]

The prohibition of expression is not limited to electioneering, however. Codes of conduct prohibit open criticisms of government policy, as well as expressions of opinion through unconventional styles of dress or items of apparel. Lettered T-shirts or buttons, for example, could be the cause of disciplinary action.

Conflict of Interest

Each department has issued guidelines that are made available through personnel officers. The major areas are disclosure and outside employment. With regard to disclosure, public servants must tell their manager about any business connections or investments that might conflict, or appear to conflict, with their official duties. These include the interests of relatives or close friends. Public servants must also refrain from sitting on a selection board where they know they would be partial to one or another candidate. Some collective agreements guarantee the individual's right to work at some other employment during off hours. Even so, any work that could lead to conflict of interest is not allowable (nor is it allowed to overlap hours of work).

Conflict of interest can extend past the period of an individual's employment with the public service. Criminal breaches will, of course, be handled by the government's security apparatus. But what of offences which are more nearly offences against "moral probity" than against the law? How to deal, for example, with a former public servant who goes to work for a company that does business with the government, and uses specialized information gained while in government work to benefit the private firm to the disadvantage of its competition? For the most part, the higher the officer's rank was in government, the potentially more significant such an offence. Some countries have ruled for a "cooling off" period, which provides that high officials, whether elected or appointed, cannot, subject to legal penalties, assume active duties with private firms that are closely related to their past competence until some specified time has elapsed. In this way, such individuals will have lost the advantage of current information, and any firm recruiting them will have to do so only on the basis of their intrinsic worth. The Canadian federal government currently has a weaker position on the issue. Its guidelines of September 1982, for the behaviour of all "holders of public office" (ministers, parliamentary secretaries, order-in-council appointees, exempt staff member or ordinary public servant), under revision in the summer of 1984, do suggest suitable cooling off periods before office holders should enter the employment of commercial firms with which they have had significant dealings, sit on boards of directors, or lobby; however, conformity with the guidelines is a "matter of honour and of personal choice." Office holders are expected to inform their seniors when they have had an offer of employment.

We have already noted that the person who sits on a selection board for a public service position knowing that he or she has a favourite candidate is in a conflict of interest situation. The best solution in terms of natural justice is for those who have a preferred candidate not to sit. Such probity depends more on morality than on formal controls, a topic of the next section on "organizational climates." Still, decisions by conflicted boards are at least potentially open for redress, because of the appeal mechanism of the Public Service Commission.

An even greyer and more complicated area is the awarding of contracts by public servants who have not followed proper tendering procedures. This is an area not usually subject to formal penalties simply because, in the absence of proper documentation, it cannot be shown whether management was objective in deciding which firm would do the best work, for the least price. It must be allowed that there are many reasons for sloppy contracting. One obvious reason is that pressures of time and lack of personnel create imperatives for managers to act swiftly: to seize the first available contractor who is familiar, so that work of acceptable quality can be available before a normal tendering procedure would even be complete. As long as it is part of the political and public mood to insist that services not be cut, but that public servants should be, we can expect this kind of action.

Yet there are undoubtedly many breaches of proper tendering that would not pass the haste test: the secretary of the Treasury Board in the federal government wrote to all deputy heads in 1983, and again in 1984, to warn them that " . . . almost one half of the departments and agencies subject to the Government Contracts Regulations had internal audit findings indicating a general lack of compliance with the basic policy of competition for contracts; poor or non-existent definitions of requirements, and poor preparation of basic documentation prior to starting."

In the same letter, the secretary regretted that Treasury Board would be unable to contemplate any further delegations of contracting authority to departments. Several months later the confidential report that had likely been the basis for the secretary's censures became public. It estimated that departments were spending almost $3 billion a year in a system riddled with deliberate abuses and "bureaucratic patronage."[24]

Deterrence: Formal Reviews

The pervasiveness of audit may well be the distinguishing characteristic of public sector employment. Everything is audited, every transaction, process and outcome, whether it deals with finances, goods or personnel. There are waves of audit that are internal to the department, reviews by the central agencies, and the ongoing financial and comprehensive audits by the external auditor, the auditor general of Canada (or the provincial legislative auditor). Even language competency, where a position requires competency in a second language to a given level, is subject to periodic testing.

Most errors or omissions in probity will be found by internal audit and will result in disciplinary action, sometimes in RCMP investigation with subsequent legal proceedings. Sometimes it will involve the calling in of Treasury Board, from which might come an eventual change of policy, for example, for proper tendering.

The other levels of audit generally concentrate more on testing systems and reviewing classes of activities and processes for their suitability and efficiency. They could lead to releases or relocations for incompetence. The RCMP, of course, can be brought in to investigate any problem where criminal activity is suspected, including suspicions of abuse of office through fraud or acceptance of gifts or favours.

Redress Mechanisms

These mechanisms can also be regarded as a system of controls on the behaviour of individuals. That is, any mechanism that is redress for the employee represents a constraint or control on the employer, and the manager of the job. Offences fall into two broad types: infractions of the human rights type and infractions related to hiring, appointments, promotion, demotion and release.

With regard to human rights, Section 3 of the Canadian Human Rights Act provides, as noted earlier, that public servants must not discriminate in the course of performing their duties on the basis of race, national or ethnic origin, colour, religion, age, sex, marital status, family status, disability or a conviction for which a pardon has been granted. Nor may they harass any other worker or employee or superior. The PSEA entitles individuals to appeal against a broad variety of personnel actions.[25]

Redress in both areas is through the appeals and investigations branch of the PSC, on the initiative of the wronged individual. (Appeals can be heard by the Federal Court.) The Human Rights Commission also establishes occasional tribunals to hear cases that break new ground in clarifying the law.

The Bureaucratic Cultures

The idea that each organization has its own culture or "climate" has been made more familiar through the recent literature on Japanese and American management techniques. The comparative success of the Japanese is often attributed, not solely to the "hard wiring" of the organization through formal controls, but also to perfection of a climate or culture that conditions employees to act sensitively, in harmony with the requirements of the organization. Breaches of rules are rare, because the individual's antennae have steered him or her clear long before impact.

Experienced observers of government will declare that each department has its own culture, its own ecology. Each agency reflects both its clientele and, one hopes, some norms representing a broader public interest. Enter the Department of Justice building and you are in the surroundings of a top-line law firm; the reception areas are a fine mix of old brass fixtures, solid wood, and rich red carpets and fabrics. At the Department of the Environment visitors might find themselves sharing an elevator with some beast or bird en route to a lab. National Health and Welfare reflects both the medical culture and a "social work" culture; its furniture is enamelled steel and arborite veneer. Treasury Board is well appointed but crowded, somewhat hurried: corridors of windowless cages house tall, clean-shaven young men wearing three-piece suits, boy scouts in mufti.

Various bureaucratic cultures also operate in the social service elements of Public Service Bureaucracy II. Thus, the medical profession has its formal codes of behaviour, some disciplinary mechanisms, and ingrained ethics of service. The teaching and related professions exude their own view of a service ethic. We point out this interplay between formal codes and bureaucratic-cum-professional cultures, not to glorify its importance, but simply to argue that workplace and discipline cultures do exert effective control above and beyond controls specified in formal rules. Indeed, it is commonplace to aver that the best form of control operates subjectively in the trained conscience of the professional.

Traditional Civil Service Culture

It is a matter of some debate as to whether an idealized mandarin class — one that embodied all the virtues of a civil service culture, did so cohesively, and shared an origin in the old social elite of the eastern provinces — ever actually existed in the federal public service.[26] We do not wish to engage in this debate, but instead to point out, on the basis of our own impressions and others' (for there is little systematic empirical research on the subject),[27] some core values of the departmental public service.

Most of the central values are dictated by the role of the civil servant in the system. They are "survival" imperatives. First among these are the group of values dictated by ministerial responsibility. To avoid charges of partisanship — resisting a ministerial policy that is not popular depart-mentally, or riding roughshod over due process and legal concerns to implement ministerial policy when it meets with his or her approval — the bureaucrat working in the traditional civil service has to cultivate a habit of even-handedness. Whatever is to be done must be justifiable from a variety of perspectives. The behaviour of long-term, successful civil servants cultivate a norm of deliberateness, which can grow into extreme caution. Experienced bureaucrats will refuse to be rushed or panicked into action, but will take a request under advisement. They want to think about what a decision will look like to hostile observers months and years down the road. As a result, error is almost always detected and punished, but great successes are few and far between.

Extreme verbal discretion is another part of this survival technique. Loose talk, and expression of preferences, draws attention to one's record and sets up incentives to other actors to initiate scrutinies. Ardently held positions can also make dispassionate analysis impossible and set one up for error. These protective mechanisms are expressed in a recognizable style in the personal conduct of the traditional civil ser-vant. One finds, in short, extreme civility in the dictionary sense of formal politeness, courtesy, guarded exchanges, and a sometimes remarkable capability and willingness to listen to others.

Another cluster of values centres on the idea of expertise. A familiar distinction is that between "process" experts and "substance" experts. Substance experts are the ones who thought they knew something before entering the bureaucracy. Process experts have frankly learned everything of use to them in their job in one position or another in the public sector: they are experts in the main structures and the tech-nicalities of the system. However, this does not mean they are mere technicians who cannot see the intent of the whole. Civil servants will often understand the spirit as well as the legalities of parliamentary government better than will elected officers: Hansard is full of examples of civil servants delicately instructing government and opposition alike in systemic imperatives.[28] In the British civil service, substance experts will generally stay within their fields, not venturing out or being accept-able to the administrative class. In Canada, employees will often be drawn from practice of their profession into management. This, and the practice of parachuting persons into high administrative jobs from outside the public service, can threaten the smoothness and cohesiveness of administrative culture and action. The outside actors, often brought in to "get something done," lack patience with the rules. Their preoccupation with results will lead to collisions with traditional bureaucrats, or to their deliberate "misuse" of the rules in end runs. In turn, this dilution of administrative culture eventually makes it necessary to have still more rules, more external, explicit controls to replace the voluntary compliance of the person who is steeped in the culture. Some observers maintain, for example, that the dismantling of the old forms (and hence the old culture) that followed on the Glassco Commission's recommendation to "let the managers manage," set up the federal bureaucracy for the proliferation of explicit, audited controls that followed at the instigation of the auditors general.

The ethic of service is another traditional civil service norm. The idealized civil servant embraces the need for anonymity with considerable grace. The notion of service is much more than masochistic self-denial. It has a positive side in that the demands of some high public service jobs can truly test the capacity of the individual. It is in this sense that the phrase "opportunity for service" is used. This ethic, too, suffers when "high flyers" are elevated quickly or parachuted in. They tend to have a more aggressive attitude toward their motives for being in the bureaucracy and their own advancement.

Connected with the idea of service to the public and the state are the old civil service norms about pay. It is common thinking that there is a trade-off between the financial rewards that a talented, energetic person will receive in the private sector, and the security and breadth of experience and personal challenge that the public sector can offer. The advent of collective bargaining in the public sector eroded this idea for employees below management level. Wage settlements now approach the levels of the private sector in most cases, and public sector workers are increasingly interested in bargaining in other areas, such as hours and conditions of work. In turn, the public sector offers less and less security, partly because of restraint and partly because managers may abuse their authority to reorganize the workplace and to declare workers surplus to needs, as an easier way to manage the human resource than individual firings.

For employees at management and executive levels, the erosion of the old civil service norms of deliberate procedure, slow advancement and opportunity for service leaves the individual surveying his or her job with a much colder eye: what about pay, conditions of work, opportunities for advancement and self-fulfilment? Once the old norms have been eroded, many of the top jobs of the civil service are not worth having. The deputy minister, for example, is thrown into a consuming and conflicting job where he or she must provide sensitive policy advice to the minister, take operating responsibility for the quality and neutrality of departmental administration, harmonize and resist the demands of the central agencies from some unifying perspective, and foster signs of talent in the lower ranks so that a new generation will be ready to take over top management positions. This work must be done in the face of the public's increasingly firm conviction that bureaucrats are lazy and self-serving, and in the midst of the multitudes of audits and checks upon their administration, any one of which can set off a disastrous chain of accusations about bad management. Surely it is to the public benefit to foster the ethic of service. But if the now battered ethic is allowed to fall even further into disrepute, what will replace it?

Advocate Agency Subcultures

The negative side of the traditional culture of the old civil service is easily seen: caution, loss of purpose through being rule- and procedure-bound, slowness, an obsession with secrecy and security, sensitivity to criticism, an extreme dislike of innovation and risk. The proponents of the subcultures of non-traditional forms — the advocacy and control bureaucracies — define themselves first in reaction to these features. They are men and women who are there to get the job done, in a timely fashion, at little cost, through being innovative, resourceful and relentlessly critical. To do their jobs, they must be in a position to make enemies in the civil service proper; therefore, their positions and prospects must be protected in a number of ways.

The particular values that they embody will depend upon the mission of their organization. Because their organization will have one main thrust, officers are able to try to maximize that value without concern for the needs of the whole service, a factor that stymies many top administrators who operate inside the civil service organization. Thus the Official Languages Commission can simply report on an organization's lack of compliance, without regard for its other constraints. The Public Service Commission can simply reprimand a manager for "crown princing"[29] without recognizing the desperation of a manager so pinched that he or she honestly believed that organizational survival dictated having a known person for the job.

In a sense, successive governments have, in setting up the control organizations, taken a selection of values and made them concrete by institutionalizing them. The values then press in on the civil service manager, sometimes reinforcing and sometimes contradicting the internalized norms discussed above. The government's choice of heads for the control organizations can be seen as an indicator of how far it wants to see them go. Thus, the commissioners of the Public Service Commission are often long-time career civil servants, imbued with the service's values, and able and instinctively willing to balance conflicting claims before coming to a decision. The last two auditors general, on the other hand, have been management consultants, and their choice probably reveals a deliberate attempt to downgrade and to energetically test old civil service norms of management and standards for procedure. In effect, such an incumbent becomes an open conduit for the norms of the private sector. These very different standards flow in to become the inspiration for the newer employees who have not already been socialized in the old norms of what it means to be an auditor of public service procedures. It means that public servants must continually explain first principles of their operations to individuals who doubt their very legitimacy.

Summary

The purpose of this chapter has been to show that in very fundamental ways organizational structure *is* political control. Detailed control elements do matter. Conflicts and confusions that reach the apexes of the various administrative hierarchies must be arbitrated by the elected political actors as a minimum condition of responsible government. We have argued that control is adequate through the departmental civil service, requiring perhaps some adjustments in the division of authority between Treasury Board and the Public Service Commission: ministers are still here the arbiters of inter-agency disputes and can intervene decisively when alerted to problems.

Even the polymorphic Public Service Bureaucracy II is nothing like the lawless wild west that it is often depicted to be. Although the respective cabinets take little interest in the day-to-day affairs of publicly owned commercial enterprises, regulatory bodies, grant-giving bodies, or even educational establishments and hospitals, they can still intervene decisively and authoritatively. What they set up may be beyond their detailed managerial direction (either because they do not have the expertise to provide precise guidance, as with hospitals, or because the organization was set up at arm's length to prevent nepotism by political actors, as with granting agencies), but cabinets nonetheless can: issue authoritative directives; replace the appointed leadership, albeit with some effort and publicity; cripple the organization financially; and, as a last resort, abolish the organization. Hence, for example, while the B.C. cabinet would properly have been powerless to change any one particular ruling of the B.C. Human Rights Commission, it was a relatively simple matter (not counting public reaction) for it to abolish the whole commission. One may not approve, but the decision was taken by legitimately elected politicians. Even school boards, which alone of all such bodies have electoral legitimacy, must bow to the power of the purse enjoyed by the provincial elected and bureaucratic actors. In essence, while Public Service Bureaucracy II may largely be unattended, even for the most part uncontrolled, it is by no means beyond control.

It also seems fair to conclude, however, that obsession with control has imported some serious deficiencies into our system of government. The structure, and hence the potential of political control, is not at all clear in the case of control agencies that are ambiguously attached to legislatures. They are, as a simple matter of fact, uncontrolled, in both daily administration and broad policy, by cabinet and backbench politicians. Parliament has demonstrated little sustained interest or capacity to provide policy leadership and to harmonize their demands. And because of the status of "Parliament's agent," it is increasingly hard to imagine that a government would act unilaterally to abolish one of Parliament's bodies, in the same way that it would restructure organizations that report through cabinet, or that a government would simply remove the appointed leadership of the control bureaucracies with the same ease that it removes and reappoints members of boards in Public Service Bureaucracy II. The control bureaucracy is both uncontrolled, then, and perhaps even beyond control.

Chapter 3

Mapping the Bureaucracy
Quantitative Trends

What's a Million?

It is clear to many Canadians that the public sector is too large. But most opinion polls ask only for the public's general attitudes toward government. They do not establish what particular part of government a person has in mind, and whether he or she has any facts that support the emotional reaction. The few studies that have tested the public's grasp of basic facts show that citizens have little knowledge on which to base opinions. For example, in a 1977 Ontario survey Auld found that fewer than 3 percent of his sample had even a rough idea of the size of the provincial government's budget. The magnitude of budgetary allocations means little to most persons, Auld notes. Fewer than 10 percent of the study's respondents had any idea of what the major items of expenditure in Ontario were, or what share the main items took of the budget. Although there was a strong feeling that too much was spent on "administration," there was a fairly general support for spending on precise programs.[1]

A review of the briefs and transcripts of hearings of this Royal Commission also shows much negative feeling against government's presence.[2] Apparently the whole is much worse that the sum of its parts, since there are few grievances against particular administrative units. The distinction between federal and provincial levels of government was rarely drawn, so that "government" in witnesses' comments and recommendations most often meant both levels.

Yet the belief that the public sector is too big, even out of control, surely requires a concept of its desirable size. After all, pathology is only defined by reference to what is normal, and deviant behaviour is only recognized in distinction to conceptions of what is desirable. To criticize the public sector as being simply too big may be good politics, but it is poor argument.

A comparative approach avoids the basic philosophical dilemmas and exaggerations that arise when we implicitly try to describe things in absolute terms. What is "tall," except in comparison to heights of other people? What is a big or small public sector except in comparison to other nations? The comparative approach, then, is a good way to begin a description of the magnitude and structure of the public service bureaucracy in Canada, because it avoids making ideological judgments about how much is "too much."

Is our public sector big? The first section of this chapter shows that it is about the same size as in most other countries. And, as with personal height, we find that wishes do not seem to affect the size of the public sector. That is, it will grow regardless of the partisan stamp or ideological preferences of the politicians in control of a particular country.[3] The next section of the chapter concentrates upon Canada. Employment is chosen as the indicator for the concentration of the public sector, after which the magnitude and distribution of employment by the federal government is described. Federal employment is then compared both with provincial public sector employment and with the limited data available from 1967 on employment in public service activities at municipal level, which is not an autonomous sector, but rather the creature of the provincial level. (Before 1967, local government employees are simply counted as provincial employees.) Finally, total public sector employment is calculated as a proportion of the total labour force. The statistical data supporting our comparative analysis will be found at the end of the chapter.

Canada in Comparison to OECD Countries

The role of government, and thus the size of the public service work force, has expanded dramatically in Canada since World War II. But the same may be said for most of the advanced industrial democracies in the same period. The growth in economic activity, associated with rapid technological change, has created the need for greater use of such systems as communications and transportation. Simple population increase has fuelled the growth of other sectors, such as those that maintain order and provide education. The accompanying social changes, such as increased mobility of populations, faster redundancy of working skills and increased divorce and family breakdown, bring their own costs. In all countries, the major component of the expansion of the public sector has been welfare expenditures.

Critics of the Canadian state contend, however, that growth in Canada has been unnaturally rapid. Yet this can be claimed only if one chooses to compare Canada to a few special cases, in particular, the United States, Japan and Switzerland. Manfred Schmidt points out that taxes and social security contributions as a percentage of Gross Domestic Product (GDP) increased less rapidly in these three countries than in Canada, Sweden, the Netherlands, Norway, Ireland, Denmark and Belgium.

In Table 3-1, Schmidt sets out the percentage share taken by the "tax state," defined in terms of the extractive capacity of general government. The picture shows that Canadian performance resembles that of most other industrial democracies. The "extractive capacity" of the Canadian state — that is, the funding provided to all levels of government for all public services — did grow quickly between 1960 and 1975 from about a quarter of GDP to a fat third. But ours was not the fastest-growing public sector: look at the Scandinavian countries, Finland, and even Austria and Australia. Nor is the bite taken by the Canadian tax state excessive in comparative terms: most states take between one-third and one-half of GDP to provide all the services of a modern state, with some social democratic governments extracting almost two-thirds of GDP. Further, most of the tax states that grew at a slower rate than did Canada's between 1960 and 1975 had had their spurt of growth earlier. In France and Britain, for example, the public sector was already at one-third of GDP as early as 1950. Canada, in its own spurt of growth, may only have been reacting belatedly to gaps in the provision of such public goods and services as have been made necessary by modern economic conditions. And indeed, the Canadian tax state, having spurted in growth, already showed signs of shrinkage by 1978. (Due to the following recession, however, this mode of analysis loses much usefulness because GDP itself drops quickly.)

It is not practical to update all aspects of Schmidt's elaborate table, but one can find the same pattern of comparisons between countries in data assembled from more recent OECD statistics by Statistics Canada presented in Table 3-2. Notice that all proportions are slightly lower than those given by Schmidt,[4] but that the relative rankings are the same. It thus confirms the interpretation offered above and extends the comparison of Canada with other nations to 1981. Canada continues to be around the median. It is even slightly below the average of 36.16. Canada maintains its position as a moderate spender even through the world-wide recession. This bird's-eye perspective on Canada is illuminating: our public sector is about as big as one would expect, given our stage of industrial development and our rather small, open economy.

In this study, we have already described the Canadian government in terms of its main bureaucratic institutions: the traditional civil service organizations, the entrepreneurial or arm's-length part of state activity, and the independent watchdog and control bureaucracies. (These last are important in a policy sense, but are not large in absolute terms; their

TABLE 3-1 The Tax State and the Political Complexion of Governments in Democracies, 1950–78

	Size of the Tax State				Expansion of the Tax State			Dominant Tendency in Government		
	1950	1960	1975	1978	1950–60	1960–75	1973–78	1950–60	1960–75	1974–78
	(percent GNP)				(percentage points)					
Australia	20.5[b]	25.5	31.6	31.9	5.0	6.1	3.2	1	2	3
Austria	28.0	31.0	39.1	44.5	3.0	8.1	6.5	3	3	5
Belgium	24.0[a]	27.5	40.6	42.7	3.5	13.1	6.3	2	2	2
Canada	**24.7**	**26.0**	**37.1**	**35.8**	**1.3**	**11.1**	**-0.4**	**1**	**1**	**1**
Denmark	21.8	27.5	45.3	49.0	5.7	17.8	3.3	3	3	4
Finland	30.4	31.6	39.8	40.2	1.2	8.2	1.7	2	2	2
France	32.8	34.0	40.5	42.3	1.2	6.5	3.7	2	1	1
West Germany	31.5	35.4	41.0	43.3	3.9	5.6	2.1	1	3	4
Iceland	27.6[b]	27.8[e]	26.6	27.9[h]	9.4[f]	-1.2[g]	1.8[h]	1	2	2
Ireland	23.4	24.5	36.8	32.2[h]	1.1	12.3	-2.7[h]	2	2	2
Israel	14.4	28.7	38.9[d]	—	14.3	10.2	—	4	4	3
Italy	1.0[b]	29.8	35.2	37.0	8.8	5.4	3.2	1	2	2
Japan	1.7[c]	20.2	23.6	24.3	-1.5	3.4	1.1	1	1	1
Luxembourg	32.5[c]	32.5	50.6	50.0[h]	0.0	18.1	9.8[h]	3	2	3
New Zealand	27.0[a]	28.4	31.4	33.6[h]	1.4	3.0	9.2[h]	2	2	3
Netherlands	32.8	33.1	52.6	54.4	0.3	19.5	5.2	2	2	2
Norway	29.7[b]	34.5	49.7	52.1	4.8	15.2	2.5	5	3	5
Sweden	25.9	34.9	52.6	60.3	9.0	17.7	11.7	4	5	3
Switzerland	25.1	25.1	32.1	34.0	0.0	7.0	5.2	2	2	2
United Kingdom	32.6	29.3	41.1	38.8	-3.3	11.8	1.9	2	3	4
United States	23.9	28.2	30.6	32.6	4.3	2.4	1.4	1	1	1

Source: M. G. Schmidt, "The Growth of the Tax State: The Industrial Democracies, 1950–1978," in *Why Governments Grow*, edited by C.L. Taylor (Beverly Hills: Sage, 1983), Table 14.1 (pp. 262–63).

Notes: Tax State = Revenues from tax and social security contribution of general government as percentage of GDP (Source: *OECD National Accounts Statistics*, various volumes, and *United Nations National Accounts Statistics*, various volumes).
Dominant tendency in government: 1 = Bourgeois hegemony 2 = Bourgeois dominance 3 = Balance 4 = Social democratic dominance 5 = Social democratic hegemony a. 1953; b. 1951; c. 1952; d. 1974; e. 1961; f. 1951–60; g. 1961–75; h. Preliminary estimates.

TABLE 3-2 Total Tax Revenue as Percentage of GDP

	1965	1971	1972	1973	1974	1975	1976	1977	1978	1979	1980	1981
Australia	24.41	25.91	24.94	26.51	28.53	29.09	29.64	29.63	28.56	29.65	30.69	31.55
Austria	34.55	36.30	36.77	37.03	38.07	38.61	38.48	39.13	41.47	41.15	41.19	42.54
Belgium	31.21	36.74	37.04	37.99	38.94	41.82	42.32	43.84	45.07	45.63	44.90	45.44
Canada	**25.94**	**31.15**	**31.80**	**31.30**	**33.90**	**32.93**	**32.51**	**31.80**	**31.49**	**31.38**	**32.65**	**34.74**
Denmark	29.90	43.52	42.87	42.39	44.22	41.35	41.55	41.99	43.38	44.76	45.36	45.26
Finland	30.13	33.62	33.81	34.51	33.70	36.15	39.94	39.50	36.41	34.89	35.14	36.82
France	34.97	35.06	35.30	35.66	36.33	37.44	39.36	39.42	39.50	41.13	42.69	42.95
West Germany	31.60	33.41	34.75	36.29	36.44	35.95	34.36	38.01	37.73	37.47	37.75	37.32
Greece	20.58	24.40	24.60	23.18	23.99	24.64	27.27	27.59	27.93	27.74	28.64	29.22
Ireland	26.03	32.37	31.00	31.20	31.67	32.09	35.64	34.59	33.07	33.10	36.51	38.44
Italy	27.25	28.66	28.53	26.28	28.32	28.98	30.27	30.89	31.26	30.22	32.87	33.74
Japan	17.75	20.02	20.72	22.47	23.01	21.01	21.90	22.47	24.24	24.81	25.93	26.86
Luxembourg	30.48	32.07	32.03	31.48	32.43	36.70	36.23	38.78	39.51	35.42	36.33	34.12
Netherlands	35.48	41.65	42.49	43.73	44.39	45.80	45.43	43.97	44.58	44.96	45.83	45.47
New Zealand	24.55	27.00	26.58	28.18	30.75	30.05	30.12	32.70	30.76	30.89	31.49	32.78
Norway	33.22	42.35	44.79	45.23	44.71	44.82	46.16	47.20	46.53	45.68	47.05	48.49
Portugal	18.46	22.79	22.51	21.99	22.52	24.79	26.91	27.39	26.45	26.10	29.27	31.11
Spain	14.73	17.43	18.37	18.98	18.24	19.60	19.61	21.54	22.88	23.44	24.16	25.24
Sweden	35.68	41.19	42.59	41.73	42.87	43.95	48.34	50.77	51.22	49.93	49.57	51.31
Switzerland	20.71	23.51	23.91	26.27	27.31	29.61	31.30	31.63	31.58	31.08	30.78	30.28
Turkey	14.93	19.43	19.08	19.60	17.91	20.67	21.03	21.61	21.26	20.78	19.07	19.29
United Kingdom	30.79	35.23	33.95	31.87	35.28	35.96	35.59	35.27	33.69	33.41	36.04	37.35
United States	26.51	28.76	29.63	29.70	30.22	30.18	29.29	30.30	30.21	31.32	30.60	31.24
OECD Total	26.95	30.98	31.22	31.46	32.34	33.14	34.05	34.78	34.73	34.56	35.41	36.16

Source: Statistics Canada, *Compendium of Statistics*, prepared for the Royal Commission on the Economic Union and Development Prospects for Canada (Ottawa: Statistics Canada, February 1984, draft edition), Table 19-13.

displaced activity is several times larger than their direct action.) We have, however, only a general idea of the relative importance of departmental structures in comparison to the enterprise sector. It will now be useful to describe the comparative sizes of the numerically largest features of the public sector landscape, and to do so in a unit of measure that has some intrinsic meaning.

Choosing an Indicator for the Public Sector's Importance: Employment versus Instruments versus Programs

There are many indicators of public sector presence. Each is revealing and limited in different ways. The proportion of the Gross Domestic Product (GDP) or Gross National Product (GNP)[5] taken by the state is a convincing comparative indicator in some regards. It is wealth taken out of the scope of the private sector's traditional property rights, where money talks for those who generate it. Secondly, it is in the form of a ratio, and is therefore suitable for concurrent cross-national comparisons. But it is less satisfactory in that the ratio of public expenditure to the total national product varies considerably over time. Public expenditure is based for the most part on long-term social programs: more than 40 percent of total public expenditure in most countries. Public expenditure thus represents a larger part of the national product in recession years. As well, as Walter Eltis notes, "Social security support for the unemployed is actually higher in a recession, which accentuates the tendency for the public expenditure cycle to fluctuate counter-cyclically."[6] The Canadian public sector may therefore appear significantly smaller in relation to GDP once the recession has ended. On the other hand, GDP share as an indicator under-represents the presence of the public sector in that it does not touch on the impact of such non-spending instruments as lawmaking or regulation, nor on the mix of services that a particular state may provide, nor the efficiency with which they are provided. Which is only to say that such a measure does not show changes within what we have called the traditional public service bureaucracy, nor changes in emphasis between the role played by the traditional public service and the newer forms of public sector activity.

Karl Deutsch has compiled a list of points it would be helpful to know in order to assess the relative importance of the public side in a country; (the list also illustrates how the various indices could be misleading if one were to rely on any taken singly):[7]

1. the total social product of society, including unpaid work such as housework, and work of those who are being educated to take on social and economic (wealth-increasing) functions;
2. the total monetized or monetizable set of goods and services, i.e., the GNP and GDP. Roughly, they are calculated by taking whatever

appears on the market and adding an estimate for the market value of goods that are consumed at home. This is the basic denominator used to compare with the proportion of the country's wealth that is recouped by government as taxes;

3. the total weight/manoeuvrability of the government sector devoted to administrative, political and military uses. We are used to the idea of discretionary income as applied to individuals (income not taken up by basic needs and obligations, which people can choose to save or to spend). Governments also have, or lack, the capacity for discretionary spending. Deutsch points out that the larger the share of the government sector and the larger the GNP, the more resources the nation can potentially reallocate for politically chosen purposes;

4. general government revenues, or the aggregate of the central government, provincial government and local government revenues, as well as expenditures for all levels. Expenditures will generally exceed revenues, if only because of inflation and loans to other governments. One must also be aware that some data will be excluded routinely as definitions are chosen or changed for ideological reasons: to look smaller or bigger;

5. the revenues of public institutions, such as the post office, health services, financial intermediaries, and so on. Whenever a government wishes to look thin, it excludes data on such institutions from its general budget, and records only the net revenue or loss. But while market-oriented regimes traditionally exclude these agencies, socialist regimes not only include them but also include any existing co-operatives such as those formed by farmers or artists, so that the shared sector is inflated; and

6. the revenues of the nationalized industries (Crown corporations in Canada) such as railroad and other transportation facilities, the national energy corporations, telephone companies, and some mining industries.

The widest conception of the public sector is as an aggregate of general government, plus public institutions, plus the nationalized industries. John Kenneth Galbraith would add to this privately owned corporations that serve only governments as customers, for example, space industries or armaments manufacturers, that is the military-industrial complex.[8] This more inclusive total should probably be set against the whole social product, rather than only the monetized portion, because the investment that a state can afford to make in its future work force is an important indicator of its real wealth.

If one were in possession of all these facts about all countries, one could draw many firm conclusions about the relative size of governments, their efficiency and relative centralization, and their discretionary incomes. Unfortunately, comprehensive revenue and expenditure data are often unavailable, or are based on different definitions. Inflation makes time-series revenue and expenditure data dubious in even one country. In international comparisons the meaning of money can be quite volatile, especially because of fluctuating exchange rates. Not least, the kinds of activities that can be more or less accurately monetized vary from country to country, as do the activities that are counted as evidence of collectivization. Hence the comparative picture as presented in Tables 3-1 and 3-2 is about as precise as is feasible, but even that should be read as an approximation.

One need not measure with dollars, of course. One could also try to measure government activity in a society. Laws, regulations, standards, guidelines, programs, are all indicators of what many people mean by bureaucracy. They represent "red tape" or "the safety net" depending on the perspective of the observer. But, as Richard Rose observes:

> Laws are far less amenable to quantitative measurement than are other major resources of government. Whereas money is fungible and public employees in the same grade or with the same function can be interchangeable, laws are not. Each statute is unique in terms of its specific content, and the specific properties of public servants or particular sums of money. Moreover laws differ greatly from each other in terms of their impact upon other resources of government.[9]

His observation is equally true of regulations and individual public programs: the meaning of any one depends on its context as well as its scope.

Still another option is public sector employment data, though this may well be the least satisfactory measure of public sector domination for purposes of comparisons between nations. The extreme variability across nations of definitions of what an employee is, and changes in all jurisdictions over time, quickly render international comparisons all but impossible. But we have already roughly examined the general size of the public sector in Canada by comparing it to other nations in terms of the proportion of GDP extracted by the state for public purposes. Our need now is to describe the relative weights of the various aspects of the public sector inside Canada, and to do so using a unit that is less subject to inflation than the dollar, but more recognizable than units of activity such as laws or regulations.

Canadian Public Employment Data

Statistics Canada collects employment data on the public sector under the two main headings, "general government" and "government enterprises." Included in the sphere of general government are the core elements of the traditional public service, the departments and ministries, and the administrative and regulatory agencies that perform functions similar to those of departments. Generally, these agencies report to cabinet ministers. There are, however, several additional forms of organization that are also classified as general government. These are: 1) government-owned institutions engaged in education, health and welfare areas, or the administration of justice, e.g., correctional facilities, residences for the handicapped, etc. (exceptions will be noted in text below); 2) social insurance plans that cover all persons in a designated category, e.g., the Canada and Quebec Pension Plans, the provinces' workers' compensation plans, and the Quebec automobile insurance plan; 3) public service pension plans operated by the government, the monies of which are available to it for financing its operations; 4) other working capital funds that are used mainly to service government departments and agencies.

Government enterprises are what we more generally call Crown corporations. Statistics Canada sets out a number of conditions that must be met before an organization qualifies to be classified here:

- a majority of its ownership must be vested in government;
- management of its affairs must be relatively independent from government;
- its primary role must be to provide goods and/or services to the private sector, not to the government; and
- the prices it sets for these goods and/or services must reflect the costs of providing them.[10]

The Statistics Canada definitions are not an exact match with our own classification of the public sector into traditional, entrepreneurial and arm's-length, and control bureaucracies. Instead, in these statistics, our Public Service Bureaucracy I and II are rolled into one, as "general government." This is inconvenient, but it is not an insurmountable problem, since we do not claim that the new control bureaucracy's importance relates to its size. Rather, we have said that its very presence indicates a new constitutional philosophy about the need for accountability and the way to achieve it. In addition, there are some complexities to do with education and health sector employees. These we touched upon earlier as part of Bureaucracy II, while here they are counted separately so far as possible. (See Table 3-15 and following.) They are counted separately in order to maintain comparability of federal and provincial employment in general government and enterprise sectors.

An employee in the Statistics Canada universe is anyone on the government payroll (whether being paid for services or for paid absence) and who files for income tax purposes. In 1983 this represented approximately 580,000 employees. (See Figure 3-1.) Also included are persons who are on unpaid absence but remain on strength, for example, people taking leave or on strike. Persons who work with government on a contractual basis, either individually or under an umbrella arrangement such as those signed with temporary help agencies, are not counted.

FIGURE 3-1   Federal Government Employment Statistics
December 1983

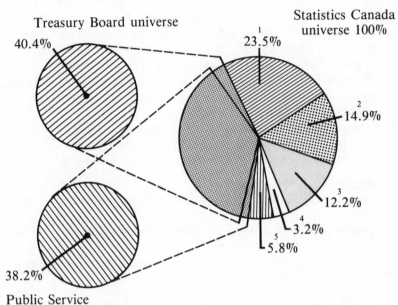

Treasury Board universe

40.4%

Statistics Canada
universe 100%

[1] 23.5%

[2] 14.9%

[3] 12.2%

[4] 3.2%

[5] 5.8%

38.2%

Public Service
Commission universe

Notes:

Statistics Canada universe:	580,731
Treasury Board:	234,866
Public Service Commission:	222,044
1 Government enterprise employees:	136,293
2 National Defence military personnel:	86,381
3 Canada Post employees:	70,829
4 Royal Canadian Mounted Police uniformed personnel:	18,603
5 Employees of other corporations and agencies for which Treasury Board is not the employer:	33,759
6 Federal public service work force for which Treasury Board is the employer (departments and agencies listed in schedule 1, part 1 of the Public Service Staff Relations Act):	234,866

Source: Canada, Public Service Commission, *Annual Report 1983* (Ottawa: Minister of Supply and Services Canada, 1984), pp. 50–51.

(This exclusion from the universe of employment is of some importance, since the "contract state" is, to some observers, not properly classified outside the public sector as private sector activity. Just as Galbraith wanted to classify the military-industrial complex as state activity, some writers believe that work generated by government, but executed by freelancers, should count as part of the public sector.)

Statistics Canada uses these definitions, so far as possible, across all levels of government. However, one must note that these definitions do not take into account differences in levels of service. A government that provides a function with proportionately fewer employees than another is not necessarily more efficient. It may be providing a lower level of service. Nor do the figures take into account the method of delivery. In some cases a service provided by a provincial government can be delivered in another region by a local government, or even involve a financial supplement paid to citizens to enable them to purchase the service elsewhere.

Let us now turn to general federal public employment data provided by Statistics Canada, and data on federal public sector employment universes reported by Treasury Board secretariat and the Public Service Commission. These organizations each report on different populations, a source of confusion when one attempts to compare data or do historical analyses.

Referring to Figure 3-1, the largest universe falls under Statistics Canada at 580,731 employees. The Treasury Board secretariat's universe totals 234,866, just ahead of the Public Service Commission's 222,044. In the simplest terms, the two smaller universes basically exclude the military, RCMP and Crown corporation employee populations, three groups which represent roughly 60 percent of the Statistics Canada universe. However, the simple becomes increasingly complex, as can be seen by the numerous notes to the tables in this chapter, when one identifies part-time and full-time, person-years or strength, Christmas and temporary help or any other tenure-related classification of the federal public service.

There are some caveats even for Statistics Canada's data. While figures for the federal public sector in total are accepted to be reliable, officials urge some caution in drawing conclusions from serial data on the regional distribution of federal public servants before 1970. Further, problems with describing the provincial public sectors are quite serious. Statistics Canada has collected data on numbers employed by provincial public sectors only since 1959, when it began rolling together the individual series of administrative data provided by the provinces (there are as many as 25 different data sources for some of the larger provinces). Reliability improved only after 1970, when Statistics Canada began aggregating payroll data. The gaps in provincial data provide a partial comment on federal-provincial co-operation: even though individuals can be required to provide information under this Statistics Act, there is no legal imperative that provinces must do so. Quebec began providing data only in the mid-1960s. British Columbia provided no data whatever on civil service employment between 1960 and 1978, and broke off data provision again between January 1983 and February 1984. In March 1984, it may be recalled, the B.C. government claimed to have reduced provincial public sector employment by a quarter during the previous year, a claim few were in a position to evaluate because of the lack of reliable data.[11] Finally, the employment picture for local governments is not studied in an energetic or exhaustive way since Statistics Canada collects and publishes only what data are sent to it.

With such problems, it is not surprising that few analysts attempt to draw out the implications of the scope of government activity. Indeed, the series on public sector employment to 1978 developed for the Institute for Research in Public Policy (IRPP) by Bird, Foot, and Bucovetsky is the only recent serious study in this country, in that it goes well beyond data in Statistics Canada publications.[12] The picture to be presented in this chapter is brought up to December 1982 in most of the tables and analyses.

Federal Government Employment

Table 3-3 shows the number of employees reported against the Statistics Canada universe on strength in all aspects of federal government employment in the month of December in each of the selected years between 1960 and 1982.[13] The table shows that while federal general government employment increased over the 22-year period, the growth in personnel was largely concentrated in the decade 1965 to 1975, and especially so between 1970 and 1975. Federal general government employment grew by roughly one-third in those five years. The federal government's employment in enterprises grew later, enjoying its fastest growth from 1975 to 1980. Federal enterprise employment grew more modestly overall than did federal general government. In fact, enterprises lose ground as a proportion of total federal government employment during the 22 years for which we have figures. This is an interesting observation, because we will see that the non-traditional forms of government (Public Service Bureaucracy II) are where growth is concentrated. It means that the federal part of the public sector is growing less than provincial public sector employment, and that, in comparison, the federal public sector remains a traditional bureaucracy in comparison to provincial public sectors, where the enterprise forms of government are growing most rapidly.

Table 3-4 shows the population figures for the whole of Canada for the selected years. (Note also that Table 3-10 provides provincial figures.) Canada's population did not grow as quickly between 1970 and 1975 as

TABLE 3-3 Federal Government Employment 1960–82: Number of Employees as at December

Year	General Govt.[a]	Percent Change	Govt. Enterprises	Percent Change	Total	Percent Change	General Govt. Percent of Total	Govt. Enterprises Percent of Total
1960	205,360		131,118		336,478		61.0	39.0
1965	214,799	4.6	129,916	– .9	344,715	2.4	62.2	37.8
1970	254,993	13.1	123,906	–4.5	378,899	6.5	67.1	32.9
1975	328,580	34.4	132,046	6.5	460,626	24.9	71.3	28.7
1980	340,305	4.2	157,988	19.6	498,293	8.6	68.2	31.8
1982[b]	355,403		138,281		493,684		72.0	28.0

Source: Statistics Canada, Federal Government Employment, cat. no.72–044 (Ottawa: Statistics Canada, 1960–82).
a. Excludes members of the Canadian armed forces and post office Christmas help.
b. Percent change is not calculated because it is a two-year period only.

did federal government employment. Thus, one can say that the federal government did not grow merely incrementally, as growth in population alone would warrant, from 1960 to 1982 (assuming that the federal government was the "right size" in 1960): while total population in 1982 was 39 percent higher than it had been in 1960, the total federal government employment had increased by almost 47 percent. It may be that the federal government was belatedly addressing the situation presented to it by the contemporary international economy.

However, the whole population is neither the only nor the best possible denominator to measure the extent of government employment. Some groups, such as the young and the old, are not potential employees of either the private or the public sector, so their inclusion in the assessment figure would effectively minimize public sector employment. On the other hand, to use only actively employed persons as a denominator magnifies the public sector's comparative share of the work force during a recession (because jobs in the private sector are more volatile during a downturn), making it appear that governments are actually quickly adding to their strengths, when in fact they are simply not shedding jobs at the same rate. We have chosen to use the more stable series, the numbers of persons available for work (although this indicator is less than perfect), to show the comparative size of the public sector's employment.

Table 3-5 shows the total size of the Canadian labour force for the selected years, plus a breakdown into male and female. The labour force grew more rapidly between 1960 and 1980 than the population of the country as a whole, particularly in female employment. For example, while the total population increased by less than 5 percent between 1975 and 1980 (Table 3-4), the labour force grew by 16 percent, with women

TABLE 3-4 National Population, Federal Government Employment

Year	Estimated Population	Percent Change	General[a] Govt.	Govt. Enterprises	Total	Percent Change
1960	17,483,000		205,360	131,118	336,478	
1965	19,644,000	12.3	214,799	129,916	344,715	2.4
1970	21,297,000	8.4	254,993	123,906	378,899	6.5
1975	22,697,100	6.5	328,580	132,046	460,626	24.9
1980	23,747,300	4.6	340,305	157,988	498,293	8.6
1982[b]	24,341,700		355,403	138,281	493,684	
1960–82 Percent Change	39.2		73.1	5.4	46.7	

Sources: Statistics Canada, Compendium of Statistics, prepared for the Royal Commission on the Economic Union and Development Prospects for Canada (Ottawa: Statistics Canada, February 1984, draft edition), Table 1-4; and Federal Government Employment, cat. no.72–004 (Ottawa: Statistics Canada, 1960–82).
a. Excludes members of the Canadian armed forces and post office Christmas help.
b. Percent change for 1982 not calculated because it is a two-year period.

taking a larger share of total employment in 1980 than in 1975 (40 percent, up from 35 percent). The growth of the labour force over the 22-year period is 83 percent, compared to the government's growth at 47 percent. (See Appendix A-5 for details of women's participation rate in the labour force and Appendix C for more on women's employment in the federal general government sector.)

A look at Canada together with a few other countries may be useful here. Table 3-6, compiled by Statistics Canada from OECD data, shows the percentage of the population that is of working age for the years 1960 and 1980, as well as the actual annual growth of the labour force between 1960 to 1970, 1970 to 1980, and the estimated growth for the period 1980 to the year 2000. Canada clearly experienced a relatively large addition to the work-force age group during that initial 20 years: in 1960 fewer than 60 percent of Canadians were in their working years, while in 1980 the proportion was closer to 70 percent. Given this great increase in the work-force age group, it is no surprise that the labour force in this country has grown annually more than in most other industrial economies, with the exception of the two other developed former dominions, New Zealand and Australia.

Let us now move from an international perspective to some interprovincial comparisons. It is interesting to distribute the federal government's employment across the country (Table 3-7) to see whether some provinces benefit disproportionately from federally provided jobs. One would expect to see the combined effect of at least four main factors, two which are centralizing and two which are decentralizing in their impact.

First, by its nature as a national government in a federal system, the federal government's employment is concentrated at headquarters, in planning, co-ordinating and negotiating, as well as running the transfer and regulation programs. Table 3-11 shows quite clearly that approximately 26 percent of the federal public service is located in Ottawa-Hull. Nor is there much leeway for the federal government to decentralize its more entrepreneurial empire. Crown corporations are by definition autonomous bodies that respond to market forces rather than to government's social policy goals. They locate where it is economic to do so, or where the industry is historically situated, and thus they do not have much redistributive effect.

Secondly, the Canadian government has long been committed to a policy of fairness in service to individual citizens, regardless of a person's province of residence. It should follow that public servants are distributed in the same pattern as the nation's population: concentrated in population centres and sparse in rural areas. If the population factor alone operated, one would expect to see federal public servants and enterprise employees resident in each province representing exactly the same fraction of total federal employment as that province's population represented of total national population.

TABLE 3-5 Canadian Labour Force: Male and Female (000s)

Year	Male	Female	Percent Female	Total[a]	Percent Change
1960	4,711	1,719	26.7	6,430	
1965	5,046	2,139	29.8	7,185	11.7
1970	5,631	2,698	32.4	8,329	15.9
1975	6,417	3,505	35.3	9,923	19.1
1980	6,909	4,613	40.0	11,522	16.1
1982	6,867	4,876	41.5	11,743[b]	

Source: Statistics Canada, *Labour Force Surveys,* cat. no. 71–001 (Ottawa: Statistics Canada, 1960–82).

a. The 1960, 1965, 1970, and 1975 totals included persons 14 years of age and older. The 1980 and 1982 totals include only persons 15 years of age and older. This should not affect the male and female breakdown, although it will cause a slight under-representation of total labour force growth.

b. Total growth over 22-year period is 5.3 million persons: an 82.6% increase. The labour force is composed of persons who are either employed or unemployed in the reference week. An unemployed person who is nonetheless a bona fide member of the labour force is someone who has looked for work in the previous four weeks, or who was on layoff status, or who had a new job to start in four weeks or less.

As an example of a service that should be delivered to the same standard across the country, and thus where staff should be distributed in the same way as concentrations of the population, we present Table 3-8 for post office personnel. In 1982, Table 3-8 shows that each province has the post office personnel that its population earns (see Table 3-10), with only a slight disproportionate concentration in Ontario.

However, not all the federal government's services and programs are applicable to all regions of the country, nor are individual citizens who make use of federal services necessarily proportionately divided among provinces. Programs to assist the less-developed regions will naturally be concentrated where they are needed. Hence, a third factor to affect the distribution of federal public servants across provinces is the federal government's commitment to an active policy of equalization. While this has primarily involved direct programs of assistance to private firms to locate in the poorer regions, one can also regard public sector employment in itself as a form of wealth that the government has in its power to distribute. As a result, one might expect to see federal employment deliberately located disproportionately in the poorest regions: the relocating of Veterans' Affairs to Charlottetown in Prince Edward Island is an example of such decentralization.

The location of National Defence bases is an example of how the federal government could in theory benefit an area. It has some discretion as to where the military personnel (excluding headquarters) will be located, and arguably could use that leeway to benefit poorer provinces. Table 3-9, showing the number of DND military personnel by province, presents a quite different pattern than did Table 3-8, for the post office.

The table indicates that Nova Scotia is a winner in terms of military stationed there (perhaps because of the Canadian commitment to NATO, British Columbia, on the opposite coast is not so favoured), and New Brunswick has slightly more military posted there than is proportionate for its share of the Canadian population. Quebec is disproportionately light on numbers of military personnel, presumably because they are predominantly English-speaking. Thus one can discern some slight redistributive effect, possibly mingled with some historical-cum-political influences.

Fourthly, when compared to the provinces, the federal government does not deliver very many labour-intensive services directly to the public. The Canada Employment and Immigration Commission, the Correctional Service of Canada and the Royal Canadian Mounted Police are examples of the handful of labour-intensive federal responsibilities. Most of the federal programs that involve a transaction between government and the individual citizen tend, instead, to be simple transfer programs. These are, by their nature, cheque-writing programs that are easily centralized. Table 3-7, Federal Government Employment: Employees by Province, distributes federal general government employment across the provinces for each of the selected years, with enterprise employment being available by province only from 1975. This table can be read in the light of Table 3-10, showing distribution of population by province. A companion table (A-1) shows percentage growth rates for population and labour force by province back to 1960. We will work with post-1975 figures, however, as many values before that year could only be estimated.

Containing 36 percent of the total Canadian population in 1975, Ontario had about 41 percent of all employment that the federal government offered. But with close to 35 percent of the total Canadian population in 1982, the province had dropped to less than 38 percent of the jobs that the federal government provides. This trend is compatible with a slight drop in Ontario's share of the labour force as of 1982, when it seemed to be levelling out at about 38 percent of the Canadian total. A review of the other provinces' standings in these two tables shows that Alberta and British Columbia have been steadily increasing their shares of population and were experiencing (at least until 1982) a comparable increase in their share of total federal government employment: 6 and 8.2 percent respectively in 1975, and 7 and 8.6 percent in 1982. The population share decreases in Newfoundland, Nova Scotia, Quebec, Ontario and Manitoba have been accompanied by similar declines in labour-force share and federal government employment share, with the exception of Quebec, where the share of federal employment increased from just under 20 percent in 1975 to nearly 23 percent in 1982. The remaining provinces, Prince Edward Island, New Brunswick and Saskatchewan, appear to have remained more stable during the period.

TABLE 3-6 Distribution of Labour Force in Industrial Market Economies

| | Percentage of Population Working Age (15–64 Years) | | Percentage of Labour Force In: | | | | | | Percentage of Average Annual Growth of Labour Force | | |
| | | | Agriculture | | Industry | | Services | | | | |
	1960	1980	1960	1980	1960	1980	1960	1980	1960–70	1970–80	1980–2000
Industrial Market Economies											
101 Ireland	58	58	36	19	25	37	39	44	(.)	1.0	1.6
102 Spain	64	63	42	15	31	40	27	45	0.2	1.2	0.9
103 Italy	66	65	31	11	40	45	29	44	-0.1	0.7	0.4
104 New Zealand	59	63	15	9	37	35	48	56	2.2	2.1	1.2
105 United Kingdom	65	64	4	2	48	42	48	56	0.6	0.3	0.4
106 Finland	62	68	36	11	31	35	33	54	0.4	0.1	0.4
107 Australia	61	65	11	6	40	33	49	61	2.6	1.8	0.9
108 Japan	64	68	33	12	30	39	37	49	1.9	1.3	0.7
109 Canada	59	67	13	5	35	29	52	66	2.6	2.0	0.9
110 Austria	66	64	24	9	46	37	30	54	-0.6	0.8	0.4
111 United States	60	66	7	2	36	32	57	66	1.8	1.5	0.9
112 Netherlands	61	66	11	6	42	45	47	49	1.6	1.3	0.5
113 France	62	64	22	8	39	39	39	53	0.6	1.1	0.6
114 Belgium	65	65	8	3	48	41	44	56	0.3	0.7	0.3
115 Norway	63	63	20	7	37	37	43	56	0.5	0.7	0.6

116 Denmark	64	65	18	7	37	35	45	58	1.1	0.6	0.4
117 Sweden	66	64	14	5	45	34	41	61	1.0	0.3	0.2
118 West Germany	68	66	14	4	48	46	38	50	0.2	0.7	(.)
119 Switzerland	66	67	11	5	50	46	39	49	2.0	0.4	0.2
Nonmarket Industrial Economies											
120 Poland	61	66	48	31	29	39	23	30	1.8	1.4	0.8
121 Bulgaria	66	66	57	37	25	39	18	24	0.7	0.3	0.3
122 Hungary	66	66	38	15	35	53	27	32	0.5	0.4	0.2
123 U.S.S.R.	63	66	42	14	29	45	29	41	0.7	1.2	0.7
124 Czechoslovakia	64	64	26	11	46	48	28	41	0.9	0.8	0.7
125 East Germany	65	64	18	10	48	50	34	40	-0.2	0.5	0.3

Source: Statistics Canada, *Compendium of Statistics*, prepared for the Royal Commission on the Economic Union and Development Prospects for Canada (Ottawa: Statistics Canada, February 1984, draft edition), Table 19-12.

TABLE 3-7 Federal Government Employment 1960–82: Distribution by Province as at December

	Nfld.	P.E.I.	N.S.	N.B.	Que.	Ont.	Man.	Sask.	Alta.	B.C.	Yukon	N.W.T.	Outside Canada	Total
1960														
General Govt.[a]	4,318	1,343	14,217	7,412	32,704	89,397	10,624	6,585	13,515	19,917		2,815	2,513	205,360
Enterprises[b]													—	131,118
1965														
General Govt.[b]	4,321	1,311	14,087	7,231	34,748	95,834	10,877	6,759	12,663	20,806		2,665	3,497	214,799
Enterprises[b]													—	129,916
1970														
General Govt.[b]	4,461	1,313	19,311	7,796	41,148	112,710	12,316	8,765	15,043	25,590	934	1,856	3,750	254,993
Enterprises[b]													—	123,993
1975														
General Govt.	6,768	1,662	21,765	9,060	55,178	151,019	14,411	10,633	19,888	30,544	1,242	1,681	4,729	328,580
Enterprises	5,735	885	5,138	6,997	36,449	36,538	12,419	4,374	7,420	7,385	259	632	7,815	132,046
1980														
General Govt.	7,581	1,818	22,622	10,039	69,335	140,437	15,496	11,624	20,885	32,729	1,294	2,000	4,445	340,305
Enterprises	4,671	855	5,121	7,299	45,248	47,081	13,350	4,541	11,401	8,504	458	469	8,990	157,988
1982														
General Govt.	8,973	2,082	22,445	10,087	71,263	147,875	15,443	11,257	22,360	34,157	1,299	2,043	6,119	355,403
Enterprises	4,159	828	4,031	6,210	41,480	38,345	12,005	3,491	12,013	8,205	460	586	6,468	138,281
Percentage Change														
General Govt. 1960–82	107	55	58	36	118	65	45	71	65	75	—	—	—	73
General Govt. and Enterprises Total 1975–82	5	14	1.5	1.5	23	1	2	2	26	12	—	—	—	47

Source: Statistics Canada, *Federal Government Employment*, cat. no. 72-004 (Ottawa: Statistics Canada, 1960–82).
a. Excludes members of the Canadian armed forces and post office Christmas help.
b. Provincial breakdown not available.

TABLE 3-8 Post Office Employment by Province

	Nfld.	P.E.I.	N.S.	N.B.	Que.	Ont.	Man.	Sask.	Alta.	B.C.	Yukon	N.W.T.	Total
1970	577	129	1,306	948	11,592	17,253	2,097	1,718	2,969	4,515	28	26	43,158
Percent of Total	1.3	0.3	3.0	2.2	26.9	39.9	4.8	4.0	6.9	10.5	0.06	0.06	
1975	1,207	174	1,835	1,342	14,699	23,991	2,553	2,283	4,466	6,584	81	21	59,236
Percent of Total	2.0	0.3	3.0	2.2	24.8	40.5	4.3	3.9	7.5	11.1	0.13	0.03	
1980	1,423	211	2,244	1,635	17,876	26,693	2,694	2,547	5,491	7,380	97	23	68,314
Percent of Total	2.0	0.3	3.3	2.4	26.2	39.1	3.9	3.7	8.0	10.8	0.14	0.03	

Source: Statistics Canada, "Statistical Papers: Public Finance Division," unpublished.
Note: Excludes Christmas help.

TABLE 3-9 Canadian Armed Forces Employment by Province

	Nfld.	P.E.I.	N.S.	N.B.	Que.	Ont.	Man.	Sask.	Alta.	B.C.	Yukon	N.W.T.	Outside Canada	Total
1970	470	1,114	13,678	4,948	11,289	26,237	5,656	1,677	8,308	7,976	0	0	8,885	90,235
Percent of total	0.5	1.2	15.0	5.5	12.5	29.0	6.0	1.9	9.2	8.8	—	—	9.8	
1975	721	1,086	11,488	3,787	8,493	22,588	3,621	1,601	7,463	7,463	8	563	10,347	79,229
Percent of total	0.9	1.3	14.5	4.8	10.7	28.5	4.6	2.0	9.4	9.4	—	0.7	13.0	
1980	851	893	12,663	4,105	10,659	23,186	3,745	1,633	7,127	8,414	6	482	7,427	81,190
Percent of total	1.0	1.1	15.5	5.0	13.0	28.5	4.6	2.0	8.7	10.0	—	0.6	9.0	
1982	840	911	12,127	4,372	10,792	24,155	3,732	1,616	7,449	8,822	6	499	7,567	82,888
Percent of total	1.0	1.1	14.6	5.0	13.0	29.0	4.5	1.9	8.9	10.6	—	0.6	9.0	

Source: Statistics Canada, "Statistical Papers: Public Finance Division" (Ottawa: Statistics Canada, CANSIM).

TABLE 3-10 Breakdown of Total Population and Labour Force
         by Province

	Nfld.	P.E.I.	N.S.	N.B.	Que.	Ont.	Man.	Sask.	Alta.	B.C.
1975										
Population	2.4	0.5	3.6	2.9	27.2	36.0	4.5	4.0	7.8	10.7
Labour Force	1.9	0.45	3.0	2.6	27.0	38.3	4.2	3.7	7.7	11.2
1980										
Population	2.4	0.5	3.5	2.9	26.7	35.8	4.3	4.0	8.6	10.9
Labour Force	1.8	0.43	3.1	2.4	25.5	37.6	4.2	3.8	9.5	11.1
1982										
Population	2.3	0.5	3.5	2.9	26.4	35.4	4.2	4.0	9.2	11.3
Labour Force	1.8	0.44	3.1	2.4	24.7	38.1	4.2	3.9	10.0	11.4
1983										
Population	2.3	0.5	3.5	2.8	26.3	35.4	4.2	4.0	9.4	11.3
Labour Force	1.7	0.45	3.1	2.4	25.0	38.1	4.2	3.9	9.9	11.2

Sources: Statistics Canada, *Labour Force Survey*, cat. no. 71–001 (Ottawa: Statistics Canada, 1975–83); and *Compendium of Statistics*, prepared for the Royal Commission on the Economic Union and Development Prospects for Canada (Ottawa: Statistics Canada, February 1984, draft edition), Table 1-4.

A slightly different picture emerges when examining the PSEA universe. Table 3-11 shows the Public Service Commission's geographic distribution of employees under the Public Service Employment Act (excluding military, RCMP and Crown corporations) for the years 1960, 1965, 1967, 1970, 1975, 1980 and 1982. The Public Service Commission, unlike Statistics Canada, has a separate classification for employees who work in the national capital region as well as the provincial breakdown. It is seen that employment in this region has dropped during the period 1960–83 from 26.7 percent to 25.9 percent, which may reflect the decentralization of some public service activities to the regions. Clearly, the areas that are benefiting the most are Newfoundland, Nova Scotia, Quebec and the western provinces, excepting Manitoba. Overall, it seems fair to say that federal employment under the PSEA in all provinces has remained markedly stable since 1960 with really only one loser — Ontario.

Thus, the data suggest that: 1) the federal government's recent efforts to decentralize its employment have, to 1982 at least, had some small effect on employment under the PSEA;[14] 2) Newfoundland is the only consistent winner since 1960 in terms of increasing its share of federal employment under the PSEA; 3) the broader universe covered by Statistics Canada (Table 3-7) shows Quebec, Newfoundland and British Columbia as having received above average increases since 1960 in federal general government employment, but since 1975 the winners have been Alberta and Quebec, with Saskatchewan, Ontario and Nova Scotia experiencing some loss in their share of federal government

TABLE 3-11 Percentage Distribution of Federal Public Servants Under the PSEA[a]

	Nfld.	P.E.I.	N.S.	N.B.	Que.	Ont.	Man.	Sask.	Alta.	B.C.	Yukon	N.W.T.	Outside Canada	Nat.Cap. Region
1960	1.7	.5	5.1	3.5	16.2	22.3	5.0	2.6	5.9	9.3	.3	.4	.6	26.7
1965	1.7	.5	5.0	3.4	16.4	19.6	4.9	2.5	5.7	9.1	.3	.4	.8	26.9
1967	1.7	.5	5.0	3.2	16.5	21.2	4.8	2.6	5.7	9.1	.3	.4	1.1	27.9
1970	1.8	.6	6.2	3.3	17.1	20.7	4.9	3.3	6.2	10.0	.4	.6	.7	24.9
1975	1.9	.5	6.1	2.9	18.0	18.9	4.3	2.7	6.2	9.5	.3	.6	.8	27.2
1980	2.2	.6	5.8	3.1	17.0	20.6	4.4	2.9	6.2	9.7	.4	.6	.6	25.9
1982[b]	2.3	.6	5.6	3.1	17.0	20.6	4.5	2.9	6.4	9.6	.4	.5	.6	25.9
1983[b]	2.3	.7	5.6	3.1	17.0	20.6	4.3	2.9	6.4	9.6	.4	.5	.6	25.9

Source: Canada, Public Service Commission, Annual Reports (Ottawa: Minister of Supply and Services Canada, 1960–83).
a. Excludes employees in Crown corporations and National Defence military personnel.
b. Post office has been included in 1982 and 1983 figures for purposes of comparison even though it was made a Crown corporation in 1981 and no longer comes under the PSEA.

employment. One can also conclude that considerable economies of scale are realized in administering the federal government's programs to the two most populous provinces.

Broad Functions Performed by Federal Public Servants

What are the main goals of the work performed by federal public servants? Statistics Canada classifies general government employees by the main function of government in which they work. With some adjustments, one can make these categories roughly comparable over the selected years. It is to be noted that the functions cut across both departments and occupational categories: they take the broadest goals of government and count under them only the employees whose work is directed to that purpose. For example, although one thinks of the Department of Justice as one entity, its strength will be partitioned among several functions. Government lawyers provide legal advice to the Crown and to departments, hence are classified under "services," while other personnel are concerned with the courts, which places them under "protection."

The human resources devoted to a function are only a rough indication of government's long-term priorities, however. The detailed classifications are filled with apparent anomalies (the Cape Breton Development Corporation is counted under "trade and industry" instead of "regional planning and development," for example), and there have been many shifts down the years as existing programs are reclassified to fit under an emerging functional heading such as "environment" or "regional industrial expansion." A description which gives the dominant flavour of the main functions is provided below:

General Services is a category incorporating public servants who perform a support or administrative function for the central managers of government and for the Governor General, Parliament, and the secretaries to cabinet. Hence the personnel who articulate and implement fiscal and budgetary decisions for the whole of government, the managers and deliverers of central services to the whole of government (such as those in supply and services, and the lawyers who provide legal services to departments and general government, and translation services), some central accounting and auditing, and some central research capacity is counted here.

Protection of Persons and Property includes, most obviously, the Department of National Defence (the armed forces are counted separately), the courts of law and the budget for the Department of Justice, the costs of running the penitentiaries (not prisons, which are in provincial jurisdiction) and parole services, and policing (including the RCMP forces leased to provinces that do not have their own police forces). Also here are the costs of administering regulatory measures for business, industry, and economic development, energy, agriculture and, in addition, the "rights-protection" industry that includes consumer affairs, women's concerns, official languages and legal and human rights.

All forms of transportation — air, road, rail and water — are in the function Transportation and Communications, as are telecommunications and the postal services.

Health, it will be remembered, is for the most part in the provincial jurisdiction. In the federal setting, it is a smaller function, reflecting the budget of the co-ordinating and research department, National Health and Welfare, the direct health services that the federal government does provide in the north, and to its own employees, the regulatory activities of the Health Protection Branch plus some preventive services including immunization. Social Services includes veterans' benefits, pensions, unemployment insurance excluding the costs of its administration, social welfare — the welfare half of NHW and the costs of the grants to the provinces to pay for individual welfare and the Department of Northern and Indian Affairs (except for education) — plus administrative costs for the Ministry that served as a secretariat to the committee of cabinet for social development and departments that administer Solicitor General, Correctional Services, and the National Parole Board.

Education, like health, is an area that predominantly belongs in the provincial jurisdiction. The federal part of the function is relatively minor in proportional terms. It includes the post-secondary education support program (the policy-making body, the Secretary of State), elementary and secondary education for native peoples, and the research councils that give grants in support of continuing higher education for individuals.

Grouped under Resource Conservation and Industrial Development are programs and administration in the fields of agriculture, fish and game, forests, mines, oil and gas, tourism, trade and industry (administration for the Department of Consumer and Corporate Affairs, the former Ministry of State for Economic Development, and the Department of Regional Industrial Expansion).

Environment, a relatively new function, includes employees working on pollution control, in departmental administration, and in conservation efforts in general.

Recreation and culture incorporates the employees (working in the Department of Environment) who administer the national parks, and the more numerous employees of the heterogeneous collection of cultural programs and agencies that make up the federal presence in the area: for example, the Arts and Culture program of the Department of Communications, the National Film Board, the Canadian Film Development Corporation, Museums, Archives, and even battlefields commissions, fitness and sports programs and programs supporting ethnic groups.

Labour and Employment and Immigration is just that: the Department of Employment and Immigration, the administration of the employment and unemployment insurance program, the Department of Labour, the Immigration Commission and Appeal Board, and the citizenship program of Secretary of State.

Foreign Affairs and International Assistance is another comparatively neat category. It includes the Department of External Affairs, the Canadian

International Development Agency, the International Development Research Centre, and the International Joint Commission that oversees administration of the Canada–U.S. boundary and adjoining waters.

Regional Planning and Development is a kind of residual category of the larger Resource Conservation and Industrial Development that is aimed specifically at assisting the less advantaged regions, or administering the federal presence wherever it provides a direct service. Here then are the Department of Public Works, the National Capital Commission which oversees the federal government's physical presence and contribution to the Ottawa-Hull area, the Department of Regional Industrial Expansion, and administration for the Atlantic Development Council and the Prairie Farm Rehabilitation Administration.

The final category, Research Establishments, includes employees working in such organizations as the Department of Energy, Mines and Resources, Atomic Energy Control Board, and in the research councils falling under the Ministry of State for Science and Technology.[15]

Table 3-12 gives the number of the federal government's employees by their function as of December of the selected years, plus the relative share of total federal government employment that that function represents for a given year, and finally, the percentage growth of that function over the previous five-year period. Thus we can see, by the final figure, the proportional amount of general government growth that each function has contributed; by the second figure, we can see whether or not a function is gaining proportionately on the other functions.

The three dominant categories of employment for federal personnel are general government, protection, and transportation and communications. General government comes close to one-fifth of employees by 1982, protection currently uses one-fifth of employees, and transportation and communications accounts for more than one-quarter. All the other functions are minor in comparison, although social services and resource conservation are the biggest of that group. Given that general government, protection, and transport functions are the most populous, it makes sense that expansion in these areas would account for the surge of growth experienced in federal employment before 1975. This is indeed the case: general services increased by nearly one-third between 1965 and 1970, protection leapt from 23 percent in 1970 to 1975, and transport and communications had rapid and steady growth from 1960 to 1975. Some of the other functions also grew fairly rapidly at some points, for example, health and social services, until 1975 (when they actually begin to shrink), foreign affairs, and regional planning (representing the establishment of DREE). But these areas are minor employers in comparison to the weight of the big three. Relative emphases among the largest functions are also interesting over time: one sees that general services have grown slowly but steadily, that protection was overwhelmingly the big service of the federal government in 1960 at a full one-third of the

TABLE 3-12 Federal Government Employment by Function[a]

	1960	1965	1970	1975	1980	1982[b]
General Services	33,276	35,204	46,755	62,561	64,028	66,956
% of Total	16.1	16.3	18.5	19.1	18.8	18.8
% Change	—	5.8	32.8	33.8	2.3	—
Protection of Persons	65,064	61,319	57,833	71,025	74,267	75,950
% of Total	32.2	29.3	23.6	21.7	21.8	21.4
% Change	—	-5.7	-5.7	22.8	4.6	—
Transportation and Communication	39,710	45,222	62,608	85,256	92,615	94,670
% of Total	19.8	21.7	25.8	25.9	27.2	26.6
% Change	—	13.9	38.0	36.0	8.6	—
Health	3,401	4,183	5,444	6,780	6,601	6,571
% of Total	1.7	2.0	2.2	2.1	1.9	1.8
% Change	—	22.9	30.0	24.5	-2.6	—
Social Services	15,308	16,207	17,623	24,970	19,108	21,915
% of Total	7.6	7.8	7.3	7.6	5.6	6.2
% Change	—	5.9	8.7	41.7	-29.7	—
Education	2,062	1,922	1,634	3,078	2,406	2,263
% of Total	1.0	0.9	0.7	0.9	0.7	0.6
% Change	—	-6.8	-14.9	88.4	-21.8	—
Resource Conservation and Industrial Development	17,192	19,430	24,726	25,576	28,089	30,254
% of Total	8.6	9.3	8.5	7.8	8.2	8.5
% Change	—	13.0	27.3	3.4	9.8	—

Environment	—	—	—	8,631	6,688	7,168
% of Total	—	—	—	2.6	2.0	2.0
% Change	—	—	—	—	-22.5	—
Recreation and Culture	4,160	5,036	4,299	8,004	8,520	8,801
% of Total	2.1	1.9	1.8	2.5	2.5	2.5
% Change	—	21.0	-14.6	86.2	6.4	—
Labour, Employment and Immigration	14,606	13,431	16,610	14,803	17,810	17,702
% of Total	7.2	6.6	6.8	4.5	5.2	5.0
% Change	—	-8.0	23.7	-10.9	20.3	—
Foreign Affairs and International Assistance	2,175	2,796	3,744	6,162	6,324	8,891
% of Total	1.1	1.3	1.5	1.9	1.9	2.5
% Change	—	28.6	33.9	64.6	2.6	—
Regional Planning and Development	550	580	3,159	3,253	3,059	3,083
% of Total	0.3	0.3	0.9	1.0	0.9	0.9
% Change	—	5.5	444.4	3.0	-5.9	—
Research Establishments	7,856	9,469	10,558	8,481	10,790	11,179
% of Total	2.5	2.8	2.4	2.5	3.2	3.1
% Change	—	20.5	11.5	19.7	27.2	—
Total	205,360c	214,799c	254,993c	328,580d	340,305	355,403
Percent of Change	—	4.6	18.7	28.9	3.6	—

TABLE 3-12 (Cont'd)

Source: Statistics Canada, Federal Government Employment, cat. no. 72-004 (Ottawa: Statistics Canada, 1960–82).

Notes: A. Functional classifications for the years 1960–75 were changed, when necessary, to reflect the classifications in the current Federal Government Employment Catalogue.

    1. 1960–70 "General Gov't," and 1975 "General Gov't Services" were renamed "General Services."

    2. 1960–75 "Social Welfare" has been changed to "Social Services."

    3. a) 1960–70 "Natural Resources and Primary Industries", 1960–70 "Trade and Industrial Development," and "Public Service and Trading Enterprises" in 1960 and 1965 were combined to form "Resource Conservation and Industrial Development."

       b) 1975 "Natural Resources" and "Agriculture, Trade and Industry and Tourism" were combined to form "Resource Conservation and Industrial Development."

    4. "Labour" and "National Employment Services" were taken out of "Social Welfare" and "Immigration and Citizenship" was taken out of "Other" and placed into "Labour, Employment and Immigration" for 1960–70.

    5. "Post Office" was taken from "Other" and placed in "Transportation and Communicatons" for 1960–70.

    6. "Civil Defence" was taken from "Other" for 1960 and 1965, as was "Defence Services" for 1960–70. They were both placed in "Protection of Persons and Property."

    7. "Veterans' Pensions and other Benefits" for 1960–70 was placed into "Social Services."

    8. "External Affairs" and "International Co-operation and Assistance" for 1960–65, and "International Co-operation and Assistance" for 1970 were renamed "Foreign Affairs and International Assistance."

    9. "Supervision and Development of Regions and Localities" was changed to "Regional Planning and Development."

  B. Adjustments were also made, where possible, to reflect the changes in the way organizations have been classified into different functions.

a. Statistics are reported at December each year. They exclude members of the Canadian armed forces and post office Christmas help.

b. Percent change to 1982 not calculated because it is a two-year period.

c. Excludes Governor General, lt. governors general and judges. Totals for 1960 and 1965 exclude employees paid from postal revenues.

d. Excludes field parties of mines and technical surveys (EMR).

personnel complement, and that it has been overtaken in the 22 years since then by transport and communication.

We can then characterize federal government employment: nearly seven out of every ten employees are working in one of three main functions. Federal government employment is mainly to provide national communication linkages, co-ordination of levels of government and its own services, and domestic law and order.

The more detailed picture of employee strength in the major federal government departments between 1960 and 1982 shown in the Statistics Canada universe (Appendix Table A-2) confirms the portrait of federal government employment that is presented in the distribution over functions. The Ministry of Transport shows big gains during the period; the two departments, of Communications, and Consumer and Corporate Affairs, which were established in 1969 and 1967 respectively, show quite steady gains, the environmental functions are established, the protection agencies of Corrections and RCMP show overall gains, and the Department of National Defence's military operations actually decrease.

Interestingly, Parliament as an organization shows astonishing gains: support personnel increased by 21 percent from 1960 to 1965, by 26 percent from 1965 to 1970, by 121 percent in the next five-year period, and by about 25 percent from 1975 to 1980. One can note, too, that the period since 1970 sees considerable growth in most of the watchdog agencies. It is to be noted that the largest of the type, the Office of the Auditor General, increased at rates of 47 percent from 1960 to 1965, 23 percent in the next five years, 50 percent in the period 1970 to 1975 when it was anticipating the new legislation which enlarged its mandate, and 34 percent in the period 1975 to 1980. If one breaks these rates down to per annum terms, it is seen that growth was still rapid, at 8 percent per annum, in the last two years we have measured. These rates of growth do not, of course, reveal the size of the contract work force, nor the amount of labour that is displaced onto departments.

Occupational Categories of Federal Public Servants

Statistics Canada also classifies federal public servants into major occupational categories which are quite different from the functional categories: a person working in the protection area, for example, can be in any of the occupational categories depending on what he or she is doing, from patrolling in a police car (operational), to heading up a division in headquarters (executive), to typing (administrative support) and so forth. Changes in the relative weights of the various occupational categories for the 12 years for which data are available (1970 to 1982) may reveal whether the federal government's work force is reflecting trends in the modern work force in general: less need for clerks as technology speeds processing, but more need for technical and management experts as computer technology and systems replace old manual systems for financial control and text production. The relative importance of the various categories will also show the extent to which employment of experts and professionals is significant in the federal government's work force.

The management of professionals in the public sector work force presents some dilemmas.[16] The idea of professional autonomy, for example, conflicts with that of the government being fully responsible to taxpayers for the use of its human resources — that is, for providing the public with a well-managed service that meets productivity norms and adequate standards or levels. To the extent that governments allow professionals the right to control conditions of entry to the profession and to control certification and the right to promotion, particularly when governments form almost the sole market for the labour of those professionals, these same governments are neither controlling nor managing their own work forces.

Statistics Canada sets out the main categories of the federal public service in its employment series as follows:

Executive: The employees in this category are involved in the development of government policy, the direction of programs, and in any other line of work that requires exceptional management qualities.

Scientific and Professional: Personnel in this category have specialist university training and/or membership in professional groups that is controlled by non-governmental but legally-established licensing bodies. Twenty-nine groups are classified under this heading. Typical are those that we normally think of as professions — lawyers, nurses, doctors, veterinarians, dentists, university teachers/professors, architects and scientific researchers. But there are many others that we may still think of as engaged in much more general kinds of intellectual work, but are nonetheless moving steadily to define their own bodies of knowledge, and which have become self-administering in imitation of the older professions. Thus we also find here groups like "social work," psychology, auditing, actuarial science, and "economics, sociology and statistics."

Administrative and Foreign Service: Here are the groups engaged in internal management in the public service, in the conduct of political and economic relations between Canada and other countries, and in some information and translation functions that link the government and citizens. It is safe to say that from this group come most of the senior managers and executives, although there are no formal barriers to movement from the professional category to executive work.

Technical: These employees are the occupational groups engaged in the conduct of analytical, experimental and investigative duties in the natural, physical and social sciences; the preparation, inspection and measurement of biological, chemical and physical substances and materials; the design, construction, inspection, operation and maintenance of complex equipment, systems and processes; and the performance of similar technical duties. Sample occupations include air traffic control, electronics, engineering and scientific support, photography and radio operation.

Administrative Support: This category is composed of the white-collar workers who come first to mind when we think of employment in government; people who work on records and push paper. Clerks, data processors, text processors and secretaries are all here.

Operational: These employees provide postal and protection services, operate machines (other than office machines), large equipment and vehicles throughout the public service, and also provide maintenance and repair for equipment and vehicles.

Table 3-13 shows how the Statistics Canada universe for the federal government's work force is distributed among these types of work. The table presents the absolute number of employees in the occupational category for the selected year, the share that category has in the same year in comparison to total federal government employment, and the growth rate of that category for the appropriate previous period.

Overall, one can say that the pattern of the types of work federal public servants perform is roughly as expected: the executive, and scientific and professional categories grow slowly but steadily over the 12-year period we can observe. Indeed, when the first three categories are summed together as the officers group, one sees that the highly trained and professional groups did gain overall at the expense of the traditional support and operational jobs. Administrative support just held its own, while the operational category, the largest single group, actually started to lose ground relative to the total. If one looks at the rate of growth for the total public service during 1970 to 1975, one sees a dramatic 22.5 percent increase that drops to roughly 4 percent from 1975 to 1980. By looking at each group during the 1970–75 period, one can see surges of growth, up to rates higher than 40 percent during the five-year period, in all groups except operational, which enjoyed its growth during the previous five-year period (as shown in the previous table distributing employees over the functions of government). Since 1975, the rate of increase for all groups has levelled off.

Unfortunately, Statistics Canada chose to combine the two highest-level groups into one category, on the reasoning that the executive employment is otherwise so small as to be trivial in comparison to the other categories. This prevents one from assessing the alleged growth of "chiefs" in an overview of the head count. However, the problem can be addressed by reviewing the Public Service Commission's distribution of employees over the classification scheme: the PSC, as noted earlier, works with a somewhat different universe than does Statistics Canada, and separates executive employment from other categories. However, the trend cannot be followed for longer than ten years, as 1981 saw a major reclassification. Before 1981, the designation in use was SX (Senior

Executive). Then, persons who were performing tasks equivalent to management and executive work, but under different job classifications, were regrouped into a broad category of SM (Senior Managers). The highest executive ranks were renamed as EX (Executive). (Some SX's were not yet reclassified into the newer EX/SM designation by December of 1982.) Table 3-14 shows the Public Service Commission's calculations of proportions of employees in each occupational category. The size of the executive category grew steadily until 1980, even though it still represented less than 1 percent of total employment to that year. The creation of the SM category brings post-1981 total management to more than 1 percent of all employment under the PSEA for the first time, reaching 1.8 percent in 1983. In the PSC's calculations, scientific and

TABLE 3-13 Total Federal Public Servants by Occupational Category[a]

	1970	1975	1980	1982
Officers				
Executives and				
Scientific/professional	16,919	25,073	24,626	28,161
% of Total	6.6	7.6	7.2	7.9
% Change	—	32.0	−0.02	—
Administrative and				
Foreign Services	25,615	48,467	52,954	58,991
% of Total	10.0	14.7	15.6	16.6
% Change	—	47.1	8.5	—
Technical	18,327	27,298	28,259	29,836
% of Total	7.2	8.3	8.3	8.4
% Change	—	33.3	3.5	—
Total Officers	60,861	100,828	105,839	116,988
% of Total	23.8	30.6	31.1	32.9
% Change	—	40.0	4.0	—
Support Staff				
Administrative				
Support	55,646	79,212	78,548	81,590
% of Total	21.8	24.1	23.1	22.9
% Change	—	30.3	−0.8	—
Operational	87,030	101,428	112,292	111,386
% of Total	34.1	30.8	33.0	31.3
% Change	—	13.8	9.6	—
Total Support Staff	142,676	180,640	190,840	192,976
% of Total	55.9	54.8	55.8	54.0
% Change	—	21.1	5.7	—
Other[b]	51,456	47,102	43,626	45,439
Total All P.S.'s	54,993	328,580	340,305	355,403
Percent Change	—	22.5	3.5	—

Source: Statistics Canada, *Federal Government Employment*, cat. no. 72–004 (Ottawa: Statistics Canada, 1970–82).

a. Statistics are reported as at December each year. They exclude members of the Canadian armed forces and post office Christmas help.

b. "Other" includes employees of "special funds" whose occupational group was not available.

TABLE 3-14 Federal Public Servants Under the PSEA:
Percentage Breakdown by Occupational Category[a]

	1970	1975	1980	1982	1983
Officers	0.3	0.5	0.6	0.9	1.0
Executives					
Senior Managers	—	—	—	0.5	0.8
Scientific and	10.1	10.5	10.2	10.1	10.1
Professional					
Administrative and	15.1	20.3	23.6	24.3	25.0
Foreign Service					
Technical	11.4	11.5	12.4	12.3	12.2
Total	37	43	47	48	49
Support Staff	32.9	32.7	31.5	31.8	31.4
Administrative Support					
Operational	30.1	23.8	21.5	19.9	19.5
Total	63	57	53	52	51

Source: Canada, Public Service Commission, *Annual Reports* (Ottawa: Minister of Supply and Services Canada, 1970–83).
a. These totals differ from Table 3-13 because it reports the smaller universe of public servants under the Public Service Employment Act (see Figure 3-1).

professional employment remains remarkably steady, while the real area of growth is in the last of the three officer groups, administrative and foreign service. As we have already seen, the support group remains roughly stable, and the operational category, the largest, declines in terms of relative share of total employment.

One can surmise, then, that the decrease in the federal government's clerical work force reflects the transformation of some routine work through new technology, and perhaps some proportional increase in officer-level employees and executives. As well, the demand for officer-level qualifications might also reflect the impact on the traditional public service of demands for more accountability made under the aegis of the select Public Service Bureaucracy III. It may be that more specialists in planning, auditing and control systems are required to respond to the mandates of these agencies. Alternately, some observers attribute the effect to "classification creep," encouraged by the individual ambitions of officers and executives.

Provincial Government Employment
We can now review provincial government employment. Tables 3-15 and 3-16 report, respectively, the numbers of general government employees in each province at December in the selected years, and the numbers of enterprise employees for the same periods. There were in 1982 some 409,000 persons employed in general government functions by provincial government enterprises. By comparison, the federal government in 1982 employed 355,000 persons in the equivalent general government functions, and had 138,000 working in its enterprises (see Table 3-7).

TABLE 3-15 Provincial General Government Employees by Province as at December, 1960–82

	Nfld.	P.E.I.	N.S.	N.B.	Que.	Ont.	Man.	Sask.	Alta.	B.C.	Yukon	N.W.T.	Total[a]
1960	6,233	1,637	10,291	8,721	39,030	46,455	6,847	9,490	14,252	18,708	165	292	162,121
% Change	—	—	—	—	—	—	—	—	—	—	—	—	—
1965	9,292	2,021	13,178	7,916	47,617	57,292	8,848	10,212	18,064	22,824	200	357	197,821
% Change	49.1	23.5	28.1	-10.0	22.0	23.3	29.2	7.6	26.7	22.0	21.0	22.2	22.0
1970	10,186	2,976	16,679	9,719	57,130	77,321	11,649	11,536	24,695	27,800	1,324	2,354	253,369
% Change	9.6	47.3	26.6	23.6	20.0	35.0	31.7	13.0	36.7	21.8	562.0	559.0	28.1
1975[c]	12,166	4,180	19,387	23,920[d]	85,465	105,304	14,742	17,125	44,510	38,921	1,485	2,655	369,860
% Change	19.4	40.5	16.2	146.1	49.6	36.2	26.6	48.5	80.2	40.0	12.1	12.8	46.0
1980	13,473	4,237	20,987	24,733	98,892	109,200	13,968	17,030	52,067	41,256	2,007	3,175	401,025
% Change	10.7	1.4	8.3	3.4	15.7	3.7	-5.2	-0.6	17.0	6.0	35.2	19.6	8.4
1982[b]	14,325	4,186	21,344	26,288	89,995[e]	109,878	14,868	15,959[f]	63,447	43,458	2,014	3,544	409,302

Source: Statistics Canada, Provincial Government Employment, cat. no.72–007 (Ottawa: Statistics Canada, 1960–82).

a. Total includes estimates for Quebec (1960) and British Columbia (1960–75) based on an average growth rate. New Brunswick was excluded after 1975 in the calculation of the rate because of the inclusion of local school teachers as provincial employees.
b. Percent change to 1982 not calculated because it is a two-year period.
c. Employees of Institutions and Special Funds are now included for all provinces.
d. New Brunswick considers elementary and secondary school teachers as provincial employees. They included 7,869 teachers in 1975; 8,207 in 1980; and 7,608 in 1982.
e. Quebec hospitals are deleted, with two exceptions.
f. University hospitals and the Cancer Foundation are excluded.

TABLE 3-16 Distribution of Provincial Government Enterprise Employees as at December, 1960–82

Year	Nfld.	P.E.I.	N.S.	N.B.	Que.	Ont.	Man.	Sask.	Alta.	B.C.	Yukon	N.W.T.	Total[a]
1960	338	48	1,243	1,740	11,811	22,549	6,373	6,356	5,913	7,028	16	29	63,444
% Change	—	—	—	—	—	—	—	—	—	—	—	—	—
1965	367	58	1,423	2,368	13,784	21,993	7,239	6,852	7,943	8,202	19	33	70,281
% Change	8.6	20.8	14.5	36.1	16.7	-2.5	13.6	7.8	34.2	16.7	18.8	13.8	10.8
1970	1,042	81	4,979	2,245	18,621	30,831	8,169	6,530	9,539	13,410	26	47	95,520
% Change	183.9	39.7	250	-5.2	35.1	40.2	12.8	-4.7	20.1	63.5	36.8	42.4	35.9
1975	2,427	257	6,824	3,609	27,047	34,809	11,819	8,949	15,589	23,120	20	43	134,513
% Change	132.9	217	37.1	60.7	45.2	12.9	44.7	37.0	63.4	72.4	-23.1	-8.5	40.8
1980	2,841	210	5,927	3,559	32,326	33,265	11,546	13,226	21,977	23,125	29	74	148,105
% Change	17.1	18.3	-13.1	-1.4	19.5	-4.4	-2.3	47.8	40.9	0.02	45.0	72.1	10.1
1982[b]	2,866	280	5,117	3,684	35,382	40,228	11,334	14,187	22,553	23,521	25	83	159,260

Source: Canada, Provincial Government Employment, cat. no.72–007 (Ottawa: Statistics Canada, 1960–82).
a. Total includes estimates for Quebec (1960) and British Columbia (1960–70) based on an average growth rate.
b. Percent change for 1982 not calculated because it is a two-year period.

Taking general government first, it is seen that the pattern of growth in total provincial jobs is roughly the same as for the federal government. There is a burst of growth to 1975, when it slackens in all but Alberta, Quebec, Yukon and Northwest Territories. It may be noted that the figure of 146 percent growth for the provincial government in New Brunswick reflects an administrative fiat rather than bureaucracy gone mad: schoolteachers were in this period reclassified as provincial government employees, a practice not followed by any other provincial government. Alberta experienced the most growth in this period from 1960 to 1982: from 14,000 to 63,000 employees.

TABLE 3-17 Summary of Provincial Total Government Growth

	General Govt.	Percent Change	Govt. Enterprises	Percent Change	Total	Percent Change
1960	162,121	—	63,444	—	225,565	—
1965	197,821	22.0	70,281	10.8	268,102	18.9
1970	253,369	28.1	95,520	35.9	348,889	30.1
1975	369,860	46.0	134,513	40.8	504,373	44.6
1980	401,025	8.4	148,105	10.1	549,130	8.9
1982	409,302	—	159,260	—	568,562	—

Source: See Tables 3-15 and 3-16.

Provincial enterprise growth begins somewhat later than general government growth, and continues somewhat longer in most provinces. Unfortunately, the data gaps for British Columbia and Quebec make it impossible to draw accurate comparisons between total provincial and total federal growth in employment. Another complexity is that Statistics Canada's general government figures include some teachers and hospital workers, making strict comparability of the federal and provincial functions less appropriate. (See Table 3-25 for estimates which exclude these workers.) One can, however, make a crude comparison by reading summary Table 3-17 alongside the table for federal employment (Table 3-3). Table 3-17 shows the rate of growth for each five-year period up to 1980, then a two-year period to 1982, for provincial general government employment totals and enterprise employment totals for all provinces for which data are available for selected years. Provincial general government growth rates were higher except for the period 1980–82: provincial employment grew at 22 percent from 1960 to 1965, 28 percent from 1965 to 1970, 41 percent from 1970 to 1975, and 8 percent from 1975 to 1980. The corresponding figures for general federal growth were 5, 13, 34 and 4 percent for each of the five-year periods to 1980. The contrast between growth in enterprise employment at the two levels of government is even stronger, with federal enterprise employment currently shrinking.

Provincial enterprise employment increased by 11 percent between 1960 and 1965, 3–6 percent between 1965 and 1970, 41 percent from 1970 to 1975, and 10 percent from 1975 to 1980. Federal enterprise rates for the same periods are decreases of 1 and 4.5 percent, then increases of 6.5 and 40 percent.

Do some provincial governments have proportionately weightier public service employment? If one were inclined to believe in the power of political ideologies, one might guess that the provinces that have been governed by social democratic parties (Saskatchewan from 1944 to 1964 and 1971 to 1982, Manitoba from 1969 to 1977 and 1981 to the present, and British Columbia from 1972 to 1975) would have proportionately larger public services. But this is not necessarily so. Table 3-18 displays the per capita figures for provincial government employment, both general government and enterprise. Alberta, notionally a conservative region, outstrips Saskatchewan in public sector employment. Quebec, now with a social democratic type of government, appears little different from Ontario, a Conservative province. Rather, a kind of regional factor is operating, which sees the Atlantic and Prairie provinces with the largest government presence. One also discerns some economies of scale, with the central and most populous provinces having the fewest provincial public servants per capita, Ontario having fewest overall (although it does have a healthy local government structure).

Distribution in Functions of Provincial Government Employment

The way that provincial governments distribute their employment over the broad functions of government has changed remarkably little over the 20-year period 1960–80. (See Appendix Table A-3 which reports available statistics for selected provinces on employment in each function as a percentage of each province's total employment.) Perhaps the most notable trend for the provincial governments is a decrease in the proportion of total employment devoted to transportation and communication (recall the federal increase here). There are also smaller decreases in health and natural resources. The largest increases are in education and social welfare. These areas are under-represented, if anything, because of the vagaries of provincial reporting to Statistics Canada. (See Tables 3-19, 3-20 and 3-21 for more comprehensive estimates of the importance of work in the health and education occupations.) The top provincial functions overall in 1980 are protection, health and education. The dominant categories for federal employment in general government were general services, protection, and transport and communications (Table 3-12).

One should also note that the 1980 proportion of total employment in general services varies considerably from province to province, with

TABLE 3-18 Per Capita Provincial Govt. Employment (per 1000)

	1960	1965	1970	1975	1980	1982
Nfld. General Govt.	14.0	19.0	20.0	22.0	24.0	25.0
Govt. Enterprise	0.7	0.75	2.0	4.0	5.0	5.0
Total	14.7	19.75	22.0	26.0	29.0	30.0
P.E.I. General Govt.	16.0	18.5	27.0	36.0	35.0	34.0
Govt. Enterprise	0.5	0.5	0.7	2.0	2.0	1.7
Total	16.5	18.9	27.7	38.0	37.0	35.7
N.S. General Govt.	14.0	17.0	21.0	23.0	25.0	25.0
Govt. Enterprise	1.7	1.9	6.0	8.0	7.0	7.0
Total	15.7	18.9	27.0	31.0	32.0	32.0
N.B. General Govt.	15.0	13.0	16.0	36.0[a]	36.0	38.0
Govt. Enterprise	2.9	3.9	3.5	5.0	5.0	5.0
Total	17.9	16.9	19.5	41.0	41.0	43.0
Que. General Govt.	7.7	8.0	9.5	14.0	16.0	14.0
Govt. Enterprise	2.4	2.4	3.0	4.0	5.0	5.0
Total	10.1	10.4	12.5	18.0	21.0	19.0
Ont. General Govt.	7.6	8.0	10.0	13.0	13.0	13.0
Govt. Enterprise	3.7	3.3	4.0	4.0	4.0	5.0
Total	11.3	11.3	14.0	17.0	17.0	18.0
Man. General Govt.	7.6	9.0	12.0	15.0	14.0	14.0
Govt. Enterprise	7.0	7.5	8.0	12.0	11.0	11.0
Total	14.6	16.5	20.0	27.0	25.0	25.0
Sask. General Govt.	10.4	10.7	12.0	19.0	18.0	18.0
Govt. Enterprise	7.0	7.0	7.0	10.0	14.0	15.0
Total	17.4	17.7	19.0	29.0	32.0	33.0
Alta. General Govt.	11.0	12.5	15.0	25.0	25.0	27.0
Govt. Enterprise	4.6	5.5	6.0	9.0	11.0	10.0
Total	15.6	18.0	21.0	34.0	36.0	37.0
B.C. General Govt.	11.9	12.7	13.1	16.0	16.0	16.0
Govt. Enterprise	4.5	4.6	6.3	10.0	9.0	8.0
Total	15.4	17.3	19.4	26.0	25.0	24.0
N.W.T. & Yukon General Govt.	12.7	14.0	70.0	66.0	78.0	80.0
Govt. Enterprise	1.1	1.3	1.5	1.0	2.0	2.0
Total	13.8	15.3	71.5	67.0	80.0	82.0

Source: See Tables 3-14, 3-15 and 3-16.
a. New Brunswick started including local school board employees in their statistics from 1975 on.

TABLE 3-19 Types of Education Employment by Province

	Canada	Nfld.	P.E.I.	N.S.	N.B.	Que.	Ont.	Man.	Sask.	Alta.	B.C.	Yukon	N.W.T.	Over-seas
Full-time Teachers in Public Schools: Elementary and Secondary Levels														
1960	153,040	4,317	969	6,664	5,866	45,694	49,292	7,460	8,638	11,762	11,868	28	103	379
1965	197,093	5,545	1,209	7,897	6,812	55,421	68,602	9,232	10,500	15,518	15,759	56	147	395
1970	262,457	6,437	1,606	9,999	7,897	77,978	93,000	11,534	10,977	20,358	21,575	223	518	355
1975	264,262	7,427	1,444	10,781	7,869	71,500	94,600	11,476	10,754	21,180	25,971	265	685	310
1979–80	276,257	7,846	1,396	10,975	7,858	76,103	96,280	12,265	11,334	23,207	27,731	263	729	270
1981–82	260,422	7,777	1,344	10,602	7,608	67,600	91,681	11,293	10,831	23,793	26,937	279	680	—
Full-time University Teachers														
1960	7,760	70	20	390	285	2,350	2,555	410	360	490	830	—	—	—
1965	14,370	170	35	635	455	4,580	4,695	715	690	975	1,420	—	—	—
1970	24,733	500	123	1,184	785	5,700	9,335	1,352	1,268	2,108	2,378	—	—	—
1975	30,858	679	121	1,549	1,030	6,860	12,290	1,573	1,360	2,574	2,822	—	—	—
1980	32,890	810	120	1,650	1,061	7,480	12,770	1,622	1,461	2,830	3,086	—	—	—
1982	33,244	866	124	1,669	1,058	7,300	12,973	1,677	1,457	2,944	3,176	—	—	—
Community College Teachers														
1970	4,434	85	10	91	69	—	2,828	120	141	738	354	—	—	—
1975–76	18,221	211	68	347	155	8,710	5,000	314	355	1,607	1,454	—	—	—
1979–80	19,828	212	65	360	213	9,400	5,215	352	360	1,892	1,759	—	—	—
1981–82	20,535	220	67	381	219	9,550	5,553	384	356	1,899	1,906	—	—	—

Sources: Statistics Canada, *Historical Compendium of Education Statistics and Education in Canada. A Statistical Review for 1979–80 and 1982–82* (Ottawa: Statistics Canada, Selected Catalogues, 81–568, 81–229, 1960–82).

TABLE 3-20 Full-time Hospital Personnel by Province[a]

Year	Nfld.	P.E.I.	N.S.	N.B.	Que.	Ont.	Man.	Sask.	Alta.	B.C.	Yukon	N.W.T.	Canada[a]
1960	3,425	1,022	7,451	6,157	44,575	68,736	9,720	11,766	14,391	15,857	24	65	183,189
1965	5,064	1,283	9,428	8,353	76,395	88,602	11,895	13,020	18,591	18,715	17	148	251,511
1970	6,718	1,485	11,305	9,593	94,896	115,827	15,263	12,284	26,027	25,778	182	428	319,826
1975	8,270	1,560	13,293	9,506	98,969	118,719	17,286	12,231	28,294	30,632	197	560	339,517
1979/80	8,205	1,418	12,134	7,836	90,211	102,951	13,076	10,886	24,656	27,487	177	351	299,388
1980/81	8,186	1,151	12,563	8,288	91,643	95,137	13,345	11,018	26,089	29,106	178	491	297,195

Sources: Statistics Canada, *Hospital Statistics: Volume I; Hospital Personnel: Volume III*, cat. no.83–227 (Ottawa: Statistics Canada, 1960–81) and *Mental Health Statistics* cat. no.83–208 (Ottawa: Statistics Canada, 1960–81).

a. Totals include federal hospital employees.

TABLE 3-21 Full-time and Part-time Hospital Employees[a]

1980/81	Canada	Nfld.	P.E.I.	N.S.	N.B.	Que.	Ont.	Man.	Sask.	Alta.	B.C.	Yukon	N.W.T.
Full-time	293,087	8,186	1,151	12,169	8,288	90,373	94,073	12,545	10,947	25,972	29,106	178	277
Part-time	94,292	1,042	382	2,346	2,460	28,208	30,916	4,570	4,856	10,589	8,921	13	56
Total	87,379	9,228	1,479	14,515	10,748	118,581	124,989	17,115	15,803	36,561	38,027	191	333

Source: Statistics Canada, *Hospital Annual Statistics 1980/81*, cat. no.83–232 (Ottawa: Statistics Canada, 1981).

a. Totals do not include federal hospital employees.

New Brunswick reporting fewest general administrators and Saskatchewan and Newfoundland most. The Appendix Table A-4 reports additional statistics to complete the national picture for Quebec, British Columbia, Yukon and Northwest Territories, but unfortunately does not cover the same period. However, it does show Quebec as the biggest general services employer of all the provinces in 1980 while British Columbia has the most employees overall in protection and social welfare. It is doubtful that these figures are more than suggestive: the divisions between functions may have been used differently from province to province.

Next we can separately review the numbers of full-time teachers and hospital workers. Table 3-19 shows the numbers of teachers in public schools and universities from 1960 through 1982, and in community colleges/CEGEPs from 1970 to 1982. (It must be noted that the reader should not add figures from Tables 3-19, 3-20 and 3-21 to the series above: the result would be inflated because of some indeterminate amount of double counting.) Teaching employment in public schools and universities generally increased quite rapidly from 1960 to 1975, when it levelled out. Public school teaching employment even dropped in a few cases. Community college/CEGEP teachers continue to grow in number through 1970 to 1982, although their absolute numbers are very small compared to other categories of teaching employment. One must also note that teaching employment is of considerable importance: totalling all teachers in Ontario, for example, shows that there are somewhat more teachers than there are workers in general government. Ontario is fairly representative of the other provinces in this regard.

Table 3-20 shows the numbers of hospital workers from 1960 to 1981. Again one sees that full-time hospital employment is large. Ontario, for example, had 95,000 full-time hospital workers in 1981 and, viewing Table 3-21, one-third again as many part-time hospital employees, although we cannot calculate the numbers of person-years contributed by the part-time workers. Table 3-25 illustrates that a single sector, such as health or education, comes close to matching and sometimes often exceeds provincial general government employment net of the overlap.

Local Government Employment

Statistics Canada has published a local general government series only since 1967, while federal and provincial catalogues have been produced since 1952 and 1959 respectively. The services provided by municipalities through their departmental organizations generally include police services, fire, road construction, street maintenance, water supply, sewage, garbage collection, health, welfare and recreation. The figures presented in Table 3-22 do not, however, include local school authorities and municipally owned hospitals, as these data are reported separately. The distribution of employment in local general government

TABLE 3-22 Provincial Distribution of Local General Government Employees as at December[a]

Year	Nfld.	P.E.I.	N.S.	N.B.	Que.	Ont.	Man.	Sask.	Alta.	B.C.	Yukon	N.W.T.	Total[a]
1967													
Total Employment	1,525	308	3,833	2,229	45,019	75,267	7,602	7,457	14,568	16,387	—	—	174,238
% Local Employment	0.9	0.2	2.2	1.3	25.8	43.2	4.4	4.3	8.4	9.4	—	—	100.0
1970[b]													
Total Employment	1,554	242	4,376	2,727	58,599	83,354	8,043	7,124	15,923	19,312	68	103	201,045
% Local Employment	0.8	0.1	2.2	1.4	29.1	41.4	4.0	3.5	7.9	9.6	0.03	0.05	100.0
1975													
Total Employment	2,730	292	5,233	3,452	64,271	105,742	10,120	8,792	20,092	25,212	160	203	247,199
% Local Employment	1.1	0.1	2.1	1.4	26.0	42.8	4.1	3.6	8.5	10.2	0.06	0.08	100.0
% Growth	75.7	20.7	19.6	26.6	9.7	26.9	25.8	23.4	31.8	30.6	135.3	97.1	22.7
1980													
Total Employment	2,338	357	6,235	3,726	63,562	120,441	9,886	10,318	28,631	28,065	163	228	274,126
% Local Employment	0.9	0.1	2.3	1.4	23.2	43.9	3.6	3.8	10.4	10.2	0.05	0.08	100.0
% Growth	-14.4	22.3	19.2	7.9	-1.1	13.9	-2.3	17.4	36.4	11.3	1.9	12.3	10.8
1982[b]													
Total Employment	2,300	332	6,576	3,931	60,112	130,775	10,334	10,956	31,126	29,725	199	737	287,103
% Local Employment	0.8	0.1	2.3	1.4	20.9	45.5	3.6	3.8	10.8	10.4	0.07	0.25	100.0

Source: Statistics Canada, *Local Government Employment*, cat. no. 72–009 (Ottawa: Statistics Canada, 1967–82).
a. Local level school authorities and municipal hospitals were not included.
b. Percent growth to 1980 and 1982 not calculated because period covered is not a five-year span.

is shown below the absolute number of employees in each province for the appropriate year, and the percent growth from period to period is shown below that. Thus, Ontario in 1970 had a total of 83,000 persons working for cities and municipalities; this number represented about 42 percent of non-enterprise employment offered by local governments in the whole of Canada, and an increase of nearly 11 percent over 1967. Overall, the pattern of growth resembles the pattern for provincial general government more than it does growth at the federal level. Growth for most provinces has been quite strong.

It is interesting to view the 1982 figures in Table 3-2 in the light of the population distribution for the time (see Table 3-10). Moving across the provinces, Newfoundland with 2.3 percent of the Canadian population provides roughly 1 percent of jobs at the local general government level; Prince Edward Island with 0.5 percent of the population provides about 1 percent of local level jobs; Nova Scotia with 3.5 percent of Canada's population offers about 2 percent of all jobs at the local level; New Brunswick has just under 3 percent of the population, and less than 1.5 percent of the jobs; Quebec has 26 percent of the population, but less than 21 percent of all jobs at the local level; Ontario has 35 percent of the country's population, but 45 percent of employment at local level; Manitoba has 4 percent of all Canadians, and provides about 3.6 percent of local employment; and British Columbia has 11 percent of the national population and about 10 percent of all local general government jobs. Assuming that the statistics are roughly accurate, and that higher proportions do not merely represent more complete reporting, it would appear that local government employment is a little light in the east and west, with Ontario quite heavily staffed at the local level, and Quebec markedly light.

The remaining universe of employment is local government enterprises (see Tables 3-23 and 3-24): municipal bodies such as utilities, transit systems, telephone, gas distribution, and so on, which are normally run autonomously and on commercial lines.[17] Unfortunately, data for enterprise at the local level have only been collected systematically since 1983–84. However, by using estimates, we have been able to create a very general picture of growth rates of employment at the local level back to 1960 (Table 3-23). We also divert to take a quick look at some available statistics on electricity-generating activities. The next table, 3-24, presents statistics on hydro-electric employment. Since 1960, the largest increases have been in British Columbia, Quebec and Ontario. These three provinces have experienced dramatic increases. In 1982, approximately 82,000 employees worked in this field, exclusive of additional numbers for Prince Edward Island and Alberta, where statistics are not available.

Because the local government sector's importance is a matter of provincial discretion, it is appropriate to round out the discussion with the aggregate picture. Table 3-25 provides a comparison of provincial and local general enterprise employment as a percentage of the provincial labour force. While the tendencies noted so far still seem to be true from this perspective, the differences noted between provinces are minimized. Overall, the prairie and Atlantic provinces have somewhat more provincial/local employment than do Quebec, Ontario and British Columbia, where the proportions seem to have remained steady. Perhaps more interesting is the contrasting approach taken to the provincial versus local mix of employment in Ontario and Quebec: local government is more important in Ontario than in Quebec.

Summary: Putting the Numbers into Perspective

This chapter has attempted to convey the message that what you can see depends, in large part, upon where you are sitting. Raw magnitudes, seen from centre stage, given an impression that governments increase in size at a wild pace. Take the absolute numbers: in 1960 there were 336,478 federal general government and enterprise employees; 22 years later, their numbers had swelled to almost half a million.

Change perspective, and what was impressive appears much less remarkable. One might ask, for example, whether the growth of the number of persons in government work has really outstripped the population increase for the same period. Table 3-4 shows that the population jumped by about seven million in the same period, an increase of just under 40 percent. On balance, then, the bureaucrats are not gaining ground as rapidly as appeared at first glance. However, are there still more of them than there "should" be — that is, more than are justified solely in terms of a greater number of citizens to look after — at standards adhered to in the late 1950s?

The world has changed since 1960. A member of today's labour force will use more public goods and services, meaning telephones, other forms of communication, transportation, regulation to support safety and health, insurance against illness and loss of wages, and so forth, than someone who is not part of the work force. Hence it might be more appropriate to gauge the growth in number of public service bureaucrats against the growth in numbers of Canadians participating in the labour force. And, when one judges the growth in the number of bureaucrats against the benchmark of 83 percent, which is our general labour force growth for the same period (see Table 3-5), the result makes the numbers of public sector workers look more routine. One does not even need to draw upon a common justification for public sector growth: that the public goods and services required in the mid-1980s are much more complex and costly to provide than the mixture that supported the work force of the late 1950s and early 1960s. The public sector, it would appear, is actually providing the modern basket of goods and services without growing disproportionately in comparison to the labour force.

What, then, could the critics of the growth of the bureaucracy be talking about? One can try to see the bureaucracy from their point of view. Don't fix upon the size of the labour force, they advise, but look instead at the numbers of Canadians who are steadily in work. Bureaucrats are paid by taxes, and if a potential worker is not receiving wages, then that worker cannot pay taxes to support a bureaucrat. And if one sets the numbers of public sector workers against fluctuations in the rate of unemployment for the total labour force, bureaucrats wax as non-bureaucrats wane. The fewer private sector jobs there are (as measured by the rate of unemployment of persons who are legitimate members of the labour force), the faster the public sector appears to grow in comparison. (One can observe that the persons who testified to this Royal Commission about the weight of the government's presence in the Canadian north were faithfully reporting the situation as they experience it: very many more of the available jobs in the north than in other regions are provided by government. See Tables 3-15 through 3-22.)

A second moral would be, however, that where one sits is not necessarily an accident that must subsequently govern all perceptions. One can choose a perspective. To this point in the chapter, we have chosen to move around a good deal, in order to encourage a flexibility of perspective. Like Lewis Carroll's Alice, we have drunk of the potions that cause explosions in size and equally violent reversals. In the conclusion to this chapter, it will behoove us to flatten and control the spectacle before us. We can do this by choosing seats high in the bleachers and far back.

Operationally, one way of choosing a long view and a moderate perspective is to look at the longest period under study that is available and choose a median indicator that splits the difference between the extremes. The longest period for which we have most of the necessary information is 1960 to 1982. (Note that, to provide the forthcoming summary, many holes have been filled through an estimating procedure, and many inconsistencies that cause double-counting of some employees have been likewise "estimated out": refer to the notes of individual tables.)

The median indicator we will use to put employment in the public sector into perspective is, as suggested earlier, the size of the total labour force. It recognizes qualitative changes in the Canadian population that have come about through longer-term demographic and social changes, but is still not so volatile and responsive to immediate economic conditions as an indicator such as total employment/unemployment.

Tables 3-26 and 3-27 present a picture of total employment by all governments in Canada from 1960 to 1982, calculated as a percentage of the total contemporary labour force. Let us take the beginning of the period. In 1960, there were about 203,000 jobs in federal general govern-

Table 3-23 Local Enterprise Employment, by Province

Year	Canada	Nfld.	P.E.I.	N.S.	N.B.	Que.	Ont.	Man.	Sask.	Alta.	B.C.
1960											
Local enterprise employment	23,718	66	12	261	166	5,740	12,001	1,020	332	3,842	285
% of Labour force	0.36	0.06	0.04	0.12	0.09	0.31	0.50	0.34	0.12	0.82	0.04
% of Population	0.13	0.02	0.01	0.03	0.02	0.11	0.20	0.11	0.04	0.31	0.02
% of Growth rate	—	—	—	—	—	—	—	—	—	—	—
1965											
Local enterprise employment	25,860	72	13	285	181	6,258	13,085	1,112	362	4,190	310
% of Labour force	0.36	0.06	0.04	0.12	0.10	0.33	0.48	0.34	0.11	0.75	0.04
% of Population	0.16	0.02	0.01	0.04	0.03	0.11	0.19	0.12	0.04	0.29	0.02
% of Growth rate	9.00	9.10	8.30	9.20	9.00	9.00	9.00	9.00	9.00	9.10	8.80
1970											
Local enterprise employment	31,976	90	16	352	224	7,738	16,180	1,375	448	5,180	383
% of Labour force	0.38	0.06	0.05	0.13	0.12	0.34	0.51	0.36	0.13	0.80	0.04
% of Population	0.15	0.02	0.01	0.05	0.04	0.13	0.21	0.14	0.05	0.32	0.02
% of Growth rate	23.70	25.00	23.10	23.50	23.80	23.60	23.70	23.70	23.70	23.60	23.50
1975											
Local enterprise employment	39,242	110	20	432	273	9,497	19,836	1,687	549	6,357	471
% of Labour force	0.40	0.08	0.04	0.14	0.11	0.35	0.52	0.41	0.15	0.83	0.04
% of Population	0.17	0.02	0.02	0.05	0.04	0.15	0.24	0.17	0.06	0.36	0.02
% of Growth rate	22.70	18.20	25.00	22.70	21.80	22.70	22.60	22.70	22.50	22.70	23.00

1980											
Local enterprise employment	43,517	122	22	479	305	10,531	22,020	1,871	609	7,049	522
% of Labour force	0.38	0.06	0.04	0.13	0.11	0.36	0.51	0.39	0.14	0.65	0.04
% of Population	0.18	0.02	0.02	0.06	0.04	0.17	0.26	0.18	0.06	0.34	0.02
% of Growth rate	10.90	10.90	10.00	10.90	11.70	10.90	11.00	10.90	10.90	10.90	10.80
1982											
Local enterprise employment	45,577	129	25	504	311	11,089	23,210	1,959	677	7,427	555
% of Labour force	0.39	0.06	0.05	0.14	0.11	0.38	0.52	0.39	0.15	0.63	0.04
% of Population	0.19	0.02	0.02	0.06	0.04	0.17	0.27	0.19	0.07	0.33	0.02

Source: Tables 3-10 and 3-25.

TABLE 3-24 Provincial Enterprise Employment (Electric)[a]

Year	Nfld.	Change %	P.E.I.	Change %	N.S.	Change %	N.B.	Change %	Que.	Change %
1960	—	—	—	—	421	—	1,099	—	8,423	—
1965	49	—	—	—	785	86.4	1,558	41.8	9,674	14.8
1970	626	1,177.6	—	—	996	26.9	1,695	8.8	14,660	51.5
1975	809	29.2	—	—	2,327	133.6	2,740	61.7	18,400	25.5
1980	930	15.0	—	—	2,576	10.7	2,794	2.0	21,779	18.4
1982[b]	981	—	—	—	2,538	—	2,832	—	24,694	—

Year	Ont.	Change %	Man.	Change %	Sask.	Change %	Alta.	Change %	B.C.	Change %
1960	15,146	—	1,669	—	2,696	—	—	—	1,100	—
1965	14,247	-6.3	2,677	60.4	2,928	8.6	—	—	6,829	520.0
1970	22,043	54.7	3,166	18.3	2,573	-12.1	—	—	7,816	14.5
1975	24,702	0.7	4,598	45.2	3,047	18.4	—	—	12,218	56.3
1980	24,702	0.7	3,673	-20.1	3,611	18.5	—	—	12,746	4.3
1982[b]	29,844	—	3,705	—	3,668	—	—	—	11,969	—

Source: Statistics Canada, "Statistical Papers, Public Finance Division" (Ottawa: Statistics Canada). Unpublished.
a. Data not available for P.E.I. or Alberta.
b. Percent change for 1982 not calculated.

TABLE 3-25 Provincial and Local General and Enterprise Employment as a Percentage of the Labour Force

	Nfld. G	Nfld. E	P.E.I. G	P.E.I. E	N.S. G	N.S. E	N.B. G	N.B. E	Que. G	Que. E	Ont. G	Ont. E	Man. G	Man. E	Sask. G	Sask. E	Alta. G	Alta. E	B.C. G	B.C. E
1960 Provincial	3.5	0.3	4.0	0.2	3.4	0.6	4.6	1.0	1.8	0.7	1.4	0.9	1.9	2.1	3.0	2.3	2.4	1.3	2.7	1.2
Local	1.2	0.1	0.9	0.0	1.5	0.1	1.1	0.1	2.1	0.3	2.7	0.5	2.2	0.3	2.4	0.1	2.7	0.8	2.5	0.0
Total	4.7	0.4	4.9	0.2	4.9	0.7	5.7	1.1	3.9	1.0	4.1	1.4	4.1	2.4	5.4	2.4	5.1	2.1	5.2	1.2
Grand Total	5.1		5.14		5.6		6.8		4.9		5.5		6.5		7.8		7.2		6.45	
1965 Provincial	5.3	0.3	5.3	0.2	4.0	0.6	3.7	1.3	2.2	0.7	1.7	0.8	2.1	2.2	2.7	2.1	3.1	1.5	2.7	1.6
Local	1.3	0.1	1.0	0.0	1.6	0.1	1.2	0.1	2.2	0.3	2.6	0.5	2.2	0.3	2.2	0.1	2.5	0.8	2.3	0.0
Total	6.6	0.4	6.3	0.2	5.6	0.7	4.9	1.4	4.4	1.0	4.3	1.3	4.3	2.5	4.9	2.2	5.6	2.3	5.0	1.6
Grand Total	7.0		6.54		6.3		6.3		5.4		5.6		6.7		7.1		7.9		6.65	
1970 Provincial	4.8	0.7	7.3	0.2	4.2	1.9	4.4	1.2	2.2	0.8	1.9	1.0	2.3	2.1	2.6	1.9	3.1	1.5	2.7	1.6
Local	1.1	0.1	0.7	0.0	1.6	0.1	1.4	0.1	2.6	0.3	2.6	0.5	2.1	0.4	2.1	0.1	2.5	0.8	2.3	0.0
Total	5.9	0.8	8.0	0.2	5.8	2.0	5.8	1.3	4.8	1.1	4.5	1.5	4.4	2.5	4.7	2.0	5.6	2.3	5.0	1.6
Grand Total	6.67		8.24		7.8		7.1		5.9		6.0		6.9		6.7		7.9		6.65	
1975 Provincial	5.2	1.3	8.4	0.6	5.1	2.3	5.2	1.4	2.4	1.0	2.2	0.9	3.2	2.8	3.7	2.5	4.0	2.0	2.5	2.1
Local	1.4	0.1	0.6	0.0	1.8	0.1	1.4	0.1	2.4	0.4	2.8	0.5	2.4	0.4	2.4	0.2	2.7	0.8	2.3	0.0
Total	6.6	1.4	9.0	0.6	6.9	2.4	6.6	1.5	4.8	1.4	5.0	1.4	5.6	3.2	6.1	2.7	6.7	2.8	4.8	2.1
Grand Total	7.0		9.64		9.3		8.1		6.2		6.4		8.8		8.8		9.5		6.9	
1980 Provincial	5.2	1.4	7.3	0.4	3.9	1.6	5.0	1.3	2.7	1.1	2.0	0.8	2.4	2.4	3.5	3.0	3.3	2.0	2.8	1.8
Local	1.1	0.1	0.7	0.0	1.7	0.1	1.4	0.1	2.2	0.4	2.8	0.5	2.1	0.4	2.4	0.1	2.6	0.7	2.2	0.0
Total	6.3	1.46	8.0	0.4	5.6	1.7	6.4	1.4	4.9	1.5	4.8	1.3	4.5	2.8	5.9	3.1	5.9	2.7	5.0	1.8
Grand Total	7.8		8.44		7.3		7.8		6.4		6.1		7.3		9.0		8.6		6.8	
1982 Provincial	5.2	1.3	7.1	0.5	3.5	1.4	5.5	1.3	2.7	1.2	1.9	0.9	2.5	2.3	3.1	3.1	3.5	1.9	2.9	1.7
Local	1.1	0.1	0.6	0.0	1.8	0.1	1.4	0.1	2.1	0.4	2.9	0.5	2.1	0.4	2.4	0.1	2.7	0.6	2.2	0.0
Total	6.3	1.4	7.7	0.5	5.3	1.5	6.9	1.4	4.8	1.6	4.8	1.4	4.6	2.7	5.5	3.2	6.2	2.5	5.1	1.7
Grand Total	7.7		8.25		6.8		8.3		6.4		6.2		7.3		8.7		8.7		6.8	

Source: Table 3-27

ment, and another 131,000 in federal enterprises. These represented, respectively, 3.2 percent and 2 percent of all workers in Canada, or a total of more than 5 percent of all workers. Summing provincial government employment with provincial enterprise employment, one finds that these represented 3.2 percent of all Canadian workers, fewer than total federal jobs. Local government jobs represented 2.7 percent of workers. As well, the provincial level was responsible for work in the education and hospital sectors: just over 4 percent and under 3 percent of workers respectively. The grand total of all workers in all public sector work came to 1,154,000. There were 6,430,000 persons in the labour force in 1960. Therefore, total public sector employment represented nearly 18 percent of all work.

By 1982, federal general government jobs represented 3 percent of all workers, and federal enterprise employment represented 1.2 percent. Provincial general government jobs had increased to 2.7 percent, and jobs in all provincial enterprises summed to 1.4 percent: a total of 4.1 percent. Adding local general and enterprise estimates, one finds that total government workers were 11 percent of the labour force. Work in the education sector had increased just slightly, offsetting a decrease in jobs in the hospital sector over the 20-year period. The result? The public sector represents about the same proportion of potential workers at the end of the period as at the beginning: 18 of every 100 would-be workers had jobs in government. Indeed, the "bureaucrats proper" — government workers excluding education and hospital workers — had remained remarkably stable at around 11 percent through the whole period.[18]

One can move through the table, across time and down the levels of government and employment in education and hospital sectors, only to find that the chart flattens any indications of change in employment share taken by all types of government in the whole of Canada over the period. Even the surges of growth in governments that we know we experienced until 1975 show only as flickers: in 1960, of every 100 persons in the labour force, just under 18 were in some kind of government work; in 1965, the figure was 19; in 1970, 20.5; in 1975, slightly fewer; in 1980, about 18; and in 1982, just under 18. The margin of fluctuation that has impressed observers so strongly over the period, therefore, is about 2.5 percent of the total work force. Certainly, the picture so described minimizes (by ignoring) the considerable variety inside the country from region to region, but this variety is described in Table 3-28.

The summary picture, broken down for provinces, is shown in Table 3-28, which should be read in a manner similar to Table 3-26. There is more variation from region to region than there is in most regions across time. In other words, with the most notable exception of Quebec, the total share of the labour force represented by jobs in all levels and all types of government tends to remain quite steady within each province. In 1960, for example, combined employment in federal, provincial and local general and enterprise government activities in Newfoundland amounted to just over 13 percent of the labour force. When employment in education and hospitals is added, public sector jobs account for about 23 percent of all workers in Newfoundland. In 1982, the total figure is about one job more. In Quebec, government jobs were held by 15.5 percent of all workers in 1960, and by 18.2 percent in 1982. The picture in Ontario was very stable in comparison. We will leave it to the reader to pursue the differences between provinces over time. The point we wish to make is merely that while the summary picture masks differences between regions, it does provide fairly convincing limits for the amounts of growth that one can claim to see for government and "bureaucracy." As a share of the total labour force, the jobs that are available in all levels of government have not changed very much over the entire generation represented by the 22-year period under review.

Indeed, it is perhaps more interesting to look at relative shares among governments. That is, we have just looked at the proportion of the total work force that is made up of bureaucrats and public sector workers at all levels, never fewer than 17.9 or more than 20.5 of every 100 members of the labour force for the whole 22-year period. Let us now look at the portion of total public sector employment for each level of government (see Table 3-29). Of every 100 jobs in the whole public sector in 1960, the federal level of government had 29. Just fewer than 18 were in federal general government employment, and more than 11 were in federal enterprise jobs. All provincial general government jobs totalled about 12, and all provinces' enterprise jobs added to just 5.5. Local general government jobs totalled fewer than 13 of the 100, and local enterprises represented only 2. The education sector, in comparison, was a big employer, with almost 23 of those 100 jobs, and the hospital sector had almost 16.

Twenty-two years later, in 1982, shares of public sector jobs have changed somewhat. Only about 23 of the total public sector jobs are held by federal government employees: it is federal enterprises that have shrunk most, general government share decreasing by only about one job. Provincial government employment has gone up, the increase shared between general government and enterprises. Local government jobs, added up across the whole country, have retained a fairly steady share of all public sector employment. The numbers of jobs in the education sector increased for a time up to 1970, and then dropped off again to about one-quarter of all public sector employment, and jobs in the hospital sector likewise increased and then decreased. To 1982 at least, then, the broad picture shows that the share of all government employment dominated by the federal level of government has dropped. Over the whole period, the federal government has tended to move out of

TABLE 3-26 Total Government Employment

	1960	%LF	1965	%LF	1970	%LF	1975	%LF	1980	%LF	1982	%LF
Labour Force (000s)	6,430	—	7,185	—	8,329	—	9,923	—	11,522	—	11,743	—
Federal												
General[a]	203,013	3.2	211,913	3.0	251,237	3.0	323,902	3.3	335,375	2.9	351,295	3.0
Enterprise	131,118	2.0	129,916	1.8	123,906	1.5	132,046	1.3	157,988	1.4	138,281	1.2
Total	334,131	5.2	341,829	4.8	375,143	4.5	455,948	4.6	493,363	4.3	489,576	4.2
Provincial												
General[b]	139,434	2.2	168,536	2.3	216,475	2.6	288,937	2.9	311,634	2.7	317,407	2.7
Enterprise	63,444	1.0	70,281	1.0	95,520	1.1	134,513	1.4	148,105	1.3	159,260	1.4
Total	202,878	3.2	238,817	3.3	311,995	3.7	423,450	4.3	459,739	4.0	476,667	4.1
Local[c]												
General	149,403	2.3	162,901	2.3	201,425	2.4	247,199	2.5	274,126	2.4	287,103	2.4
Enterprise	23,187	0.4	25,860	0.4	31,976	0.4	39,242	0.4	43,517	0.4	45,577	0.4
Total	173,121	2.7	188,761	2.7	233,401	2.8	286,441	2.9	317,643	2.8	332,680	2.8
Total Government												
General	491,850	7.6	543,350	7.6	669,137	8.0	860,038	8.7	921,135	8.0	955,805	8.1
Enterprise	218,280	3.4	226,057	3.2	251,402	3.0	305,801	3.1	349,610	3.0	343,118	2.9
Total	710,130	11.0	769,407	10.8	920,539	11.0	1,165,839	11.8	1,270,745	11.0	1,298,923	11.0

Education Sector

Teaching	160,800[d]	2.5	211,463[d]	2.9	291,624	3.5	313,341	3.1	328,975	2.9	314,201	2.7
Non-teaching[e]	99,696	1.6	131,107	1.8	180,807	2.2	194,271	2.0	203,965	1.8	194,805	1.7
Total	260,496	4.1	342,570	4.7	472,431	5.7	507,612	5.1	532,940	4.7	509,006	4.4
Hospital Sector[f]	183,189	2.8	251,511	3.5	319,826	3.8	339,517	3.4	299,388	2.6	297,195	2.5
Grand Total	1,153,815	17.9	1,363,488	19.0	1,712,796	20.5	2,012,968	20.3	2,103,073	18.3	2,105,124	17.9

Source: Tables 3-3, 3-5, 3-15, 3-16, 3-19, 3-20 and 3-23.

a. Excludes federal hospital care workers. They are reflected in the hospital sector totals.
b. Excludes provincial hospital care workers. They are reflected in the hospital sector totals. Also excludes local school teachers from New Brunswick who were included 1975–82. Excludes teachers from CAATs (Ontario) and CEGEP (Quebec) who were included from 1975–82. Public college teachers who were included in 1975 are excluded from provincial totals. These employees are reflected in the education sector totals. Estimates for Quebec in 1960 and B.C. from 1960–75 are included in the totals.
c. Local general employment totals for 1960 and 1965 are estimated. Local enterprise totals are estimated for 1960–82.
d. Excludes Community College teachers.
e. Non-teaching personnel are estimated for 1960–82.
f. The 1979–80 hospital statistics were used for 1980 total. The 1980–81 statistics were used as estimates for 1982 total.

TABLE 3-27 Percentage of the Labour Force Employed by Government

	1960	1965	1970	1975	1980	1982
Federal						
General	3.2	3.0	3.0	3.3	2.9	3.0
Enterprise	2.0	1.8	1.5	1.3	1.4	1.2
Total	5.2	4.8	4.5	4.6	4.3	4.2
Provincial						
General	2.2	2.3	2.6	2.9	2.7	2.7
Enterprise	1.0	1.0	1.1	1.4	1.3	1.4
Total	3.2	3.3	3.7	4.3	4.0	4.1
Local						
General	2.3	2.3	2.4	2.5	2.4	2.4
Enterprise	0.4	0.4	0.4	0.4	0.4	0.4
Total	2.7	2.7	2.8	2.9	2.8	2.8
Total Government[a]						
General	7.6	7.6	8.0	8.7	8.0	8.1
Enterprise	3.4	3.2	3.0	3.1	3.0	2.9
Total	11.0	10.8	11.0	11.8	11.0	11.0
Education Sector						
Teaching	2.5	2.9	3.5	3.1	2.9	2.7
Non-teaching	1.6	1.8	2.2	2.0	1.8	1.7
Total	4.1	4.7	5.7	5.1	4.7	4.4
Hospital Sector	2.8	3.5	3.8	3.4	2.6	2.5
Grand Total	17.9	19.0	20.5	20.3	18.3	17.9

Source: Table 3-26.
a. Totals exclude DND military personnel. In 1960 they represented 1.8 percent of the labour force; in 1970, 1.1 percent and by 1980, 0.7 percent.

large-scale employment in enterprises. The federal level of government remains a traditional bureaucracy in comparison to the provincial level of government, where employment in enterprises has increased roughly in tandem with increases in general government employment. If one considers everything that is not in the federal government's jurisdiction to be in the provincial sphere, it is seen that the federal to provincial ratio dropped from 29 percent federal versus 71 percent provincial in 1960, to about 23 percent federal versus more than 77 percent provincial in 1982. The margin of change is therefore about 6 percent of the whole public sector pie.

Thus, if one conceives of bureaucracy as represented by jobs in any level of government, excluding teachers and hospital workers, it is fair to say that it has not run mad. Indeed, even including these sectors, the proportion of the labour force that is in government work has not increased alarmingly. Rather, the size of the labour force has increased by 82.6 percent over the 22-year period (see Table 3-5), and the total size of the aggregated governments has kept pace. Nor is it the federal government in particular, as much comment would lead one to believe,

TABLE 3-28 Percentage of Public Employment/Labour Force Employed by Government, by Province

	Nfld.	P.E.I.	N.S.	N.B.	Que.	Ont.	Man.	Sask.	Alta.	B.C.	Canada
1960											
Total government	13.2	11.8	13.6	14.7	8.8	10.9	13.9	11.7	12.1	11.2	11.0
Hospital sector	3.1	3.2	3.3	3.6	2.5	2.9	3.2	4.4	3.1	2.8	2.8
Education sector	6.5	5.0	5.0	5.8	4.2	3.6	4.2	5.4	4.2	3.6	4.1
Total	22.8	19.0	21.9	24.1	15.5	17.4	21.3	21.5	19.4	17.6	17.9
1965											
Total government	14.5	12.9	14.3	13.8	9.2	10.3	13.6	10.4	11.1	11.2	10.8
Hospital sector	4.4	3.9	4.1	4.6	4.0	3.2	3.6	4.0	2.9	2.9	3.5
Education sector	8.1	6.1	6.0	6.5	5.2	4.4	4.9	5.7	4.7	4.4	4.7
Total	27.0	22.9	24.4	24.9	18.4	17.9	22.1	20.1	18.7	18.5	19.0
1970											
Total government	12.7	14.3	16.5	14.2	9.3	10.7	13.0	10.4	11.6	10.4	11.0
Hospital sector	4.7	4.4	4.2	5.0	4.2	3.7	4.0	3.6	4.0	3.0	3.8
Education sector	8.1	8.3	6.8	7.4	6.0	5.4	5.5	5.9	5.8	4.6	5.7
Total	25.5	27.0	27.5	26.6	19.4	19.8	22.5	19.9	21.4	18.0	20.5
1975											
Total government	14.5	15.3	18.3	14.5	9.7	11.4	15.3	12.9	13.1	10.8	11.8
Hospital sector	4.4	3.5	4.4	3.7	3.7	3.1	4.2	3.4	3.7	2.8	3.4
Education sector	7.1	5.8	6.8	5.8	5.3	4.7	5.2	5.5	5.4	4.4	5.1
Total	26.0	24.6	29.5	24.0	18.7	19.2	24.7	21.8	22.2	18.0	20.3

TABLE 3-28 (Cont'd)

	Nfld.	P.E.I.	N.S.	N.B.	Que.	Ont.	Man.	Sask.	Alta.	B.C.	Canada
1980											
Total government	13.7	13.7	15.0	14.0	10.3	10.4	13.3	12.7	11.6	10.1	11.0
Hospital sector	4.0	2.8	3.4	2.8	3.1	2.4	2.6	2.5	2.3	2.2	2.6
Education sector	7.0	5.2	5.8	5.2	5.2	4.2	4.8	4.9	4.2	4.2	4.7
Total	24.7	21.7	24.2	22.0	18.6	17.0	20.7	20.1	18.1	16.5	18.3
1982											
Total government	13.7	13.8	14.1	14.1	10.3	10.4	12.8	12.0	11.6	10.0	11.0
Hospital sector	3.8	2.2	3.5	2.8	3.2	2.1	2.7	2.4	2.2	2.2	2.5
Education sector	6.7	4.8	5.7	5.0	4.7	4.0	4.4	4.5	3.9	3.8	4.4
Total	24.2	20.8	23.3	21.9	18.2	16.5	19.9	18.9	16.7	16.0	17.9

Source: Tables 3-3, 3-5, 3-15, 3-16, 3-19, 3-20, 3-23 and 3-26.
a. The notes of explanation on Table 3-26 apply to the statistics on this table.

that increases apace. Of every ten public sector employees, only two of them are working for the federal government in either general government work or enterprise, while the other eight are not under general control, but are under provincial government jurisdiction as either provincial or local public sector employees. And while the federal government has lost ground over the 22 years in comparison to the provincial jurisdiction, the shift is in the range of 6 percent of total government employment. This is a change, certainly, but not a revolutionary change.

If we are seeking to discern significant changes in the nature of government in our society, we will not find them reflected in the sheer number of government employees, or even in the relative importance of work as a regular government employee as a ratio of the labour force. We will have to look at what governments do, and not at how massive they have become, for as we have seen, they have remained quite trim in terms of this chapter's findings.

TABLE 3-29 Level of Public Sector Employment/Total Public Sector Employment

Level	1960	1965	1970	1975	1980	1982
	(percent)					
Federal General	17.6	15.5	14.7	16.1	15.9	16.7
Federal Enterprise	11.4	9.5	7.2	6.6	7.5	6.6
Total	29.0	25.0	21.9	22.7	23.4	23.3
Provincial General	12.1	12.4	12.6	14.4	14.8	15.1
Provincial Enterprise	5.5	5.2	5.6	6.7	7.0	7.6
Total	17.6	17.6	18.2	21.1	21.8	22.7
Local General	12.9	11.9	11.8	12.3	13.0	13.6
Local Enterprise	2.1	1.9	1.9	2.0	2.1	2.2
Total	15.0	13.8	13.6	14.3	15.1	15.8
Total Government						
General	42.6	39.9	39.1	42.7	43.7	45.4
Enterprise	18.9	16.6	14.7	15.2	16.6	16.3
Total	61.7	56.5	53.8	57.9	60.3	61.7
Education Sector						
Teaching	13.9	15.5	17.0	15.6	15.6	14.9
Non-teaching	8.6	9.6	10.6	9.7	9.7	9.3
Total	22.5	25.1	27.6	25.3	25.3	24.2
Hospital sector	15.8	18.4	18.7	16.9	14.3	14.1

Source: Table 3-25.
a. The notes of explanation on Table 3-26 apply to the statistics on this table.

Chapter 4

Public Service Bureaucracy
as the Object of Public Policy

Rather than simply functioning as the means through which public policy is implemented, public service bureaucracies have become the object of public policy as: 1) social policy laboratories, 2) economic management targets, and 3) experimental subjects for new instruments of indirect managerial control by all elected political officials. To understand the evolution of Canada's public service institutions, one must therefore examine in some detail the different ways in which they have served as such an object of policy.

Public Service Bureaucracy as Social Policy Laboratory

Public service bureaucracies have increasingly become social policy laboratories in the sense that they are required by statute, or expected by declaratory intent, to deal with a range of social issues encompassing various rights and concepts of equity, equality and fairness. This is not to suggest that they had no similar obligations in the past, but rather that newer examples have been added to the list of obligations, using both federal and provincial policies. Our intent here is to demonstrate the broad cumulative effects of these social obligations and the values and ideas they encompass. These obligations are reflected in: 1) conflict of interest provisions; 2) collective bargaining; 3) language policy and rights; 4) affirmative action and broader views of a representative bureaucracy; 5) human rights legislation; and 6) the Canadian Charter of Rights and Freedoms.

Initially, however, it is useful to affirm that the oldest social policy obligation is reflected in the merit concept and the merit system itself. Since this is a central element of Public Service Bureaucracy I and is discussed in Chapters 1 and 2, we need only stress here its essential social meaning. Merit was a response to the excesses of political patronage. The merit principle initially embraced two interrelated concepts: the selection of the person most qualified for the job, and the right of all qualified Canadians to apply for the job. The first concept does not concern us here, since its very purpose was to build a modern rational bureaucracy. The second concept was a social one, however, since it implied the need for a sense of fairness. The merit idea gave birth to the merit system, that is, the administrative procedures necessary to give meaning to these concepts.

Closely related both in time and concept were the principles and systems intended to ensure the proper acquisition of goods and services as well as people. The system of competitive bidding instituted in all governmental jurisdictions was intended to produce honesty and probity as well as fairness. Combined with the merit system, it produced a system of management that today goes to the core of the public service bureaucracy as a modern rational organization in the Weberian sense, but one with social obligations rooted in a concept of equity and fairness. From the outset, procedures were put in place in public institutions that were not required in private institutions. These procedures immediately broke the mould of the pure hierarchical model of management where the manager goes out and obtains the people and goods he or she needs, in order to realize organizational goals.

Attempts to produce mechanisms that would reduce or eliminate real or perceived conflicts of interest are among the newer efforts that continue these earlier historic concerns. Guidelines rather than rules[1] have been the norm here. They have been instituted in some jurisdictions to ensure that ministers and senior officials cannot reward either themselves or their relatives and former business associates via the contracting or hiring process. Large problems remain as to how much honesty and probity can be secured.

Beginning essentially in the 1960s, public service bureaucracies were endowed with a newer genre of social obligations. Chief among these was the establishment of collective bargaining, including the right to strike. While we examine collective bargaining later in this chapter in relation to the bureaucracy as an entity for economic management, our focus here is on its role as a further manifestation of the social obligations of the government as a progressive employer.

In the full flush of the social reformist 1960s, expanded public sector collective bargaining (a phenomenon that did not have a parallel in the United States) was seen as the extension of the social obligations to be met within bureaucracy. The wide-scale introduction of collective bargaining at the federal and provincial levels represented an increased recognition of the public servant as both citizen and employee. Granted in the midst of the rapid growth of white-collar, middle-class and professional employment in the public sector, the extension of rights also reflected the political pressure that these groups were able to bring to bear in the heady optimism and prosperity of the 1960s. These pressures were not all uniform, however.

For example, the expansion of collective bargaining in Quebec, and the later extreme form of centralized bargaining that occurred there, was linked to the overall transformation of Quebec society in the Quiet Revolution.[2] The existence of language barriers in the English-dominated private sector in Quebec meant that the Québécois saw the state sector as their main avenue of mobility and identity. Thus, the development of collective bargaining in Quebec took on a larger sense of collective justice, rather than the more confined sense of furthering progressive employment rights that characterized its expansion in the federal government and in the other provinces.

It is well to remember, especially in the light of our later discussion of the bureaucracy as the target of economic management policies, that collective bargaining rights in the public sector were never the full-blown rights that characterized the private sector system.[3] It must be said, in addition, that the right to strike was not initially generously given at the federal level. Rather it was given in the wake of a postal walkout which seemed to show that even if the right did not legally exist, it would be exercised. The methods of selecting the right to strike, the absence of lockout provisions, the items that could be bargained, the definition of the bargaining unit, and the designation of employees eligible to go on strike, were all constrained by law. In short, bargaining in the public sector was much less free than in the private sector.

Hard on the heels of the introduction of collective bargaining in the federal government came the Official Languages Act of 1969, which ushered in the era of official bilingualism. The federal government's language policy was intended to ensure that Canadians of either official language group could obtain access to the basic services of the federal government in the official language of their choice. As such, it embraced as a social policy a doctrine that went to the very foundation of the contemporary definition of Canada as a political society.[4] That it was both basic and controversial there can be no doubt. There were many threads to the language policy in terms of its expectations about bureaucracy as a social policy laboratory. First, it made more explicit the reality that language competency was to be part of the definition of merit. Secondly, it involved the accelerated recruitment and advancement of francophone Canadians for senior public service positions and the development of a massive language training enterprise. Thirdly, over time it profoundly affected the structure of provincial education systems through language grants and the development of French immersion programs. This is perhaps its most fundamental effect, since not only did it alter education to help generate a future cadre from which bilingual officialdom could be selected, but it also produced in some quarters a strong resentment of a perceived new elitism in future intergenerational career changes. Indeed, October 1984 saw Manitoba MP Dan McKenzie persisting with complaints to the Canadian Human Rights Commission alleging discrimination against English-speaking Canadians in federal government hiring.[5] The goal of McKenzie's efforts is to have the Canadian Human Rights Act amended to include discrimination on the basis of language.

In the 1970s, language legislation and its effects were increasingly accompanied by a larger array of social pressures to have the bureaucracy play a leading role in helping to resolve inequalities other than the status of francophones. Sometimes expressed in the concepts of a "representative bureaucracy"[6] or as a commitment to affirmative action, these inequalities were centred on the role of women but they also dealt with the handicapped, native Canadians, and what were increasingly called the visible minorities.[7] There are now 65 such visible minorities that have advocacy for a share of jobs in the federal bureaucracy. Also at the federal level, the Public Service Commission's programs were supplemented by a new, almost "central" agency, the Office of the Status of Women. (Various similar offices or units were set up at the provincial and urban levels. See the Appendices.) No one, in the face of the evidence, could seriously dispute the inequality factor in these cases or fail to argue that reform had to start somewhere. In each case, the answer to the "somewhere" was the public service. Little sustained attention was given to the possibility that inequities in participation of some groups might most significantly stem from social and economic inequalities that prevented members of such groups from acquiring employment qualifications. In a sense, the bureaucracy assumed a burden for the whole society, policies on employment in public service jobs substituting for basic social, economic and education policy. It is not our intent here to assess the actual degree of progress made in the bureaucracies' social laboratory role; indeed, the record seems to be spotty at best. (See the Appendices on the record.[8]) Rather, we merely wish to show the grafting onto the public service bureaucracy of these additional social expectations.

The 1970s also saw the introduction of human rights legislation. Indeed, in some provinces such legislation dates back to the late 1960s. Intended to provide procedures to redress discrimination in hiring and related practices, the legislation was accompanied at the federal level by the establishment of the Human Rights Commission, again, as an agent of Parliament as well as of the executive. It should be noted that the Official Languages Act also brought with it the Commissioner of Official Languages, another direct agent of Parliament, as was the historic protector of merit, the Public Service Commission. None of these bodies is a large bureaucratic structure when compared to the main line departments of government. In relation to our presentation of Public Service Bureaucracy III, however, it is important to stress the degree to which these small units, these "rights ombudsmen," add an institutionalized presence for the ideas of equity and equality. They do so out of a recognition that parliaments and legislatures, as an assemblage of elected politicians, do not in themselves have a sustained organizational capacity to persistently fight for or monitor these rights in the day-to-day settings in which their infringement is likely to occur. As we have already suggested in earlier chapters, however, we believe that Parliament to an excessive degree has absolved itself of a responsibility to monitor this collection of rights agencies.

Last, but hardly least, in this brief chronological treatment of the bureaucracy as social policy laboratory was the constitutional entrenchment in 1982 of the Canadian Charter of Rights and Freedoms. The effects of the charter on public service bureaucracies can only be guessed at this early date. Suffice to say, however, that it institutionalizes even more some of the rights that had evolved in the 1970s. Moreover, it brings into play a potentially far greater role for the courts[9] to police the bureaucracy itself or, alternatively, to assist the bureaucracy in the enforcement of rights, including the implementation of various affirmative action programs.

Public Service Bureaucracy as the Target of Economic Management Policy

As we have stressed in the previous section of this chapter and in the Introduction to this study, a key event in changing the government's approach to the bureaucracy was the emergence of collective bargaining rights and the concurrent growth of public sector unions. This was especially the case at the provincial level. For most of the 1960s and in the early 1970s, there was no apparent conflict between the role of government as a manager of the public service and as a manager of the economy.[10] From then on, however, the conflict between the two roles increased greatly. Public service bureaucracies became the target of a newer array of economic management policies in several different ways and contexts and, in some instances, sought to end or reduce "rights." Once again, it is important to stress that this is not an inherently new phenomenon, since controlling the size of government and wage levels has been a part of implicit or explicit theories of fiscal prudence and fiscal expansion. We trace these newer developments here under three headings: 1) direct efforts to control public sector wages; 2) various public sector retrenchment and restraint strategies; and 3) more general efforts to restrain the use of aggregate governing instruments, such as regulation and Crown corporations, in the general pursuit of economic management objectives. By economic management objectives, we refer to the pursuit of policies and actions designed to promote economic growth and greater price stability in some overall fiscal strategy. In this sense, we argue that both the federal and provincial governments practise some kind of overall economic management function, recognizing at the same time that the federal level has a greater arsenal of tools at its disposal.

Although extensive political debate about public sector wages and public service strikes began to occur well before the mid-1970s, the two major instances of direct wage control are the 1975–77 anti-inflation program and the 1982–83 "6 and 5" program. The former imposed controls on the public sector and major sections of the private sector and sought to control both wages and prices.[11] It applied at both the federal and provincial levels. The "6 and 5" program, on the other hand, applied only to federal public servants.[12] The tentacles of the program, however, stretched out in an effort to extend its coverage, albeit episodically, to other sectors via vigorous exhortation of those who were the recipients of federal grants. Selected provincial control programs are listed in the Appendices.

Two elements of the origins of these programs deserve particular emphasis. Both programs were preceded by strenuous efforts to characterize the then-increasing rates of inflation as being led by public sector wages, despite evidence, over the last decade as a whole, that was either opposed or decidedly unclear. The variability in the evidence is found in Gunderson's conclusions,[13] which showed a strong upward public sector wage bias in the 1960s and 1970s but a dissipation of it in the late 1970s. The advantage is larger for females and low-wage workers. Indeed, in the early years of bargaining, their wage increases involved a catch-up situation vis-à-vis the private sector. There is a wage disadvantage for the high salary levels, despite the common portrayal of the latter as "fat cats" in the 1970s. In 1975, this did not produce a policy targetted only at the public sector, but by 1982, it was so targetted. The policy was the combined result of: 1) explicit pressure from key business organizations that public sector wages be controlled; 2) the federal government's need to recover politically from the debâcle of its November 1981 budget; and 3) the fact that public opinion polls showed an intense resentment against bureaucrats, in part because, in the midst of a deep recession, bureaucrats apparently had job security.[14]

While these were the most visible examples of bureaucracy becoming a direct target of economic management policy, they were by no means isolated instances. One must relate them to a series of smaller steps that were occurring as governments sought to rein in on the bargaining rights previously granted. At the federal level, for example, the Treasury Board began to take a much tougher stance regarding the numbers of workers designated as essential during a strike. This weakened the impact of strike action and the board's practice was later upheld by the courts.[15]

At the provincial level, there emerged a strong pattern of the increased use of back-to-work legislation. This increased practice of "permanent exceptionalism" meant that bargaining rights continued to exist only as long as they were not practised too often.[16]

Also swept into this burgeoning anti-public service bureaucracy ethos were a variety of provincial retrenchment and restraint programs. These are the subject of a separate study by the Commission, so for our more limited purposes, one or two examples are sufficient.[17] The most stridently anti-bureaucracy and anti-public sector program was that launched in 1983 by the Bennett Social Credit government of British Columbia. It attacked the notion of civil service tenure, sought to limit collective bargaining rights and eliminated both public service jobs and programs. The program cuts were primarily those involving small "rights" agencies, including a human rights agency and the Office of the Rentalsman. A sharply contrasting, but nonetheless equally real, restraint program was that instituted by the Parti Québécois government of Quebec. Instead of rolling back programs or engaging in massive layoffs, the Quebec government, despite its close political links with the public sector labour movement, rolled back public sector salaries.

Somewhere in between these basic restraint strategies was a range of other practices and political circumstances. Alberta, Saskatchewan and Quebec cut back on public service positions much later than other provinces, notably between 1980 and 1982. Ontario professes to have practised responsible restraint for much of the post-1975 period and there is some evidence presented in Chapter 3 that supports this claim. (Ontario, however, now has a rather large local government sector.) At the federal level, signs of restraint showed up in two ways in the late 1970s. First, rates of growth in the traditional public service were cut back. Secondly, term appointments increased as a proportion of all appointments, in effect creating a more manoeuvrable public sector labour force than has historically existed.[18]

Another way in which public service bureaucracy became the target of economic management policy in the late 1970s and early 1980s was in the debate about, and periodic action on, the reform of regulation and Crown corporations.[19] By the mid-1970s, these appendages, which had grown in importance as employers mainly at the provincial level, were the object of debate in two interrelated senses. The first dealt with general problems of accountability, both to legislative bodies and to those producer and consumer interests affected by their decisions. Of more importance in this section of our analysis, however, was the link between the economic debate about these instruments and the neo-conservative demands for less government as the ultimate cure for a stagnating economy.

Once again the debate was not a uniform one, nor did it necessarily result in action. The regulatory reform debate, in one sense, crystallized around the work of the Economic Council of Canada's regulation reference.[20] The council argued that excessive regulation in some sectors was costing the economy billions and reducing its capacity to be competitive and efficient. There were, however, few outright instances of deregulation resulting in lost public sector jobs at the federal or provincial level. Here again, various practices were in evidence. British Columbia established a minister for deregulation. Ontario established various task forces that eliminated some of the so-called paper burden of government (but presided over an increase in numbers of boards and agencies). By the early 1980s, however, the debate shifted to the regulatory context in specific sectors. Thus, energy regulation actually increased but there was simultaneous pressure to deregulate parts of the industry, such as gas exports. Prospects for a form of airline deregulation increased by 1984 but were counterbalanced in part by demands for more regulation to ensure airline safety.

A similar mixed bag of debate and practice accompanied the issue of Crown corporations. At a general level, debate initially focussed on the speculations of the short-lived Clark Conservative government about privatizing several federal Crown corporations. Attention then shifted to the Liberals' establishment of the Canada Development Investment Corporation, which was formed both to divest the government of certain firms or assets but also potentially to establish others. Meanwhile, despite the general bias against Crown corporations, the Liberals concurrently strengthened Petro-Canada and established new Crown enterprises such as Canertech and Canagrex.[21] The newly elected Mulroney Conservative government renewed its promise to sell off some Crown enterprises, but none had been sold up to early 1985. At the provincial level, the most concrete manifestation of an economic desire to alter the role of Crown corporations was found in Saskatchewan. There, the newly elected Conservative government, under Grant Devine, sought to restructure the stable of Crown corporations constructed by successive NDP-CCF governments.[22] Even here, however, there were no major privatization measures.

Thus, from the mid-1970s on, public service bureaucracies became the target of economic management policies in a variety of ways, but with decidedly mixed results. When viewed as "unions and wage demanders," the policy makers became increasingly accurate in hitting their bureaucratic target. When viewed as "programs or bundles of regulatory and Crown corporation activity," public service bureaucracies, as befits their ambivalent role as both implementor of policy and object of policy, proved to be more elusive. Nonetheless, in the last decade or so, there has clearly emerged a climate of criticism and cynicism in which bureaucracy in all its manifestations is seen to be part of the problem rather than the solution.

Public Service Bureaucracy as the Object of New Measures of Political Control

Interwoven with, but partly distinguishable from, the twin notions of bureaucracy as the object of social policy and as the target of economic management, are a number of innovations to improve the influence of the political level over bureaucratic management. In each case, the dilemmas at the federal level are better known but the provinces had many counterparts. Several measures intended to exert some version of greater political control were adopted throughout the 1970s and into the 1980s in the apparently never-ending search for ways to ensure that the public servants remain servants of the public and of the elected political system. These include: 1) strengthened central agencies; 2) value-for-money auditing and other budgetary reforms; 3) ombudsmen and access to information legislation; and 4) decentralization and/or the geographic dispersal of government offices.

Central agencies were strengthened and grew in size, in part, out of a desire to enhance control over the bureaucracy, especially the line departments, but also the independent agencies.[23] In part, they were strengthened to produce greater horizontal co-ordination among departments, drawing a constitutional justification from a novel application of the idea of collective cabinet responsibility as distinct from the traditional doctrine of individual ministerial responsibility. While such central agencies grew markedly, they were still, in the grand scheme of things, quite small units of government that built on already existing agencies.

Increasingly, however, such agencies, especially in the federal government, came in the late 1970s and early 1980s to epitomize the triumph of "out of touch" bureaucracy. The coteries of so-called super bureaucrats were perceived to be the opposite of the old-style neutral public servant.[24] Any useful role that central agencies may have played became submerged in the general perceptions of bureaucratic excess. The line bureaucrats and ministers of the traditional departmental public sector came to increasingly resent the analysts at the centre. Departments could not recognize that their needs had really been "harmonized" by their processing through the eye of the needle at the centre. Expanded central agencies were an innovation nominally to improve cabinet's management capabilities, We have seen also innovations to improve the capacity of backbench parliamentarians to intervene in issues of the management type.[25]

As concerns about accountability increased, various budgetary reform measures were introduced. The auditor general of Canada, with an undoubtedly sincere concern about the growth of expenditure, transformed his office between 1977 and 1984 from that of a traditional "honesty and probity" auditor, who usefully based his work largely on financial accounts and records, to that of a "comprehensive auditor," in effect a management consultant,[26] who formed opinions not only about financial transactions and systems but also about the overall quality of non-financial management, the quality of policy advice to ministers, and the revenue budget. Since policy cannot legitimately be directly criticized by public servants, the new management auditors justify their work by resorting to a complicated rationale that they are merely concerned with the appropriateness of the government's "systems." Apart from assessing whether the auditor general was still functioning correctly as an agent of Parliament and a servant of the public accounts committee, it remains genuinely debatable whether the new focus on systems helps or hinders the elected MP. The latter is now deluged by information, much of it in a form that, precisely because it is comprehensive (but supposedly only about systems), is incomprehensible in practical political terms. When MPs push for an interpretation by the OAG, the office is led willy-nilly into policy areas; when they do not, the office operates without guidance from the body that it nominally serves, the public accounts committee. There have been, to be sure, some improvements in the form of presentation of the Estimates which can be attributed to the OAG's missionary work, but this ultimately must be related to whether the consumer, that is, the MP, can make use of it.

The phrase "intellectual imperialism" can be used to depict the tendency of key knowledge groups to define new tasks for themselves. This applies not only to accountants in the sense described above but, more generally, to the recent growth of the professional evaluation industry.[27] Thus, economists' and other social scientists' support of cost benefit analysis and scientific program evaluation often suffers from a failure to appreciate that cerebral forms of evaluation, as opposed to those forms that occur through political and social interaction and pressure, are only one mode of evaluation. It is not certain that formal evaluation leads inexorably to more perfect public policy or more rational behaviour by elected ministers.

It is in this sense that we have included, albeit somewhat hesitantly, in our characterization of Public Service Bureaucracy III the notion of new forms of what we have called "acceptable professional patronage," in the more polite sense of the state as patron. It is not the dastardly, blatant patronage about which reformers were exercised in the early decades of this century (and during the federal election campaign of 1984) and for which the merit system and the sealed contractual bid were the central reforms. This new quasi-patronage is more subtle. Moreover, it is not necessarily confined to Public Service Bureaucracy III, since there are earlier examples — for example, the practice of hiring lawyers in the Justice and Attorney General's departments at both levels of government as well as media specialists, communications experts, auditors and evaluators and management consultants by other departments. Indeed, many will object even to calling it patronage. These latter-day "public servants" are part of the larger contract state.[28]

Professionally educated and upwardly mobile, many of those who practise these technical and evaluative arts, especially private firms who do most if not all their business in the public sector, or academics who derive steady supplementary contract income, would not even view themselves as public servants. But in reality, they are heavily dependent on the public sector. Moreover, they often idealize themselves as progressive reformers, especially of Public Service Bureaucracies I and II.

While central agencies and the professional evaluation industry in general try to oversee contemporary substantive issues of policy and management, the other three examples of control measures are to be found on the outer edges of the political system. Ombudsmen, for example, began to be established in Canada in the provincial governments in the late 1960s and early 1970s (see the Appendices).[29] Once again, they were usually independent officers of the legislative branch intended to handle various grievances by citizens against the decisions and non-decisions of bureaucrats and governments. They were considered a form of redress for the average citizen, less expensive than the courts, but at the same time an implicit acknowledgment that the elected MP, the democratic front-line grievance handler, could not fully cope with demands.

In the early 1980s, access to information legislation was passed and new "rights" commissioners were established to resolve differences of view as to the release of information.[30] The legislation sought to increase the rights of citizens, the private sector and the media to government information. There are a wide range of exceptions or categories of information to which the right to information does not apply. These include matters of commercial privilege, international relations and national security, federal-provincial relations, and intra-cabinet policy formulation. But the central point for the purposes of our analysis is that the evolving state of bureaucracy had produced the need for new measures to control Leviathan, whether the latter was viewed as bureaucracy or as big government in general.

Efforts in the 1970s to decentralize bureaucracies were also an important, though elusive, manifestation of a political desire to make them more amenable to control in the sense of enhanced sensitivity to diverse local conditions and geographic areas.[31] Although two-thirds of all federal government employees are traditionally located outside the national capital region, the federal government still felt the need to visibly alter the field/headquarters balance. Here, one must distinguish real decentralization of decision making from the mere geographic dispersal of activity. There are few genuine examples of the former in that the acid test of real geographic decentralization is the capacity of regional officials to make major resource allocation decisions. Perhaps the closest example of this was the effort to decentralize the decisions of the former Department of Regional Economic Expansion (DREE) by placing assistant deputy ministers in each of the main regions. A more frequent occurrence was the geographic dispersal of government operating units, affecting about 4,500 jobs to date. This was done in part to act as an economic stimulus to some of the country's smaller urban centres. While this practice was in one sense justifiable, the actual process of moving often created chaos for the department and employees concerned. As a single event, this would not have been unmanageable, except that it was one of many such reforms going on concurrently.[32]

The provincial parallel to DREE was often found in concerns about the delivery of programs in the northern parts of each province. The provincial level was also subject to the not inconsiderable pressure from municipal and city governments to decentralize, and to demands for public hearings in the environmental assessment process. Thus, no matter what configuration of programs exists at either level of government, there is always a geographical and spatial dimension to organizational structure, decisions and "presence." In this sense, too, bureaucracy became the object of policy to control it, even when the nature of control norms and values was imprecise and partly contradictory.

Summary

By focussing on how the evolving bureaucracies of the past two decades have increasingly been the object of public policy, one can see the nature of the changes that have been attempted. As shown, they have been the object of policy in three senses: 1) as a laboratory for social policy; 2) as a target of economic management policy; and 3) through renewed efforts to impose control by a variety of political actors.

In retracing our steps in this way, we can see more starkly why public service bureaucracies cannot be viewed only as a constitutional means for the delivery of public services and programs. The modern public service obviously continues to deliver programs and must be judged accordingly, but the reality of the 1980s is that it has become a composite summary of both the basic means and the ends of Canadian political life. As such, it has become a partially contradictory mix of the social and economic policies of the public sector. This is not to suggest that Canadians have knowingly planned what they have now inherited.

While the analytical models we are using suggest an overall uniformity to the patterns of change portrayed, it is necessary also to distinguish among the provinces, since the very nature of diverse provincial political systems and regional economies produces varied outcomes. For some aspects, the vast differences in the scale of government alone will produce differences. For the smallest provinces, for example, the resort to ponderous control structures in the form of central agencies was not needed nor necessarily even considered. In other cases, such as Quebec, public service bureaucracy can scarcely be understood without reference to the links between the modernization of Quebec and state employment, and between the Parti Québécois and the public sector labour movement.

What do these three narratives tell us about the manner in which elected governments in Canada have chosen to act upon the public sector work force? One can draw out a number of problems.

First, where governments treat their public sector work forces as test cases for the development of social policy, we should be safe in assuming that politicians are acting from a view of what the outcome should be. That is, if the public sector is to bear the burden of advertising particular values even as it tries to do its other work, then someone, somewhere, must take responsibility for the priorities among those values, for the trade-offs between them, and for recognizing unacceptable social outcomes. A responsible government should be responsible for the capacity and quality of the public sector work force.

It is easily recognized, and understood, that some of the social policy goals will work against some of the economic goals. As we argued in the Introduction, due process is not always the quickest and cheapest way of operating. As a society, we prefer to operate fairly in our public institutions, agreeing to pay the "overhead" on fairness and equity. Fairness is to operate as a constraint upon managerial goals of efficiency.

But even the social policy initiatives, when isolated from the economic policy initiatives, conflict with each other. One can use merit, the most central value of the public service as an institution for the past 75 years, as an example. The merit principle is an individualistic, "small-l" liberal value: the person who is most qualified for a position is the one who will get it. On the other hand, the idea of affirmative action is a collectivistic value. It says that, if one does not see the visible minority/ groups present in the public service in the same proportion that one sees them in the population as a whole, there is some injustice afoot.

Under the most simplified affirmative action ideas, the public sector management tries to achieve social fairness by building a work force that will eventually be representative of all the visible elements in society. The reformed public service aggregate will eventually be what it should have been, had social forces operated as if they were completely blind and absolutely neutral. Yet under such policies the state does not grapple with the social forces and institutions that continually create the initial "unfair" representation out of the fabric of the society. For example, the contingent bias of the education system which affects who can qualify for certain jobs is left to operate as it will. Thus, even while public sector employers establish targets for hiring (for example) women in non-traditional management and scientific and technical jobs, the social and educational systems continue to operate on traditional lines, and few women qualify for newly available jobs in these areas. The theory is apparently that demand will eventually restructure supply, even in the face of formidable barriers, and despite the weakness of the new demand.

There are problems other than ineffectiveness with the administration of affirmative action programs, whether the value being affirmed is language, territory, gender, age or minority race. It must first be said that the question of whether individual members of the visible minorities can in principle be fully suitable for their share of jobs is no problem whatever. Of course they can. The real issues are, in no particular order of importance and with no claim to exhaustiveness; 1) whether personnel can meet all the requirements for staffing on a timely basis from among those individuals who are able to meet job requirements and decide to put themselves forward; 2) whether the sheer proliferation of values that must be satisfied leads to arbitrary staffing because the complexity is not auditable, and hence, to the eventual demise of a merit system; 3) whether persons who possess a characteristic will eventually be compelled (perhaps to their distaste) to describe themselves as part of a group defined by that characteristic in order to make a contribution to some target or quota; and 4) whether the representatives of various groups in the public service will begin to doubt each other's merit for positions and perhaps evade the control of some incumbents of office. The danger here is that the management milieu will lose its rational rule-bound character.

Still more important questions stem from the political history of the languages policies. The contemporary policies are ostensibly about language, but they found their political energy in the fact that they held the promise of lessening alienation from the federal government of citizens based overwhelmingly in one territory — Quebec. One can then ask, first, whether the initial political thrust to build up francophone representation and, thus, national unity is trivialized by the proliferation of goals for representation of so many other groups, constituted on such diverse social principles. As a subsidiary, one can next inquire whether it is fair not to give regional groups other than the francophone groups at the territorial centre an explicit share of the employment, and so on. The sense of being excluded from employment at the national centre is surely one source of western alienation. Overall, it is plausible to claim that the policies of the last 20 years have partly federalized the bureaucracy, placing on it demands for representations in order to shore up national unity. It also seems fair to say that whether or not the merit system actually works is now incomparably more difficult to establish, since it is now in such complex balance with the other rights criteria.

In the control bureaucracy seen in the aggregate, a still greater va
of values is embodied in institutions which work single-minded
maximize the particular value(s) that they stand for. They monitor,
badger, hound and coax the public service into compliance with their
policies. In short, they are hardly monitoring and advisory agencies of a
passive kind. Each situation, meaning the resolution of strong demands
from a variety of sources, is left to chance and the relative powers of the
opposing forces. When the result is the almost inevitable compromise,
the individual control agencies often tend to resort to rhetoric and
pressure tactics to raise the costs of non-compliance for the organization
resisting them. What one control agency does, so must the others, or
else the measures of their own performances indicate deterioration. The
performance of the public service must be painted as terrible beyond
belief, in order to "improve" it on the next round.

There is no harmonization of these disparate tunes from on high. We
are not saying there can be. We suspect that it would be impossible to
develop a formula for reconciling so many disparate economic and social
goals, that is, so many "goods" for which no standards have been set.
We are saying, rather, that if the bureaucracy is to be used for symbolic
purposes, then these symbols should be few, and powerful, so that the
observer can at least see what the lesson is meant to be. To establish any
semblance of increased control, fewer ad hoc control bureaucracies will
yield more control provided they are accompanied by suitable changes
in the over-arching elected representative institutions. In short, the
cluster of bodies in Public Service Bureaucracy III should be brought to
account before some single elected body for continuous scrutiny. So also
should the cluster of abstract "goods" being sought by the programs
designed to improve the representation of various minorities in public
sector work forces. From one perspective, these are social and political
policies that are being sought by the instruments of government employment targets on the one hand and individual rights on the other, the latter
now more readily enforceable under the Charter of Rights. The problem
is that the "laboratory" in all cases is an organization that is also
intended to be the work force that directly delivers all programs to the
public. Surely the responsibility of the elected government ought to be
weighed constantly in matters of such importance.

Political Parties as Public Service Control Institutions and as Reform Advocates

We have now examined the evolution of Canada's public service bureaucracies through the framework set out in the Introduction and in Chapter 1, mapping them both quantitatively and in relation to specific control regimes and to the trend toward making bureaucracy an object of public policy. Before we can take the analysis further, we must link what we have learned to, first, the role of political parties as a real or potential control institution; and, second, the ideas that parties embody and articulate about bureaucratic reform, both as governing parties and in opposition.

The first analytical task of this chapter is to explore the role of parties as a primary institution for the control of public service bureaucracy. In this context, we will examine the specific ways in which political parties do or could operate as more successful control institutions. More specifically we look at a political party when it functions: as an electoral vehicle; as a democratic forum in convention; when it is preparing for a transition to power; and when it functions as a caucus in Parliament. This focus arises out of our view that political parties too often see reform as it relates to the bureaucracy in the context of other institutions and not in relation to themselves as institutions. This is not to suggest that political parties have not developed some views about bureaucracy and the reform agenda.

The second analytical task of the chapter is thus to explore the nature of these views. Our focus here is on the last decade, when concern about bureaucracy has escalated. Before embarking on this dual analytical task, however, we will present an historical setting on some of these issues. Clearly, they have arisen before and political parties have had to deal with them.

Parties and Bureaucracies in Historical Context

Four main issues relevant to this study have evolved out of earlier historical periods of Canadian politics. These are: 1) the relationship between merit, patronage and parties; 2) the concern of early socialist parties about the power of bureaucrats; 3) the World War II experience with an influx of businessmen (the so-called dollar-a-year men); and 4) more general concerns expressed about the problems of transition to power. Each of these is discussed briefly.

The initial reforms which led to the system-wide adoption of merit had a profound effect on political parties. In an era when parties were elitist and bore little resemblance to modern, more democratic organizations, government jobs were an important basis for securing political support and party activists. When in power, however, these political civil servants did not produce very good administration.[1] As stressed in Chapter 1, the trade-off for parties in the adoption of the merit system was a loss of patronage leverage in exchange for a better quality of government and a public service that would implement the will of the governing party. There has always remained, however, a tension between merit and patronage. The amount of political control over staffing has been reduced, but the growth of government in absolute terms means that there are still several hundred patronage positions (filled by the governor-in-council), as well as the forms of modern quasi-patronage referred to in our discussion of Public Service Bureaucracy III.

The second historical issue to concern us (though now more likely to be raised by conservative parties) arose out of the deep concerns of early socialist thinkers and parties that, even if they won electoral power, they would face an array of officialdom fundamentally opposed to their views. In the United Kingdom, this took on particular class connotations, but it also occurred in the early evolution of the Co-operative Commonwealth Federation (CCF) in Saskatchewan. Lipset's account of the CCF's rise and assumption of power shows these concerns.[2] The CCF government of T.C.Douglas put in place a fairly elaborate central cabinet planning machinery, in part from its concern to control a civil service that had long served a Liberal administration. The CCF's unabashed presentation of party manifestos was also related to this issue.

The influx of businessmen into senior positions during World War II, many as dollar-a-year men to lead the civilian war effort, is of considerable importance in a party/bureaucracy sense.[3] While obviously a broader phenomenon tied to the very exigencies and patriotic environment that only wartime induces, there is here an important connection between party and bureaucracy in two respects. First, the influx led to a close association between the governing Liberal party and businessmen throughout the postwar period and into the 1950s, in terms of direct recruitment into both the party and the public service. It also implanted or reinforced the notion that business experts could be relied upon to offer private sector ideas on how to run government like a business. The latter did not necessarily take on a deep ideological flavour, since it was a view that powerful Liberal ministers such as C.D.Howe applied to running the new stable of wartime Crown corporations.

The general sense of wartime spirit and co-operativeness, coupled with Canada's considerable emergence in the postwar decade as an influential middle power, meant also that the interdependence of the Liberal ministers and key senior officials was taken for granted. The mythical notion of the mandarins as part of the seamless structure of power was fostered in this setting. This link is of some contemporary importance as a supposed benchmark of what the neutral Canadian public service ought to be.[4] While some of this neutrality ethos was true, some of the practical links of senior officials to the governing Liberals (such as speech-writing during elections) involved a politicization that would exceed that practised today. Yet, ironically, the overwhelmingly fond memory of this era is that of the mandarin heyday, while the decade ending with 1984 is labelled as having introduced the excessive politicizing of the public service.

These three historical threads can be said to lead to the fourth, namely, the more general evolving concern about the transition to power by opposition parties. Given that merit plus an expanding bureaucracy was producing an increasingly institutionalized centre of power based on expertise and permanence, and given the dominance of the Liberals, there was a dual problem for opposition parties. Did they have the level of expertise to prepare for the takeover of power, and would there be a core of senior officials who would be sympathetic and supportive of their core values and priorities? It was the Diefenbaker Conservatives who first faced this double-barrelled task. At the provincial level, several parties faced it in different party configurations. These are explored further below.

Political Parties as Public Service Control Institutions

Political parties (or the party system) have evolved as political institutions. We do not propose to examine them in detail, but rather to focus on their contemporary links to the topic at hand, namely their current and possible future role as essential institutions for the control of public service bureaucracies.[5]

The assumption of democratic elections is that the winning party will carry out a policy plan that has been seriously considered and approved by the electorate — the mandate.[6] Even taking into account the normal excesses of electoral debate, there is at least a minimum expectation that governing parties assume power with a more or less coherent view of what they wish to do on a list of key items. The notion of a politically neutral public service is essential in this parliamentary concept of democratic politics, since it presumes that it is the duty of the public service, especially at the senior bureaucratic levels, to serve the wishes of any party that is elected to govern, tendering its considered advice in a responsible way sensitive to the priorities enunciated by the party in power. It should not engage in anything that compromises its partisan neutrality. As for opposition parties, the system also presumes that criticism will be directed to the cabinet, in part at least, on the assumption and expectation that one of the opposition parties may one day form a government, and hence will need and want an expert public service that may serve its needs as well.

If there are overriding institutional impediments to the democratic political control of the public service's policy role, they are partly attributable to the extremely uneven way in which the party system functions in the electoral context. There are certainly examples where parties have made their key positions clear, but also many where electoral tactics were based on the classic perceived need to be vague so as to assemble a coalition of aggrieved voters and interests (the "outs") who would turn out the "ins." In still other cases, the winning party took actions directly opposite to their campaign promises. While there is a strong tendency to label parties as being only vehicles for electoral mobilization and elections as being the politics of "leadership" and not "issues," the actual record is a mixture of these, since some issues and priorities are closely linked to leaders. This kind of evidence must then be linked to the actual pattern of electoral results and to party competition.

In national politics, the Canadian party system has exemplified what could easily be regarded as almost a textbook scenario for reduced policy control of the public service. Until the recent victory of the Mulroney Conservatives, Canada has had one-party dominance by the Liberal party for all but nine months of the past 20 years, and for 22 of the previous 27 years as well. The party system has, moreover, been highly regionalized, with neither the Liberals nor the Progressive Conservatives in a position over those two decades to be a truly national party.[7] The longer the Conservatives were out of power, the more suspicious and distrustful they became of the neutrality of the senior public service.[8] The Liberals have aided and abetted this perception by politicizing the public service to some degree. This was not a wholesale politicization, but rather one in which appointments of some high-profile persons, with direct partisan connections, to the deputy minister level and to some boards and agencies, led to the suspicion that the ideal of the political neutrality of the public service was being significantly eroded.[9] In the context of the sheer longevity in power of the Liberals, this ensured that the perception of public service neutrality, one of the main institutional devices that control its policy role, was partially compromised. Given the historical antecedents discussed above, there is at least some ambivalence on what is the dominant value. Neutrality is preferred in one sense but, on the other hand, putting trusted partisans in key positions can mean greater control for the governing party.

It is obvious, however, that it is not just the lack of alternation of the parties in power that affects the democratic control of bureaucracy. The way in which parties go about developing party policy is itself a factor. The parties in convention (annual, leadership review, or leadership meetings) do discuss policy but it is much more in the form of aggregating a wish-list of resolutions. There are examples of what might be called benchmark conventions, such as the Liberals' 1960 Kingston Conference, which helped set the agenda of the Pearson Liberals when they assumed power in 1963. But the two major parties are not known for developing a platform on the basis of elaborate party processes. Only the NDP pays sustained attention to mechanisms for generating, testing and consolidating policy. Neither of the two parties that can seriously expect to hold office have processes in their riding or national meetings or conventions that produce sustained concern for the policy mandate. By this we do not mean that every policy adopted by the party must eventually be adopted by the government (the party in office). Rather, we have in mind the main broad mechanisms through which accountability and control operate. That is, if ministers face on the one side a Parliament that does not function as a check because it is not organized around any clear principles, and on the other side a party lacking any apparatus to check on the progress of agreed policy strategies, conditions are ripe for maximizing both de facto bureaucratic power and the perception of bureaucratic power.

In this regard, the connection between party and Parliament is absolutely crucial and usually overlooked. Within the House of Commons, the party is the caucus. The ways in which ministers are accountable to the caucus is yet another point at which the party can exercise more control in the sense of exerting steady pressure on ministers. Caucus meetings are held weekly when Parliament is in session. Many government party MPs stress the importance of caucus as their prime arena for getting answers from ministers. One could argue that more frequent caucus meetings, both during sessions and when Parliament is not in session, would increase the points of pressure on ministers and thus help counterbalance the daily pressure of bureaucratic advice. Special caucus measures could be used in pre-budget and similar major occasions. But there are limits to this too, not the least of which is ministerial time and the time of MPs who have other committee duties, and constituency responsibilities as well. There may also be some constitutional improprieties involved if the government gives too much advance information to its own caucus and not to the House of Commons as a whole.

Our explicit treatment of these key arenas of party activity is not to suggest that any one of them is "the solution" to bureaucratic control. It is the total array of points of leverage and contact that can add to the potential for greater control. Thus the party is: 1) the membership at large in democratic meetings; 2) the cabinet as the fulcrum of governing; and 3) the caucus in day-to-day, week-by-week interaction. When dealing with their remedies for taking control of policy by exerting better control of the bureaucracy, Canadian parties have too easily ignored their own potential role at each of these three points. They have too easily succumbed to managerial "reformism," as a substitute for hard thought about their own institutional role. Canadian federal Liberal politicians have seemed to be endlessly fascinated by the machine at their disposal, disappearing under the hood of the bureaucracy to play with tappets while the basic questions about the political party as an institution go unasked. (The extent of the changes made to the machine are discussed in Chapters 1, 2 and 4.) While the situation is obviously different in some degree for the opposition parties, since by definition there is no consolidation of the party into a governing cadre (and the duty to oppose certainly affects their agendas), it does not fundamentally affect the verdict we reach about the degree to which the party system forgets about itself when it thinks of reform of the bureaucracy and of government.

Thus far, we have spoken only of the federal party system, and in general terms. Since the provincial sector generates ten different intra-provincial party systems, it is more difficult to generalize about them.[10] Some of the provinces replicate the features of the national scene. Ontario has had one-party dominance of an even more entrenched, uninterrupted kind under Tory rule. Alberta has had long periods of one-party dominance both under the Conservatives and under the preceding Social Credit regime. In both jurisdictions there have been charges about the politicization of the public service. Lest there be any hidden assumption in our analysis to date about the invariable superiority of competitive two-party systems, it should be noted that the recent experience, since 1970, with the alternation of NDP and "small-c" conservative parties in Manitoba, British Columbia and Saskatchewan has produced quite deep-seated controversy about the neutrality of the public service.

Beyond these aggregate features, there are some elements of the provincial party systems which perhaps encourage closer scrutiny of the bureaucracy by way of greater countervailing pressures on ministers. In some provinces, such as Alberta, the role of the government caucus is more developed than that in evidence in the national system.[11] However, this effect is likely cancelled by the inherent weaknesses of the legislature itself, which has a bare handful of members of the opposition party. There is little real evidence that provincial legislatures are better equipped to play their role than is Parliament.

All of the above deals with the party system as a whole. While we believe the parties themselves contribute to the problem, it is not sufficient to leave our analysis at this level. Political parties and their leaders have obviously had to deal with bureaucracy both in general and as individual policy proposals, such as those surveyed in Chapter 4, emerged on the agenda. Let us now look at what political parties and their leaders say and do about the bureaucracy both as governments and as opposition entities. What ideas do they bring to bear on the subject? Which of the three public service bureaucracies do they wish to reform? What is it that they wish to control?

The Liberal Party and Managerial Reformism

Given their dominance in the seat of federal power, the Liberals' views and actions vis-à-vis the public service constitute much of the history we have presented in previous chapters. However, the Liberal party, as an extra- parliamentary apparatus, has expressed few overall views about the public service. The closest it came was on those periodic occasions during the Trudeau era when resentment was expressed about the power of the prime minister's inner circle of PMO and some PCO advisors. This involved his political advisors such as Marc Lalonde, Jim Coutts and Tom Axworthy, and sometimes included public servants such as Michael Pitfield. In most respects, however, the actions of the Liberal party are the actions of the Liberal cabinet. These actions and the ideas behind them need not be repeated here, since the earlier chapters fulfil this task. Rather, what is essential in the present context is to draw out key features of the overall Liberal view.

As befits a middle-of-the-road party with strong instincts for political adaptability and survival in power, the Liberals' cumulative history is not consistent. One must also differentiate the levels of bureaucracy and the attendant accountability regimes to which Liberal positions and actions were addressed.

In a general sense, the Liberals have been content to hold a mirror to the times. In the 1960s and early 1970s they were willing experimenters, making the bureaucracy a laboratory for social policy. From the mid-1970s on, they acceded, albeit reluctantly, to using the public service as a target of economic management. Because of their essential easiness with the reins of power, however, they presided over and indeed essentially reinforced an almost casual, ad hoc view of bureaucratic reform. That is, one "reformed" and "controlled" the public service by creating more organizational appendages rather than by encouraging use of the basic institutions that were already in place. The Liberal legacy was to have engaged in permanent experimentalism. Each separate experiment could be justified by reference to a present shortcoming, real or only perceived. As each led to another, the cumulative effect was not reassessed.

Within the executive in the Trudeau Liberal era there was the array of central agencies, that is, new or expanded bureaucratic agencies to help control the civil service proper. Within the ambit of Parliament, there was erected a new parliamentary civil service, an array of devices that included more research support for the opposition parties, more staff for committees, more rights commissioners and watchdogs and their staff, and advisory bodies. Some of these were no doubt useful. Still, the cumulative judgment that emerged is that none fundamentally assisted the elemental focal points of democratic life, such as ministers themselves, MPs and the caucus, political parties, and Parliament as an assemblage of elected politicians rather than just a team of disciplined troops. It was as if the Liberal view was to trust the managerial/organizational trappings of democracy, but not its essential elected and representative underpinnings.

While the comments above focus properly on the federal Liberals, one should also examine the other political parties, federal and provincial. In several important respects, they too have supported this view, if not always by their words, then certainly by some of their actions, both as governments and as opposition entities that vote on such measures in the House of Commons and in provincial legislatures. In the case of both the Liberals and other political parties, the practical conundrum is a real one: the ambivalence we have about delegating power to the bureaucracy on the one hand, and the need to maintain the pace of the overall policy agenda on the other, which makes increased delegation inevitable. Even though it may be known that a host of individual issues affect the bureaucracy and other core political principles, one is in fact usually looking at them one at a time. Moreover, there are other value-laden disputes about each issue, meaning that the impact on core institutions is only one among many concerns.

The Progressive Conservatives and Other Conservative Regimes

The harsh reality facing the federal Progressive Conservative party prior to its massive 1984 election victory was that it had been out of power for most of the past four decades.[12] For that reason alone, it had grown increasingly more suspicious of what it perceived as a Liberal-infested, self- perpetuating, and increasingly interventionist bureaucracy. From the mid- 1970s onward, this critical analysis of bureaucracy has been aided by the generation and propagation of a core of theoretical ideas that have been aggressively presented and in part acted upon. The latter ideas are reflected in what might be called Parkinsonian-cum-public choice theory applied directly to the behaviour of bureaucracy as well as other public institutions.[13]

Generally, these ideas represent a concerted promotion of market mechanisms and an attack on the expansionary habits and waste of bureaucracies. Rooted in a long-standing conservative ideology but brought to the fore in the 1970s by the realities of economic decline, these views have been systematically articulated by some private sector bodies that study public policy, such as the Fraser Institute in Vancouver, and have entered the debate within federal and provincial Conservative parties as well as the Social Credit party in British Columbia. The ideas have also been sympathetically viewed by the conservative wing of the Liberal party. In essence, the pro-market stance is suspicious of the claim that the public sector does behave "in the public interest," and is strongly inclined to attribute the expansion of government to the automatic empire-building habits of self-interested bureaucrats and their ministerial allies.

There was some evidence supporting this critique of bureaucratic expansion in the documented rapid growth of senior executive positions in the federal public service in the early 1970s and in such tendencies as the proliferation of Crown corporations through the creation of subsidiaries. Some saw the penchant for reorganization as further evidence of expansionary motives. The "horror stories" of the auditor general's annual reports were also often read as proof that the bureaucrats' minds were less on their jobs than on self-aggrandizement. While no one can convincingly deny the existence of some expansionary habits, the evidence on program growth and on actual growth in numbers of bureaucrats is dubious on two grounds. First, in the areas where programs grew and hence reflected the growth of governments, the history of virtually all of them suggests that they cannot be causally attributed to the initiatives of bureaucrats. Far larger social, economic and political factors account for their emergence and growth.[14] Secondly, the growth of federal bureaucratic employment levelled off, as we saw in Chapter 3, from the mid-1970s. While one observer might say that this restraint was in part because of the pressure brought to bear in a very general way by the overall conservative critique, another might believe that it simply showed the bureaucracy responding as usual to direct instruction from the political masters.

This conservative critique has led, in addition, to the advocacy of deregulation, the privatization of Crown corporations, strict expenditure control, and flat-rate tax systems — in short, less government — and also to the advocacy of revoking the right to strike by public servants.

This increasingly clearly articulated set of ideas has not, however, been the only conceptual influence upon the federal Conservative appreciation of the bureaucratic beast. The Conservatives also pay strong homage to the traditional underpinnings of parliamentary government, including the ideal of a neutral public service. This has been demonstrated in concrete terms on the previous two occasions when they have assumed power and, hence, relates to the issues of transition discussed at the beginning of the chapter.

The stance taken by both prime ministers John Diefenbaker and Joe Clark was informed by a respect for tradition.[15] Despite the strong urging of their Conservative colleagues and supporters, both leaders resisted the temptation to make major new appointments at the senior levels of the bureaucracy. Clark made more changes in his short tenure in power than did Diefenbaker, but even these were few in number. Adherence to these traditional views was also reinforced by the Conservatives' dependence on the expertise of the civil service about how to govern. The experience here is a mixed one. For example, the first year of the Diefenbaker government did involve a strong ministerial/political push to impose its then-new populist program. The Clark government, which was functioning in a minority context, seems to have been not at all well prepared to govern, despite having established a transition team.

The Mulroney Conservatives, at least in comparison to the Diefenbaker and Clark teams, were much better prepared for transition to power, but vis-à-vis the control of the bureaucracy, the transition measures reflect a melding of concerns. Thus, Prime Minister Mulroney reassured senior public servants that he wanted a neutral public service and that they would be fired only for incompetency. At the same time, he instituted the highly paid position of ministerial "chief of staff," allowing each minister to hire a senior policy advisor with sufficient knowledge and authority to challenge the deputy minister and provide competitive policy advice. While he had criticized Liberal patronage in the realm of order-in-council appointments, Mr. Mulroney's own actions were ambiguous: first, he made a few non-partisan placements such as former Ontario NDP Leader Stephen Lewis, but followed that with a host of new appointments sympathetic to Conservative views. Later, he announced quite strict rules regarding public servants and the media. These required public servants to speak only about facts and not to explain policy. Discussions would be "on the record" and the public servant would be named.

In much of their opposition party role, the federal Conservatives, since the mid-1970s in particular, did increasingly take up the banner of the neo-conservative critique of government, both at a rhetorical level and in some of their actions. For example, they strongly supported the conservative "value for money" ethos of the auditor general and his demand for greater expenditure control, fewer expenditures, more productivity measures, more policy and program evaluation, and reduction of the national debt.

In a speech to the Progressive Conservative Canada Fund in April 1984, Brian Mulroney promised to instil a "positive approach to productivity management that will permeate the whole government," led by cabinet ministers who would themselves "spell out the objectives and intended outcomes of any program." He pledged also to create "a budgetary structure that will challenge existing programs" through such mechanisms as sunset provisions (where ongoing programs are given specific termination dates so that they will automatically die unless the legislature, i.e., the government, intervenes to vote funds specifically for them), the role of the comptroller general and zero-based budgetting techniques. At the same time as resource control would be centralized, human resource planning would be decentralized, he said, to the work-place. More complete ministerial and parliamentary control would be exerted over Crown corporations. Again, following Conservative tradi-tion, he asserted allegiance to a parliamentary form, pledging to "bring back" the principle of ministerial responsibility.[16]

This hard-nosed business ethic moderates, however, when federal Conservatives move from the realm of the abstract and into that of the concrete. For example, the Conservatives objected strongly when pro-ductivity measures were instituted by the Department of National Reve-nue to improve efficiency in the tax collection process. Here, efficiency was perceived to clash with fairness and equity. Yet the Conservatives' solutions to the problem involved more bureaucracy when they even-tually advocated both more tax auditors and more appeal mechanisms.[17]

In other realms, the federal Conservatives pushed hard for the control of Crown corporations and for the privatization of some of them. The Tory view of privatization has not been a uniform one, in that support for the privatization of Petro-Canada, a key 1979 election promise, had by 1984 been changed to a policy of qualified support for the national oil company. Similarly, in the controversy over government-owned Cana-dair and de Havilland, the Conservatives, while wishing to sell the companies, give no indication that they will stop supporting these indus-tries.

As to other tactics to control the bureaucracy, the Conservatives were in the forefront of the battle to secure passage of access to information legislation, and they have enthusiastically supported federal human rights legislation. Their caucus was divided over language policy, but a strong majority of Tory MPs supported the policy and its objectives for a bilingual public service.

At the provincial level among Conservative governments, the experi-ence varies considerably, both among provinces and over time. The long-entrenched Ontario Conservative government adopted many of the provincial equivalents to those measures adopted in Ottawa, sometimes leading the way and at other times following the federal lead. Ontario, however, can claim, with some justification, that it has not succumbed to the federal excesses in the expansion of the executive category. It does not suffer from anything like the same perception that its public servants are "out of control." This is no doubt partly because the Ontario

Conservative leadership, party and caucus have exercised considerable control. It also stems partly from the fact that: 1) one of the opposition parties, the NDP, would not, in principle, campaign against public sector workers in the same way as a Conservative party would; 2) no single province has to contend with criticism to the same degree that Ottawa's bureaucrats do; and 3) the legislative auditor has not interpreted his mandate in the same way as his federal counterpart. Ontario Tories pride themselves on being good and sound managers in both the organizational and political sense of the word. On the other hand, they are subject to the same charges as the federal Liberals when it comes to patronage in appointments to agencies, boards and commissions; in short, in Ontario's Public Service Bureaucracy II.[18] In both cases, the criticism is deserved, all the while evincing the inherent ambivalence to which patronage issues give rise.

The election of the Conservative government of Premier Grant Devine in Saskatchewan produced a quite different variant. For the first time in any significant way, a political battle arose over the public service. Its senior mandarins had been used to decades of primarily NDP/CCF rule which strongly supported state expansion. The quality of its senior officials was praised throughout the 1960s and 1970s by the larger national network of official bureaucratic and ministerial opinion. The Devine government, however, came to power with several key activists who were operators of small businesses and who were strongly resentful of bureaucratic power, of big government, and of "socialist" bureaucrats in particular. This was a role reversal, certainly in relation to the historic CCF concern about bureaucracy alluded to at the beginning of this chapter. During the election, a few Saskatchewan public servants actively supported the NDP, angering Conservative partisans even more. Immediately after its election, the Devine government took decisive action. Many senior officials were ousted or pressured into leaving. Even in this instance, however, the anti-bureaucratic, anti-statist instincts of the new government were not uniformly put into action. For example, the Devine government did not make a fundamental attack upon the stable of Saskatchewan Crown corporations, most of which were politically popular. Instead, it took steps to ensure that they were "better managed," that is, managed along more commercial lines.[19]

Without doubt, the most significant concerted generalized attack on statism and its bureaucratic appendages is to be found in the Bennett Social Credit government's package of "restraint" measures announced in July 1983, just after an election.[20] In contrast to the Saskatchewan case, the British Columbia situation did not involve an assault on the "mandarins"; rather, it brought the elimination of some services and agencies, the privatization of others, actual reductions of several thousand public sector positions and limits on public sector collective bargaining. It also cut into levels of service of institutions such as hospitals, leaving them understaffed. As well, it attempted to establish more centralized control over the heart of the provincial version of Public Service Bureaucracy II; namely, the education system. Thus, it was a comprehensive attack directly influenced by the neo- Conservative ideology.

"Small c" conservative party views of public service bureaucracy necessarily cover a wide spectrum, depending on the particular political economy and jurisdiction which they occupy, or in which they are competing for power. As a whole, however, it is fair to say that Conservatives, of all party representatives, are the most inherently suspicious and critical of bureaucracy. In addition, and in common with other parties, they often do not specify which bureaucracy they are criticizing, nor do they openly acknowledge the basic ambivalence that is a part of their historical record.

The New Democratic Party and the Political Left

We have already referred to the early concerns of the CCF about controlling unsympathetic bureaucrats. In some respects, however, especially since the mid-1970s when the impression of a general malaise of government became more widespread, the NDP and left-of-centre parties such as the Parti Québécois faced the greatest intellectual dilemmas about bureaucracy and government. At the heart of the left's traditional critique of capitalist society has been the recommendation that only action by a socialist democratic state can remedy the failures of the market. For the PQ in Quebec, as we have seen in Chapter 4, the state is doubly necessary: not only must the excesses of capitalism be rectified, but the excesses of English-dominated federalism must also be overcome. When evidence mounts that the state has failures too, and can produce, moreover, a stifling kind of impersonal society, the gap between ideology and reality is especially difficult to resolve. This tension is amplified even further by strands in the Canadian left which are rooted in populist concepts such as co-operatives and other voluntary citizen-based ways of solving problems. These instincts and traditions that imply decentralization also suggest disapproval of impersonal bureaucratic modes of response.

The NDP and the political left have accordingly also exhibited their own array of responses. At one level they have practised the art of studied silence, much of the time trying to avoid active participation in, or encouragement of, debates over items such as the auditor general's reports or criticisms of spending. In the June 1984 leaders' debate, however, Ed Broadbent did speak out in support of spending, frankly doubting that a new prime minister would discover great savings in the existing federal program array. At another level, the NDP has been the most active protector of public sector collective bargaining rights. This is a matter of both genuine belief and necessity. The belief is historically well established even when one notes the periodic support of wage control programs by provincial NDP governments. The necessity arises from the fact that, in the 1970s, public sector unions were the fastest growing element of the Canadian Labour Congress, whose support for the NDP was a crucial base for the party, if not in votes then certainly in organizational and financial resources. At still another level, the NDP has supported all the major "rights" reforms and has joined enthusiastically in criticism of patronage and conflict of interest issues, and has supported the auditor general's quest for access to cabinet documents on general grounds.

It is useful also to draw attention to one feature of the NDP as a governing party, namely, its close attention to the party's policy resolutions and the potential of this connection to control the bureaucracy along the lines discussed. The NDP prides itself on the democratic nature of its party processes and on its serious debate of policy. NDP governments in Manitoba, Saskatchewan and British Columbia lend some credence to the view that they enter power with more detailed and coherent platforms derived from the party, and with a party that understands the program and wants to see it implemented. Still, there is no conclusive evidence that this, in itself, translates more exactly into the action ultimately taken by the public services over which they take charge. This is because there is inevitably a large gap between the process of being a party and that of being a government; hence, the gap between actually having to govern on behalf of the entire electorate, as opposed to only that part which supports the party, and doing so in the face of many new and unforeseen circumstances.

Because of its two-pronged rationale of the state, the PQ government encounters a double dilemma when the state does not deliver. The PQ's support was firmly rooted in white-collar, public sector, professional workers in the education and other departments of Quebec's Public Service Bureaucracy II. In Quebec's system of highly centralized collective bargaining, the PQ government of René Levesque granted generous wage increases in the late 1970s, partly to buy support or, at least, a favourable climate for the sovereignty-association referendum of May 1980. Later, when the recession hit, the PQ was forced to roll back public sector wages, and thus lost a great deal of its support. The PQ approach, however, did not take the form of a concerted attack on particular programs or on the bureaucracy as the mandarin class. It made its savings in an across-the-board rollback of wages.

Summary

We have drawn attention to the role of political parties both as real or potential institutions for bureaucratic control and as ambivalent bureaucratic reform advocates. The former implies a need to specify the party role in elections, in convention, in caucus and in transition to power. We conclude that, within limits, there is room for parties to look more to themselves as core institutions to deal with bureaucratic control. While we have seen some improvements in the state of preparedness for power, weaknesses exist in the other realms in which parties are present. Reforms to party, however, are invariably linked to other core institutions such as Parliament and federalism. Parties, moreover, deserve some sympathy because keeping rein on the modern agenda is no easy task.

The main federal parties are, in part, prisoners of both their own rhetoric about the bureaucracy and the economic and social pressures that buffet government. As brokerage parties in a highly regionalized country with a complicated division of powers between provincial and federal governments, they appreciate "safe" issues, those on which they can afford to commit themselves before they have tapped public opinion. In the 1984 federal election, platforms were being put together on a running basis. Both major parties attempted to tailor statements for enough narrow special interests to add up to a winning coalition.[21] The public, however, being an aggregate, can register temperatures only on issues taken one by one. This means that nothing necessarily follows from any one commitment. There are no logically grouped "families" of issues that fall into place when one priority is stated, because the public is not one mind operating by logical and conventional principles of what goes together. The party thinkers do less thinking than diagnosing of the public's many moods: they must be ever watchful for almost any winning cluster of issues. In such a volatile environment, it is no wonder that the main parties have embraced the motherhood issue that the bureaucrats should be forced to efficiency, and have geared important parts of their campaigning to promoting their own images as managers. Yet, however attractive to voters the idea may be that the country should be "well managed" and however feasible this may seem, it is a potential minefield.

Even the notion of reforming the bureaucracy is not the comprehensible issue that it seems at first glance. For the most part, when members of the public criticize government or bureaucracy, they do not have a particular level of government or agency in mind. They often mean the vague total of local, provincial and federal officialdom as it affects them. The major federal parties (and some provincial parties) play to this vagueness of public expression in their campaigns, and inadvertently offer an impression that their party, if elected, can affect a correspondingly broad, virtually jurisdictionless redress for general grievances. In short, politicians make an implicit promise that extends well beyond the capacity of their own jurisdiction. Further, provincial and federal politicians tend often to play to the confusion by blaming many of their own sins of commission and omission on the other level of government in their own election campaigns.

In power, not being a "national" government in the sense of being a superior level of government, but only a federal government in the sense of being one government in a near-dozen, federal politicians find that their substantive initiatives are easily lost. Nevertheless, tinkering with the machinery of the state does get results and innovations accumulate, simply because the public service takes action (whether or not the exact intended action) when instructed. It sets up agencies, revises legislation, and occasionally sends parts of itself packing. One of the main effects of the long Liberal rule, set in an evolving period of significant change, has been the blurring of lines of accountability that are natural to a parliamentary system by an array of devices that have in many ways attenuated it. The tendency to add controls has in at least one major case been accelerated by the opposition's desire for short-term partisan advantage. The Conservative opposition's whole-hearted use of the strengthened Office of the Auditor General to discredit the Liberals' managerial capacity can partly be understood from the perspective of a party mentally in permanent opposition. In assisting the OAG to expand its mandate, it seemed not to consider that an executive has some legitimate prerogatives. Only the NDP, with no hope of governing, has taken a matter-of-fact attitude toward the public service, but one not without its own set of ambivalent components.

The various parts of the Canadian public sector, we suggest, have been in the limelight over the past decade, often for the wrong reasons. The real record does not justify the kind and level of negative rhetoric that is a normal part of any Canadian federal electoral campaign. Taking a swipe at the bureaucracy solves few of the ills that impinge from all directions. Inevitably, even robust organizations will become unable to work well under such conditions, and the best parts of the leadership will drift away. The danger is the erosion of quality in top ranks through constant vituperation for partisan advantage: as sure a route to the destruction of the merit principle at the top of the bureaucracy as is outright use of patronage.

Not a major villain, the permanent machinery of the state is not a potential miracle worker either. It is fundamental, however, that public service mechanisms cannot be created to routinely generate political control. It is the task of political parties to assign value and priorities to possibilities — in other words, to aggregate and articulate goals.

Chapter 6

Conclusions

The remaining task is to draw together the threads of our analysis. To do so, we will first summarize the findings of the foregoing chapters, then suggest broad lines of reform for refreshing the capacity for control and oversight of the various bureaucracies by elected officials, and for rejuvenating the ideas of merit and of responsible citizenship in a mature bureaucracy set in Canada's evolving constitutional framework.

The Introduction to this study presents a framework for differentiating major aspects of the evolution of the public service bureaucracy in Canada. It argues that bureaucratic development can be described as evolving in three overlapping phases: 1) the traditional departmental public service that administers the basic functions of government and for which ministers are accountable; 2) a somewhat independent division that embraces a range of regulatory boards, Crown enterprises and many of the institutions of the so-called welfare state, all characterized by a greater preference for collective leadership and a loose kind of representativeness through this leadership, and by indirect accountability; and 3) a set of expert agencies that we also call the control bureaucracy, whose members are intended to exercise surveillance of the traditional public service bureaucracy in a variety of ways.

Chapter 1 examined the evolving constitutional rationales for the various aspects of the conglomerate depicted in the framework. It portrayed the idealized controls and the secondary or "auxiliary" controls of cabinet government, then described the main features of the Canadian adaptation of the genius of the Westminster system. It is important not to be captured by romantic notions about parliamentary democracy, because the Canadian system has never functioned as an ideal parliamentary system. When the nation was established, the structures of federalism were as important as the parliamentary institutions. In the decades since, the Canadian system has been influenced by underlying social and economic changes. It has also been attracted by the American congressional example, and influenced by the political agenda flowing from south of the border. Nowhere is this mixed and sometimes contending set of influences more clearly seen than in the methods at play in Canadian government for handling the relations of political actors to the various bureaucracies, and in the conceptions that have guided the evolution of the internal structures of the public service bureaucracies.

The chapter proposed that the important ideas from the British influence are those of responsible and representative government, and the main supplementary ideas coming in significant ways, but certainly not exclusively, from the United States are pluralism and efficiency. The chapter attempted to demonstrate that the net effect of this particular mix has been a paradoxical weakening of the exercise of responsible government; in the Canadian context, a weakening of the capacity and will of political actors to set goals for bureaucratic actors and to control the implementation of those goals. This weakness is most in evidence in the newest distinguishable aspect of the public service bureaucracy, Parliament's control bureaucracy.

We argued that traditional ideas of government by responsible ministers are likely as adequate as they ever were for understanding the main lines of functioning of the departmental public service. This is not to denigrate the very real tensions that do exist. For example, newer themes that emphasize the collective responsibility of ministers for the quality of management, implemented through the central control agencies, have made the system considerably less comprehensible, if only in mythical terms, without demonstrable gains in either the quality of government or in efficiency.

The non-departmental segment, Public Service Bureaucracy II, is less accountable/responsible than the traditional bureaucracy, but has its own rationales that emphasize a form of representation and arm's-length ministerial responsibility. Further, the scope of operation and the policy significance of any one element of Public Service Bureaucracy II is limited; it does not, as a rule, have the opportunity to advocate values that are of society-wide significance.

Public Service Bureaucracy III is different again. The contemporary Canadian control bureaucracy embodies, in part, the modern U.S. influence on our constitutional framework, but it also reflects important domestic social and economic changes. The former consists of a pronounced emphasis on managerial efficiency as an important agenda-setting value, separate strong advocacy for other rights-oriented values from other fragments of government, and a belief that there is a need to control the power of the executive by resort to expertise and the legislature, either jointly or separately. One can summarize these themes by reference to the primary U.S. values of efficiency and pluralism. But the Canadian Public Service Bureaucracy II that is loosely attached to Parliament rather than to the executive does not embody the particular genius of U.S. congressional democracy, which is electorally representative pluralism. Because of the emphasis on "independent" leadership, the current norms of parts of our control bureaucracy do pose a partial acceptance of alternative sources of energy and power to that of the cabinet. Most significantly, the cabinet does not take responsibility for harmonizing the demands of the various parts of Parliament's control bureaucracy. Thus, even though the various agencies of Parliament's control bureaucracy affect policy of great scope, sometimes from a basic adversarial position, and can be charged with the duty of interpreting their own founding legislation, they have neither an independent electoral foundation nor a comprehensive set of links to a minister or a parliamentary body. They are thus not fully founded democratically in either British or U.S. constitutional rationales.

In effect, therefore, Chapter 1 proposed that the basic control theory of the place and role of bureaucrats in our constitutional framework is generally adequate to the two largest kinds of bureaucracy, but not to significant parts of the newest, Parliament's control bureaucracy. It has become a kind of wild card in our mixed system that, to the extent that it has power to affect outcomes, demands to be given either its own electoral base or a link back to responsible government.

The control bureaucracy is, however, only one source of pressure of control (other than the control of party which operates mainly through the agency of the minister and the scrutiny of the House of Commons) that guides and influences the traditional public service. Chapter 2 showed what it means to be part of the bureaucracy that is at the centre of the Constitution and is thus regulated by law and ongoing central agency surveillance. The chapter described these controls, taking a perspective from inside the bureaucratic structures.

Chapter 3 presented evidence bearing on the question of bureaucratic growth from a single perspective, employment across all levels of government. One of the ideological threads that wove its way through the 1970s, in part to counter the entrenchment of social programs in the welfare state, was a claim that bureaucracies grow inexorably, that there is a Malthusian aspect to officialdom that is distinguishable from the size and kind of program being administered. With regard to the federal bureaucracy, this general fear of a self-aggrandizing bureaucratic energy was melded into a more focussed critique of the Trudeau era's emphasis on central agencies, and its related indulgence of growth in senior executive ranks through both upward classification of existing functions and tolerance of "classification creep." To the extent that data on employment can address such complex concerns, it would appear, to the contrary, that general government growth was fairly well controlled, and that some "Trudeaucrat" growth was evident but was not a major trend. The proportion of the work force that is made up of bureaucrats and public sector enterprise workers at all levels of government has remained at around 20 percent for the past two decades. This is very similar to the public sector presence of other nations, with the possible exceptions of the United States and Japan, whose public sector employment is atypically small. If one takes the total of employment by all governments as a universe in itself, at the beginning of the 1960s the federal level of government held almost 30 percent, while 22 years later it had dropped to about 23 percent. Most of the loss in the federal share appeared to be due to loss of impetus in the federal enterprise sector. Hence, the big picture is generally soothing, at least to the extent that it says there are no runaway trends toward inexorable growth in bureaucracy.

We do not argue that there is no connection between the growth of government, expressed as programs or instruments, and bureaucracy. The evidence is more persuasive, however, that the big programs (expenditure and regulatory) that have emerged and incrementally expanded are due much more to political forces rather than to bureaucracy itself. This is all the more apparent when one looks carefully at the two major issues of Chapters 4 and 5, issues which we believe have not been fully examined in either existing literature or debate.

Chapter 4 focussed on the ways in which our nation's political actors have treated the public sector work force as a captive, or, more neutrally, as an object, and have acted upon it for experimental and demonstration purposes as well as to fulfil various kinds of representational needs. For example, the method by which a state takes on personnel and acquires goods, through merit or through patronage, can be seen as either a principle of management or as a social policy. The chapter was concerned with the second aspect, where the government acts on the public sector work force to make a statement about its values, or perhaps to set an example, so as to exhort the rest of society. Our analysis suggested that Canadian politicians too often act indirectly upon a bureaucracy, rather than attempting to effect more direct kinds of change on the problem they have targetted.

Chapter 5 both continued the thrust of the analysis, examining those senses in which the public service bureaucracy is controlled or not, especially as regards policy control, and pointed to the obligation of political parties to fulfil their traditional control responsibilities. That is, although partisan politics is at the heart of our maintaining a democratic system, parties too seldom look at themselves, after the cabinet, as the single most important source of control over the policy directions that a bureaucracy can take, or get away with taking. While this lack of perspective on themselves is understandable, because the whole panorama is accessible only to hindsight, it nonetheless dilutes the political influence that is brought to bear on official action. The chapter described the general approaches of the parties to the permanent officials, and suggested that parties should methodically refresh the mechanisms at their disposal for influencing and guiding the bureaucracy in all arenas in which they operate — electoral, convention, and caucus.

The potential directions for change are implicit in this analysis. Our opinion is that there are obvious imperatives for the federal government at two points: 1) the constitutional framework; and 2) inside the bureaucracy, with an emphasis on a simpler view of merit in a mature, maximally autonomous work force.

The reader will not be slow to grasp that our operating preference for Canadian institutions is the parliamentary, rather than the congressional system. Our reasons for this choice of values are: 1) we believe that our institutions are still closer to basic parliamentary forms than to congressional forms. Consequently, we think political control will be easier to re-establish along parliamentary lines than by a leap to a frank separation of powers system where the fragmentation of power to contending actors is substituted for parliamentary centralization of power; and 2) we believe that parliamentary government has some advantages in that it provides the citizens with a clearer focus for grievance in the person of the minister, and in that it is a manoeuvrable form of government suited to a middle power that must be able to accommodate to the imperatives posed from outside. Doubtless, however, some observers will prefer lines of change leading to congressional forms. What follows is a concluding sketch of what we think are the main directions that emerge from the analysis.

Reassertion of Political Control

The analysis suggests a need to clarify the main lines of accountability to political actors and ultimately to the electorate. Most generally, this implies some pruning back to the main design of the system, which has become unnecessarily overwhelmed by other rationales and auxiliary control institutions. Specifically, in our view, direct political control would be enhanced by close political attention to the following points:

- *The current lack of political leadership for the various agencies of the control bureaucracy*. The non-democratic/non-electoral-based pluralism exemplified in the autonomous operations of some of these agencies is an anomaly. Even if one accepts that parliamentarians require institutionalized assistance to monitor the adherence of general bureaucracy to certain politically stipulated values and goals, democratic norms would dictate that politicians should continually "face the music" with regard to ranking and melding the values that now can come into conflict through the current pluralistic operation of these agencies. It would be in keeping with the logic of a parliamentary system if the various audit criteria pursued by these agencies acting independently of one another were to be placed together in one body, perhaps a parliamentary committee, and if one minister were to take responsibility for the policy that emerges as a result of their combined impact. The Office of the Auditor General especially, being the largest and the most powerful of these bodies, as well as the most ambitious and independent, requires responsible monitoring, leadership and restraint, and a balancing of its corporate views and demands with those of other centres, which pursue other values and standards. In essence, politicians should be responsible for establishing a more explicit hierarchy of values and standards as pursued by these agencies collectively. They would be in a much better position to identify conflicts of values and standards than at present. Finally, in no case should an "independent" control bureaucracy be allowed to wedge itself between cabinet and its advisors on a pretext of scrutinizing the calibre of advice.

- *A need to re-invigorate political parties as the most crucial part of the circle of control beyond cabinet and Parliament.* Related, a need for somewhat less "managerialism" from parties in power, and for less dramatizing of managerial-type values like efficiency. This is because the pursuit of efficiency, like the pursuit of economy and probity, can easily become a substitute for goal-setting and thus stand in the way of political, as opposed to managerial, interpretations of the effects of policy. Since there is no firm principle for dividing "administration" from "politics" that holds for more than one case at hand, it becomes a question of continual balance. Nonetheless, our analysis has led us to believe that Canadian politicians by habit and inclination retreat to managerialism too readily. We think that if parties were re-invigorated, they might take a more value-oriented interest in bureaucratic action. But the reform of parties in this context is multi-dimensional and would have to occur in all of the arenas in which they function.
- *Possible benefits to be realized from scaling down some of the most dramatic myths about how parliamentary institutions operate.* Conventions of confidence are an obvious example. While the idea of confidence in the sense that the cabinet must be responsible and accountable in the House of Commons and to the House's membership is essential, it is a fact that political common sense mediates the application of the convention, and governments, in fact, often choose when they will ignore a vote against them in the House on the grounds that it was an accident of attendance, or an item that is not a "matter of confidence." It might be possible to use this adaptation of the convention more constructively, rather than purely defensively. By this, we mean that under a more generous confidence convention,

MPs might be capable of more substantial investigations than at present, because the government would feel able to share more information (without fear of a partisan use that could lead to its defeat). This is a familiar enough recommendation and really only implies that the government might forecast the issues on which it will be sensitive so that it could allow more of a contribution from the membership of the House, while retaining the capacity to control or deny any given initiative through use of the vote when necessary.

There is obviously an important connection between these three points and the full agenda of parliamentary reform. We have not examined the full array of issues on the latter agenda, in part, because of the internal division of labour within the present Commission's research program. Accordingly, we see the three directions for reform itemized above as flowing from a focussed analysis of public service bureaucracy as such.

Reinforcing Merit, and Maturity in Management of the Work Force

The conclusions about the quality and character of the Canadian bureaucracy, particularly the federal bureaucracy, that emerge from our work, are somewhat more general. Our assumptions are that the Canadian public service bureaucracies are mature institutions and that, at least for the near present, the gains that were made in the fight for merit in personnel appointments and for probity in procurement still exist. Likewise, since bureaucratic growth has been at the same rate as that of the labour force over two decades, and since most economic analysis shows that public sector wages are, in general, responsive to market forces, there is no reason to regret the existence of collective bargaining rights. It is perhaps time to move on to broader issues and new challenges for the development of an expert, efficient, loyal and fairly managed work force consonant with the changes in Canadian society that have occurred in the past three decades.

We view the existing tension between governor-in-council/"political" appointments and "merit"/PSEA appointments as natural, inevitable and even desirable. After all, merit and patronage are both, albeit different, systems for making appointments that assist the politicians to achieve some element of control over their bureaucratic instrument. It is again, like the policy administration debate, a question of continual balance rather than a question of setting inexorable rules and limits. Our analysis has suggested, however, that the upper ranks of the federal public service, at least, have become somewhat too heavily politicized, and that, furthermore, this politicization at the top had not (to early 1985) been matched by a liberalization of rules that guide the conduct of rank-and-file bureaucrats. That is, even while some very prominent political appointments have been made that violate the ideal of a non-partisan public service, fairly strong sanctions are continually threatened and sometimes levelled against comparatively minor forms of political activity when the offenders are lower-grade public servants. Hence, even while it is the right of the government to place partisans in key positions and, in addition, to be served neutrally by the permanent officers, the current practice still has an air of saying that might makes right. Other countries, notably Britain, manage systems that allow more freedom of expression to rank-and-file public servants who are not in sensitive positions.

In addition, one must take into account the increasing complexity of the public service environment, and its differentiation into quite distinct aspects and kinds of work, many of which bear no relation to policy or advisory roles nor involve positions of any sensitivity regarding fair dealing with members of the public. Accordingly, our general assumptions are that both citizen rights to collective bargaining and partisan political rights are in principle compatible with most forms of rank-and-file work in the various public sectors, but that they are generally unsuitable for senior bureaucrats and officers working in sensitive public positions. The lines of reform that we think should be examined are as follows:

- An all-party group might review the current use of governor-in-council appointments in the foreign service, the judiciary, top-level departmental appointments, and ministers' staffs, with a view to identifying positions where the advantage of a partisan sensitivity is obvious. Our view is that the process should be continuous and that appointments of no clear partisan value should revert to the merit system so that the total of such appointments does not grow overall. We suggest in addition that the role of merit appointees in ministers' offices is currently undervalued. In other words, career civil servants have a role to play in serving as links to the instrumental bureaucracy, and service in a minister's office could be a crucially important developmental experience for a potential deputy minister.
- Further, governor-in-council appointments might benefit from a more open process. The right of the executive to make these appointments in a parliamentary system is beyond dispute, but some consideration might be given to putting potential appointments to a parliamentary committee for exposure and information. While it might not prove useful to engage in public discussion of individuals, open discussion of the general criteria that should guide selection would seem particularly valuable for both senior policy advisory positions and the control positions.
- A mechanism similar to that in the collective bargaining system for determining and designating categories of employees might be of use for the purpose of allocating specific kinds of political rights to public

servants. Our view is that senior policy bureaucrats (those in the permanent public service) should have no rights to engage in partisan political activity other than the simple acts of gathering information on which to base a vote and then voting, and should have neither the right to run for office while on a leave, nor the right to donate money to a political party. The rights of all officer-level appointments to an organization of the control bureaucracy should be similarly limited, because of the sensitive nature of the work. Rank-and-file workers, on the other hand, should be free to engage in the full range of expression, subject only to the stricture that it should not affect their capacity to perform their work without bias, or put them in a position in which they would be open to suspicion of bias in workplace decisions.

In conclusion, we believe that proposals for changing the bureaucracy should be reviewed against two basic criteria: first, whether or not they will increase the leverage of elected representatives on the bureaucracy while preserving the basic features of cabinet-parliamentary government; and secondly, whether they increase the fairness and maturity with which the work force is managed in light of the values inherent in a more rights-oriented society, while maintaining the ideal of a neutral, loyal, non-partisan bureaucracy in its fundamental policy advisory role.

Appendix A: Appendix to Chapter 3

TABLE A-1 Population and Labour Force Growth Rates

	Canada	Change (%)	Nfld.	Change (%)	P.E.I.	Change (%)	N.S.	Change (%)	N.B.	Change (%)
					(000s)					
1960[a]										
Pop.	17,870.0	—	448.0	—	103.0	—	727.0	—	589.0	—
L.F.	6,430.0	—	109.0	—	32.0	—	225.0	—	173.0	—
1965[a]										
Pop.	19,644.0	9.9	488.0	8.9	109.9	5.8	756.0	4.0	615.0	4.4
L.F.	7,185.0	11.7	115.0	5.5	33.0	3.1	230.0	2.2	180.0	4.0
1970										
Pop.	21,297.0	8.4	517.0	5.9	110.0	0.9	782.0	3.4	627.0	2.0
L.F.	8,329.0	15.9	142.0	23.5	34.0	3.3	267.0	16.1	192.0	6.7
1975										
Pop.	22,697.1	6.6	549.1	6.2	117.1	6.4	819.5	4.8	665.2	6.1
L.F.	9,923.0	19.1	189.0	33.1	45.0	32.4	299.0	12.0	254.0	32.3
1980										
Pop.	23,747.3	4.6	563.5	2.6	122.0	4.2	841.8	2.7	691.9	4.0
L.F.	11,522.0	16.1	206.0	9.0	50.0	11.1	361.0	20.7	281.0	10.6
1982										
Pop.	24,341.7	—	567.7	—	122.5	—	847.4	—	696.4	—
L.F.	11,743.0	—	215.0	—	52.0	—	364.0	—	283.0	—
1983										
Pop.	24,634.2	—	569.2	—	122.8	—	852.2	—	699.1	—
L.F.	11,949.0	—	206.0	—	54.0	—	376.0	—	285.0	—

	Que.	Change (%)	Ont.	Change (%)	Man.	Change (%)	Sask.	Change (%)	Alta.	Change (%)	B.C.	Change (%)
1960[a]												
Pop	5,024.0	—	5,969.0	—	891.0	—	907.0	—	1,248.0	—	1,567.0	—
L.F.	1,813.0	—	2,379.0	—	302.0	—	266.0	—	463.0	—	572.0	—
1965[a]												
Pop	5,685.0	13.2	6,788.0	13.7	965.0	8.3	950.0	4.7	1,450.0	16.2	1,797.0	14.7
L.F.	1,904.0	5.0	2,738.0	15.1	331.0	9.6	320.0	20.3	560.0	21.0	640.0	11.9
1970												
Pop	6,013.0	5.8	7,551.0	11.2	983.0	1.9	941.0	−1.0	1,595.0	10.0	2,128.0	18.4
L.F.	2,274.0	19.4	3,173.0	15.9	383.0	15.7	341.0	6.1	650.0	16.1	858.0	34.1
1975												
Pop	6,179.0	2.8	8,172.0	8.2	1,013.6	3.1	907.4	−3.6	1,778.3	11.5	2,433.2	6.4
L.F.	2,679.0	17.8	3,804.0	20.0	416.0	8.6	363.0	6.5	765.0	17.7	1,110.0	29.4
1980												
Pop	6,338.9	2.6	8,501.3	4.0	1,028.0	1.4	951.3	4.8	2,052.8	15.4	2,589.4	6.4
L.F.	2,932.0	9.4	4,334.0	13.9	482.0	15.9	434.0	19.6	1,089.0	42.3	1,275.0	14.9
1982												
Pop	6,438.2	—	8,624.7	—	1,026.2	—	968.3	—	2,237.3	—	2,744.2	—
L.F.	2,895.0	—	4,475.0	—	499.0	—	456.0	—	1,171.0	—	1,333.0	—
1983												
Pop	6,482.4	—	8,715.8	—	1,035.2	—	979.4	—	2,317.0	—	2,790.1	—
L.F.	2,991.0	—	4,551.0	—	507.0	—	469.0	—	1,179.0	—	1,339.0	—

Source: Statistics Canada, *Labour Force Survey*, cat. no.71–001 (Ottawa: Statistics Canada, various years) and *Historical Labour Force Statistics*, cat. no.71–201 (Ottawa: Statistics Canada, 1974 and 1983).

a. 1960 Labour Force statistics breakdown for all provinces is estimated. The Atlantic Provinces and the Prairie Provinces for 1965 are also estimated.

TABLE A-2 Population of Federal Departments

Department or Departmental Agency	1960	% Change	1965	% Change	1970	% Change	1975	% Change	1980	% Change	1982
Agriculture	8,711	—	8,682	-0.3	8,524	-1.8	10,024	17.6	9,597	-4.3	10,163
Communications	—	—	—	—	1,622	—	2,166	33.5	2,038	-5.9	2,318
Consumer and Corporate Affairs	—	—	—	—	1,531	—	2,565	67.5	2,275	-11.3	2,475
External Affairs	2,105	—	2,790	9.0	3,245	16.3	5,490	69.2	5,312	-3.2	7,584
CIDA	—	—	—	—	—	—	989	—	1,010	2.1	1,165
Finance	—	—	398	—	597	50.0	949	59.0	875	7.8	1,083
Fisheries[a]	2,241	—	2,499	11.5	—	—	—	—	5,325	—	6,708
Forestry	556	—	1,281	130.0	—	—	—	—	—	—	—
Fisheries and Forestry	—	—	—	—	4,983	—	—	—	—	—	—
Economic Development	—	—	—	—	—	—	—	—	94	—	183
Environment	—	—	—	—	—	—	14,665	—	10,575	-27.8	11,261
Energy, Mines and Resources[b]	2,666	—	3,224	20.9	5,100	58.2	3,759	-26.3	3,697	-1.7	4,822
Indian Affairs	2,560	—	3,079	20.3	—	—	—	—	—	—	—
Northern Affairs and Natural Resources	4,838	—	4,712	-2.6	—	—	—	—	—	—	—
Indian Affairs and Northern Development	—	—	—	—	8,643	—	6,993	-19.1	6,244	-10.7	6,209
Industry	—	—	472	—	—	—	—	—	—	—	—
Trade and Commerce[c]	1,497	—	2,040	—	—	—	—	—	—	—	—
Industry, Trade and Commerce	—	—	—	—	2,685	—	2,875	7.1	2,930	1.9	2,229
DREE	—	—	—	—	1,729	—	1,971	13.9	2,026	2.7	1,843
Statistics Canada[d]	1,830	—	2,485	35.8	4,657	88.5	5,196	11.6	4,544	12.5	4,774
Justice	351	—	345	-1.7	572	65.8	1,736	203.0	2,200	26.7	2,494

Labour	580	900	55.1	743	-17.4	835	12.4	953	14.1	1,017
UIC[e]	11,511	11,542	0.2	6,498	43.7	11,577	78.1	—	—	—
Citizenship and Immigration	4,876	5,272	8.1	—	—	—	—	—	—	—
Manpower and Immigration	—	—	—	9,026	—	13,234	46.6	—	—	—
Employment and Immigration	—	—	—	—	—	—	—	25,099	—	27,608
National Defence (civilian)	53,218	48,094	-9.6	37,684	-21.6	38,425	2.0	36,912	-3.9	37,405
National Defence (military)	—	—	—	90,238	—	79,229	-12.2	81,190	2.5	82,888
National Health and Welfare	4,788	5,212	8.9	7,582	45.5	10,085	33.0	9,499	-5.8	9,548
National Revenue	13,762	14,366	4.4	17,065	18.8	22,369	1.1	25,497	14.0	26,518
Public Works	8,694	8,942	2.9	8,210	-8.2	9,108	10.9	8,819	-3.2	10,404
Post Office[f]	26,005	29,382	13.0	43,165	46.9	59,236	37.2	68,314	15.3	68,885
Science and Technology	—	—	—	—	—	188	—	284	51.1	159
Social Development	—	—	—	60	—	—	—	—	—	77
Solicitor General	—	—	—	—	—	225	275.0	230	2.2	280
Correctional Services	2,368	3,724	57.3	4,654	25.0	8,386	80.2	9,936	18.5	10,002
RCMP	7,664	9,160	19.5	13,381	46.1	18,792	40.4	21,233	13.0	22,437
National Parole Board	—	—	—	382	—	242	-36.6	290	19.8	307
Secretary of State	726	910	25.3	1,330	46.2	3,852	-8.9	3,486	-9.5	3,431
Transport	13,466	15,088	12.1	17,889	18.6	20,371	13.9	20,487	0.6	21,796
Veterans' Affairs	13,512	13,403	-0.8	11,327	-15.5	8,046	-29.0	4,867	-77.8	4,999
Parliament	921	1,121	21.7	1,414	26.1	3,132	121.5	3,909	24.8	4,011
Governor General and Lt. Governors General	15	29	93.3	40	37.9	86	115.0	101	17.4	94
Privy Council Offices[g]	163	133	-18.4	355	167.0	386	8.7	301	-22.0	390
Treasury Board	—	—	—	482	—	846	75.5	878	3.8	987
Public Service Commission[h]	673	930	38.2	1,352	45.4	3,932	191.0	2,653	-33.0	2,641

TABLE A-2 (Cont'd)

Department or Departmental Agency	1960	% Change	1965	% Change	1970	% Change	1975	% Change	1980	% Change	1982
Auditor General	131	—	193	47.3	237	22.8	358	51.1	480	34.1	556
Economic Council of Canada	—	—	—	—	107	—	134	25.2	154	14.9	137
Chief Electoral Office	43	—	18	-58.1	28	55.6	37	32.1	51	37.8	71
Chief of Official Languages	—	—	—	—	12	—	76	533.0	102	34.2	136
Public Service Staff Relations Board	—	—	—	—	84	—	142	69.0	162	14.1	169
Federal-Provincial Relations Office	—	—	—	—	—	—	50	—	70	40.0	66
National Library	41	—	124	202.0	271	119.0	473	74.5	493	4.2	550
Public Archives	114	—	199	74.6	340	70.8	686	102.0	735	7.1	784
National Museums	79	—	147	86.1	390	165.0	1,062	172.0	993	-6.4	1,021
Atomic Energy Control Board	8	—	18	125.0	38	111.0	84	121.0	196	133.0	249
Canadian Grain Commission[i]	1,049	—	1,001	-4.6	974	-2.7	873	-10.4	903	3.4	877
Canadian Radio-television and Telecommunications Commission[j]	25	—	36	44.0	167	364.0	421	152.0	392	-6.9	425
Canadian Transport Commission[k]	227	—	263	15.6	456	73.4	820	79.8	769	-6.2	818

Department or Departmental Agency	1960	% Change	1965	% Change	1970	% Change	1975	% Change	1980	% Change	1982
National Energy Board	38	—	85	124.0	155	82.3	323	108.0	358	10.8	452
National Film Board	707	—	767	8.5	961	25.3	838	−12.8	1,285	53.3	1,128
National Research Council	3,052	—	3,351	9.8	3,454	3.1	2,945	−14.7	3,078	4.5	3,315

Source: Statistics Canada, Public Accounts Division Reports and *Federal Government Employment*, cat. no.72–004 (Ottawa: Statistics Canada, 1960–82).

a. In 1980 and 1982 it is called Department of Fisheries and Oceans; Forestry moved to Environment by 1975.
b. Formerly Department of Mines and Technical Surveys.
c. Excludes Dominion Bureau of Statistics.
d. Formerly Dominion Bureau of Statistics.
e. Includes National Employment Services. Note also that UIC combines with Employment and Immigration between 1975 and 1980.
f. Excludes Christmas workers. Since 1981 Canada Post Corporation.
g. Excludes various royal commission employees.
h. Prior to 1967 Civil Service Commission.
i. Formerly Board of Grain Commissioners.
j. Formerly Board of Broadcast Governors.
k. Formerly Board of Transport Commissioners.

TABLE A-3 1960–80 Function Breakdown of Selected Provincial General Government Employment[a]

Function	Nfld. (Fb PT)[b]	%	P.E.I. (F PT)	%	N.S. (F PT)	%	N.B. (F PT)	%	Ont. (F PT)	%	Man. (F PT)	%	Sask. (F PT)	%	Alta. (F PT)	%	Total	F PT %
General Services																		
1960	594	9.5	238	14.5	255	2.5	433	5.0	3,795	8.2	524	7.6	787	8.3	2,296	16.1	8,922	8.6
1980	1,620	12.0	456	10.7	1,071	5.1	1,105	4.5	9,492	8.7	1,540	11.0	2,116	12.4	6,033	11.6	23,433	9.2
Protection of Persons																		
1960	534	8.6	61	3.7	350	3.4	253	2.9	6,949	15.0	864	12.6	778	8.2	2,046	14.4	11,839	11.4
1980	1,399	10.4	200	4.7	1,289	6.1	903	3.7	19,260[c]	17.6	1,767	12.7	1,562	9.2	6,996	13.4	33,376	13.1
Transportation & Communications																		
1960	1,079	17.3	522	31.9	4,706	45.7	5,102	58.5	13,575	29.2	1,548	22.6	2,005	21.1	3,076	21.6	31,613	30.4
1980	1,851	13.7	558	13.2	3,761	17.9	2,681	10.8	12,940	11.8	2,144	15.3	1,847	10.8	3,800	7.3	29,582	11.6
Health																		
1960	3,071	49.3	528	32.3	3,435	33.3	1,479	17.0	12,420[d]	26.7	2,064	30.1	2,788	29.4	2,883	20.2	28,668	27.6
1980	3,378	25.1	922	21.8	8,240	39.2	3,136	12.7	16,622	15.2	1,908	13.7	2,113	12.4	15,718[e]	30.2	52,037	20.4
Social Welfare																		
1960	316	5.1	82	5.0	137	1.3	62	0.7	536	1.2	211	3.1	461	4.9	324	2.3	2,129	2.0
1980	1,943	14.4	865	20.4	708	3.4	846	3.4	7,192	6.6	1,162	8.3	1,492	8.7	3,766	7.2	17,974	7.0
Education																		
1960	174	2.8	91	5.6	454	4.4	241	2.8	2,294	4.9	—	—	—	—	—	—	3,254	3.1
1980	1,389	10.3	510	12.0	2,733	13.0	13,331[f]	53.8	27,452[g]	25.1	1,478	10.5	1,709	10.0	4,469[h]	8.6	53,051	20.7

Function	Nfld.	F[b] PT %	P.E.I.	F PT %	N.S.	F PT %	N.B.	F PT %	Ont.	F PT %	Man.	F PT %	Sask.	F PT %	Alta.	F PT %	Total	F PT %
Natural Resources																		
1960	249	4.0	22	1.3	609	9.9	881	10.1	3,909	8.4	684	10.0	687	7.2	1,450	10.2	8,491	8.2
1980	925	6.9	168	4.0	1,326	6.3	868	3.5	5,134	4.7	1,143	8.2	942	5.5	2,517	4.8	13,023	5.1
Agriculture																		
1960	77	1.2	63	3.8	216	2.1	206	2.4	1,111	2.4	403	5.9	734	7.7	647	4.5	3,457	3.3
1980	370	2.7	297	7.0	675	3.2	592	2.4	2,413	2.2	1,124	8.0	1,539	9.0	2,236	4.3	9,246	3.6
Environment																		
1960	—	—	—	—	—	—	—	—	—	—	—	—	—	—	—	—	—	—
1980	38	0.3	28	0.7	187	0.9	113	0.5	2,232	2.0	187	1.3	153	0.9	1,116	2.1	4,054	1.6
Recreation & Culture																		
1960	88	1.4	29	1.8	57	0.6	14	0.2	723	1.6	—	—	34	0.4	137	1.0	10,082	1.0
1980	364	2.7	139	3.3	288	1.4	522	2.1	2,954	2.7	369	2.6	213	1.3	1,869	3.6	6,218	2.6
Labour																		
1960	14	0.2	—	—	35	0.3	40	0.5	223	0.5	55	0.8	64	0.7	94	0.7	524	0.5
1980	33	0.2	21	0.5	47	0.2	267	1.1	625	0.6	281	2.0	107	0.6	634	1.2	2,015	0.8
Supervision																		
1960	15	0.2	1	0.06	17	0.2	1	0.01	207	0.4	102	1.5	147	1.5	312	2.2	802	0.7
1980	163	1.2	73	1.7	535	2.5	290	1.2	1,310	1.2	510	3.7	1,615	9.5	922	1.8	5,418	2.1

TABLE A–3 (Cont'd)

Function	Nfld. F[b] PT	%	P.E.I. F PT	%	N.S. F PT	%	N.B. F PT	%	Ont. F PT	%	Man. F PT	%	Sask. F PT	%	Alta. F PT	%	Total F PT	%
Other																		
1960	15	0.2	—	—	19	0.2	5	0.5	33	0.07	—	—	83	0.9	44	0.3	199	0.2
1980	—	—	—	—	127	0.6	81	0.03	—	—	—	—	233	1.4	609	1.2	1,050	0.4
Total																		
1960	6,233		1,637		10,291		8,721		46,455		6,847		9,490		14,252		103,926	
1980	13,473		4,237		20,987		24,733		109,200		13,968		17,030		52,067		255,695	

Source: Statistics Canada, *Provincial Government Employment*, cat. no.72–007 (Ottawa: Statistics Canada, 1960–80).

a. Statistics were not available for Que., B.C., Y.T. and N.W.T. for the period reported.
b. Function over Provincial Total.
c. Increase attributable to initiatives in Correctional/prison services.
d. Mental Retardation Centres now divided between Health and Social Welfare functions.
e. Special Funds were added for new programs.
f. Local school boards were added.
g. CAATs were added.
h. Public colleges were added.

TABLE A-4 1980–82 Function Breakdown of Selected Provincial General Government Employment

Function	Que.	$\frac{F^a}{PT}$ %	B.C.	$\frac{F}{PT}$ %	Y.T.	$\frac{F}{PT}$ %	N.W.T.	$\frac{F}{PT}$ %	Other Provinces	$\frac{F}{PT}$ %	Total	$\frac{F}{PT}$ %
General Services												
1980	14,933	15.1	2,944	7.1	204	10.2	987	31.1	23,433	9.2	43,121	10.8
1982	15,253	17.1	3,253	7.4	288	14.3	1,128	31.8	25,909	9.6	45,813	11.2
Protection of Persons												
1980	15,625	15.8	7,009	16.9	156	7.8	156	4.9	33,376	13.1	56,322	14.0
1982	16,213	18.1	7,181	16.5	200	9.9	199	5.6	35,518	13.1	59,311	14.5
Transportation and Communications												
1980	12,559	12.7	7,325	17.8	323	16.1	130	4.1	29,582	11.6	49,919	12.4
1982	10,188	11.4	6,978	16.1	255	12.7	149	4.2	27,489	10.4	45,059	11.0
Health												
1980	11,274	11.4	9,510	23.0	10	0.5	21	0.7	52,037	20.4	72,891	18.2
1982	2,253[b]	2.5	9,989	23.0	13	0.6	61	1.7	63,360	23.4	75,676	18.5
Social Welfare												
1980	6,725	6.8	4,413	10.7	205	10.2	242	7.6	17,974	7.0	29,559	7.4
1982	5,053	5.7	5,197	12.0	209	13.3	269	7.6	19,342	7.2	30,070	7.4
Education												
1980	19,788[c]	20.0	593	1.4	878	43.7	1,123	35.4	53,051	20.7	75,433	18.8
1982	20,473[c]	22.7	574	1.3	767	38.1	1,203	39.4	54,816	20.3	77,833	19.0
Natural Resources												
1980	4,351	4.4	6,293	15.3	51	2.5	109	3.4	13,023	5.1	23,827	5.9
1982	4,226	4.2	6,421	14.8	46	2.3	131	3.7	13,635	5.2	24,459	6.0
Agriculture												
1980	5,340	5.4	1,060	2.6	36	1.8	104	3.3	9,246	3.6	15,786	3.9
1982	4,899	5.5	969	2.2	65	3.2	116	3.2	10,210	3.8	16,259	4.0

TABLE A-4 (Cont'd)

Function	Que.	$\frac{F^a}{PT}$ %	B.C.	$\frac{F}{PT}$ %	Y.T.	$\frac{F}{PT}$ %	N.W.T.	$\frac{F}{PT}$ %	Other Provinces	$\frac{F}{PT}$ %	Total	$\frac{F}{PT}$ %
Environment												
1980	1,384	1.4	380	0.9	—	—	—	—	4,054	1.6	5,818	1.5
1982	1,284	1.4	806	1.9	—	—	—	—	4,525	1.7	6,615	1.6
Recreation and Culture												
1980	2,571	2.6	861	2.1	42	2.1	31	1.0	6,718	2.6	10,223	2.6
1982	2,833	3.2	554	1.3	43	2.1	31	0.9	6,771	2.6	10,232	2.5
Labour												
1980	2,670	2.7	461	1.1	—	—	110	3.5	2,015	0.8	5,256	1.3
1982	4,093	4.6	668	1.5	—	—	116	3.3	3,069	1.2	7,946	1.9
Supervision												
1980	1,286	1.3	395	1.0	—	—	128	4.0	5,418	2.1	7,227	1.8
1982	1,197	1.3	868	1.0	68	3.4	141	4.0	5,092	1.9	7,366	1.8
Other												
1980	—	—	12	0.02	—	—	—	—	1,050	0.4	1,062	0.3
1982	—	—	—	—	—	—	—	—	1,203	0.5	1,203	0.3
Total												
1980	98,982		41,256		2,007		3,175		255,695		401,025	
1982	89,995		43,458		2,014		3,544		270,291		409,302	

Source: Statistics Canada, *Provincial Government Employment*, cat. no. 72–007 (Ottawa: Statistics Canada, 1980–82).

a. Function over provincial total.
b. Includes only two of the provincial hospitals.
c. CEGEPs were added.

TABLE A-5 Canadian Labour Force: Male and Female (000s)

	Male	% Male	Female	% Female	Total	Participation Rate Male	Participation Rate Female	LF Pop. Total
1960	4,711	73.3	1,719	26.7	6,430	79.5	28.8	54.1
1965	5,046	70.2	2,139	29.8	7,185	76.7	31.9	54.1
1970	5,631	67.6	2,698	32.4	8,329	74.8	35.2	54.8
1975	6,417	64.7	3,506	35.3	9,923	75.4	40.3	57.6
1980	6,909	60.0	4,613	40.0	11,522	78.3	50.3	64.0
1982	6,867	58.5	4,876	41.5	11,743	75.0	51.2	62.8

Source: Table 3-5.

Appendix B
Comparisons of Provincial Organizations and Their Responsibilities

Where we could not establish the relevant information, a blank space has been left. The variety of organizational forms and inter-relationships may make some comparisons tenuous. Most of the provincial bodies have had a number of name changes which could not be accommodated in the tables. Therefore we have reverted to using a generic title for the relevant function, which will be more or less close to the actual, current title in use in any one province to designate the organization.

TABLE B-1 Provincial Status of Women Offices

	Nfld. Provincial Advisory Council on the Status of Women	P.E.I. Advisory Council on the Status of Women	N.S. Advisory Council on the Status of Women	N.B. Advisory Council on the Status of Women	Que. Conseil de statut de la femme	Ont. Ontario Women's Directorate	Man. Advisory Committee on the Status of Women	Sask. Advisory Council on the Status of Women	Alta. Alberta's Women's Secretariat	B.C. British Columbia Women's Office
Year established	1980	1975	1977	1975	1973	1983	1972	1976	1981	1980
Reports to	Premier	Designated minister	Designated minister	Designated minister	Designated minister	Deputy premier	Minister of Labour	Minister of Labour	Designated minister	Minister of Labour
Provides:										
Policy advice (ID issues + priorities)	Y	Y	Y	Y	Y	Y	Y	Y	Y	Y
Information/education	Y	Y	Y	Y	Y	Y	Y	Y	Y	Y
Referral service	N	N	N	N	Y	Y	N	N	Y	Y
Research/grants	Y	N	Y	N	Y	N	Y	Y	Y	N
Counselling	N	N	N	N	Y	N	Y	Y	N	Y
Training	N	N	N	N	N	N	N	Y	N	Y
Liaison and co-ordination with other groups	Y	Y	Y	Y	Y	Y	Y	Y	Y	Y

Sources: Telephone interviews and/or correspondence with: B.C. House (Ottawa); Ontario Women's Directorate; Nova Scotia Advisory Council on the Status of Women; Provincial Advisory Council on the Status of Women, Newfoundland and Labrador; Saskatchewan Advisory Council on the Status of Women; Conseil du statut de la femme, Quebec; New Brunswick Advisory Council on the Status of Women; and various annual reports.

Notes: This is not an exhaustive list of provincial women's organizations. Some provinces, particularly Ontario and Quebec, have other advocacy groups which fulfil other specific roles.

TABLE B-2 Provincial Civil Service Commission/Central Personnel Agencies' Responsibilities

	Nfld.	P.E.I.	N.S.	N.B.	Que.[h]	Ont.	Man.	Sask.	Alta.	B.C.
Reports to	Public Works and Services	Designated minister	Designated minister	Finance	President of National Assembly	Chairman of the Management Board of Cabinet	Designated minister	Designated minister	Designated minister	Provincial Secretary and Minister of Government Services
Provides:										
Recruitment and selection	Y	Y	Y[b]	Y[c]	N	Y	Y	Y	Y[f]	Y
Training and development	Y	Y	Y	N	N	Y	Y	Y	Y	Y
Advice on matters of personnel administration	Y	Y	Y	Y	N	Y	Y	Y	Y	Y
Development of equal opportunity programs	Y	N	Y	N	N	N	N	Y	Y	N
Delegation of some staffing authority	Y	N	N	Y	N[a]	Y	Y	N[e]	Y[f]	N
Classification	N	Y	Y	N	N	Y	Y	Y	N[f]	N
Agent of employer in collective bargaining[d]	N	Y	Y	N	N	Y	Y	Y	Y	N[g]
Appeals (on staffing matters)	N	Y	N	Y	Y	N	Y	N	N	N

TABLE B-2 (Cont'd)

Source: Telephone interviews with the commissions, supplemented by annual reports and an examination of the appropriate legislation. J.E. Hodgetts and O.P. Dwivedi's *Provincial Governments as Employers* (Toronto: Institute of Public Administration of Canada, 1974) provides an excellent, but dated, survey of personnel administration in the provinces.

a. Participates on negotiating committees with Treasury Board.

b. Employees of central body are seconded to departments to act as personnel directors.

c. Proposed reform legislation, if passed, will see the staffing function move to an expanded Treasury Board which will be reconstituted as a board of management.

d. The CSC would retain the responsibility for preserving the merit principle through the audit function.

e. Currently undertaking a six-month pilot project for delegating staffing and classification responsibility to a few departments.

f. Some authority has been decentralized to departments; the Personnel Administration Office retains responsibility for management level employees.

g. The Government Employee Relations Bureau, established in 1976, is the industrial relations arm of Treasury Board. It is also responsible for job classification and evaluation.

h. Commission de la fonction publique hears appeals brought by civil servants, and audits the staffing process to ensure that impartiality and fairness are maintained. The Office des ressources humaines assumes the responsibilities of the former Office du recrutement et de la sélection du personnel in matters of recruitment and selection. The Office also provides services and gives advice to departments and agencies on matters of personnel management, and may delegate its staffing responsibilities.

TABLE B-3 Provincial "Treasury Board" Responsibilities

	Nfld.	P.E.I.	N.S.	N.B.	Que.	Ont.	Man.	Sask.	Alta.	B.C.
	Treasury Board	Treasury Board	Management Board	Treasury Board	Conseil du trésor	Management Board	Treasury Department	Treasury Board	Treasury Department	Treasury Board
Classification	Y	N	N	Y	Y	N	N	N	N	N
Collective bargaining	Y	Y	N	Y	Y	N	N	N	N	N
Sets mandate for collective bargaining		Y			Y					Nᵃ
Sets terms and conditions of employment	Y	Y	Y	Y	Y	Y	Y	Y	Y	Y
Personnel policy	Y	Y	Y	Y	Y		Y			
Creating and abolishing positions	Y				Y					Y
General management practices policy	Y	Y	Y	Y	Y	Y		Y	Y	Y
Organizational structure		Y			Y	Y		Y		Y
Budgeting systems and procedures	Y		Y		Y	Y	Y			Y
Co-ordinating the budgetary process	Y	Y	Y		Y	Y		Y	Y	Y
Reviews estimates	Y	Y	Y	Y	Y	Y	Y	Y	Y	Y
Evaluates programs	Y		Y		Y	Y		Y		Y

Sources: Telephone interviews with the staff and the various boards, supplemented by an examination of the appropriate financial administration legislation.

a. Strictly speaking, B.C. established the Government Employee Relations Bureau in 1976 as the industrial relations arm of Treasury Board.

TABLE B-4 Provincial Human Rights Agencies' Responsibilities

	Nfld.	P.E.I.	N.S.	N.B.	Que.	Ont.	Man.	Sask.	Alta.	B.C.
Year established	1970 Justice	1975 Designated minister	1969 Designated minister	1967 Labour and Human Resources	1975 President of the national Assembly	1962–81[a] Minister of Labour	1974 Attorney General	1947–79[e] Minister of Justice	1972 Minister of Labour	1979–84[d] Minister of Labour
Functions of Commissions:										
Investigates complaints of discrimination	Y	Y	Y	Y	Y	Y	Y	Y	Y	Y
Public information	Y	Y	Y	Y	Y	Y	Y	Y	Y	N
Public education	Y	Y	Y	Y	Y	Y	Y	Y	Y	N
Advice	Y	Y	Y	Y	Y	Y	Y	Y	Y	N
Approves and monitors affirmative action programs	Y	Y	Y	Y	Y[c]	Y	Y	Y	N	N
Orders affirmative action programs	N	N	N	N	Y[c]	N	N	N	N	N
Research	Y	Y	Y	Y	Y	Y	Y	Y	Y	N
Failing settlement, directs the minister to convene board of inquiry	Y[b]	Y[b]	Y[b]	Y	Y	Y	Y	Y	Y	Y[b]
Initiates own investigations	N	N	N	N	Y	Y	Y	Y	N	N

Sources: Telephone interviews with all of the provincial human rights commissions, supplemented by their annual reports and legislation.
a. Human Rights Code of 1981 consolidates previous 20 years of statutes.
b. Commission makes a report to the minister who decides whether case goes to a board of inquiry for settlement or that proceedings are discontinued.
c. As of October 1984, these provisions were not yet in force.
d. The 1979 act was repealed and B.C. Council of Human Rights takes the former Human Rights Commission's investigatory responsibilities.
e. In 1947, the CCF government in Saskatchewan passed the first Bill of Rights in Canada, which remained in effect until 1979, when the Saskatchewan Human Rights Code became law.

TABLE B-5 Provincial Ombudsman Responsibilities

	Nfld.	P.E.I.[e]	N.S.	N.B.	Que.	Ont.	Man.	Sask.	Alta.	B.C.
Year established	1970[a]	—	1971	1967	1968	1975	1970	1972	1967	1975[b]
Officer of the legislature	Y		Y	Y	Y	Y	Y	Y	Y	Y
Committee of the legislature on ombudsmen	N		N	N	N	Y	N	N	Y	N
Responds to complaints	Y		Y	Y	Y	Y	Y	Y	Y	Y
Initiates own investigations	Y		Y	Y	Y	Y		Y	Y	Y
Investigates decisions, acts, recommendations of commissions of:										
Departments	Y		Y	Y	Y	Y	Y	Y[c]	Y	Y
Agencies	Y		Y	Y	Y	Y	Y	Y[c]	Y	Y
Municipalities	N		Y	Y	Y[d]	N	N	N	N	Y
Courts	N		N	N	N	N	N	N	N	Y
Cabinet	N		N	N	N	N	N	N	N	N
Investigates matters referred to its office by:										
Legislature	Y		Y	N				Y		N
Governor-in-council				N				Y		Y

Sources: Telephone interviews with the provincial ombudsman offices, supplemented by annual reports and an examination of the appropriate legislation.

a. Not proclaimed until 1975.
b. Office established in 1979.
c. Unable to investigate decisions of deputy ministers and other permanent heads.
d. Decisions of this Quebec municipal commission are subject to investigation.
e. PEI does not have an Office of the Ombudsman.

Appendix C
Equality of Participation and the Merit System

In his 1972 discussion of the merit principle in operation in Canada,[1] J.E.Hodgetts outlines what he sees as the meaning of the ideal of merit. First, all Canadians should have "reasonable opportunity" to be considered for appointment; and secondly, the decision to appoint should be based solely on an individual's fitness for the job. It is in the administration of the merit system that he sees problems emerging. He identifies the treatment of French-Canadian civil servants and females as two major areas where the merit system has demonstrably failed to provide the framework in which equity of participation could be ensured.

More than a decade later, the problem largely persists that the neutral application of a rule of appointments and promotions by merit (as defined by the PSC) simply does not guarantee proportionate representation of identifiable social groups. This persistence is in spite of the Public Service Commission's known care in interpreting the merit principle in operational terms, and despite programs such as Equal Opportunity for Women[2] and strong efforts to support francophone recruitment. To use the phrase of these jargon-ridden times, it has become clear that "systemic discrimination" has operated below the surface to deprive certain groups of their job opportunities and the merit administrators of their goals. More recently, since 1983, the Treasury Board secretariat has initiated "proactive" policies to increase the representation of visible groups through affirmative action policies, leaving the Public Service Commission responsible for auditing departments and agencies for compliance with these new policies, as well as for the traditional merit audits.

REPRESENTATION OF WOMEN

In general terms, there is evidence of a dramatic increase in the participation of women in the federal public service. Whereas in 1965, only 26.9 percent of full-time employees under the Public Service Employment Act (PSEA) were women, by 1982, the figure had climbed to more than 40 percent; in 1982, women represented 41.5 percent of the labour force (see Table C-1).

TABLE C-1 Percentage of Males and Females Employed Under the Public Service Employment Act

	1965	1967	1970	1975	1980	1982
Male	73.1	72.7	71.9	67.4	62.2	59.6
Female	26.9	27.3	28.1	32.6	37.8	40.4

Source: Public Service Commission, Annual Reports.

However, the almost 90,000 women enumerated in the Public Service Commission's universe of federal government employees (that is, falling under the provisions of the Public Service Employment Act) are not distributed proportionately throughout all the occupational categories. Nearly 71 percent are working as support staff in either the administrative support or operational categories, with only 29 percent working at officer levels. In 1982, only 172 women, less than one-quarter of 1 percent of officers, were working as executives (see Table C-2). The proportions of women who work at these heights are therefore so tiny that great improvements can be made to the absolute numbers of women employed without much affecting the male-female ratio; see below for more on women at executive ranks.

Of the total of men, 61 percent are at officer levels, and 2.8 percent are executives. Statistics Canada's figures[3] actually show a decline in the proportion of women employed at higher levels since 1970. Then, women were nearly one-quarter of their grouping "executive, scientific and professional" which combines executives with the other two groups, while in 1982 their proportion had declined to just under 21 percent (Table C-3). The increase in proportions of women in public service employment is preponderantly due, then, to their increased presence in the administrative support category: in 1970, women were 67 percent of all workers here, while in 1982 they were more than 82 percent of all workers in these lower-paying support jobs. (Some improvement has, however, occurred in the administrative and foreign service category; while in 1970 women were only 12 percent of officers here, by 1982 they were nearly 32 percent. Improvements can also be seen in the technical category.)

The government has demonstrated concern over this apparent lack of progress in the integration of women into all ranks of the public service. In June of 1983, Treasury Board President Herb Gray announced an affirmative action program to begin in 1985: "a comprehensive systems-based approach" to "ensure equitable representation" of women, handicapped and indigenous people.[4] The goal is to create a work force "representative of the Canadian people," from among the "available, qualified and interested people." Gray claimed that equitable representation "can only be achieved through strong proactive measures." His affirmative action strategy is in essence a work-force audit and analysis of policies, practices and procedures. It is designed to eliminate barriers in employment (systemic discrimination), to establish "temporary special measures" to facilitate entry, along with corresponding support in development and promotion. Each department and agency, as defined in Schedule 1.1 of the Public Service Staff Relations Act (PSSRA), is responsible for undertaking this analysis and for preparing "action plans" that include goals and timetables before the end of 1984.

TABLE C-2 Participation of Women Under the PSEA by Occupational Category

	1972			1975			1980			1982		
	W	T	%W	W	T	%W	W	T	%W	W	T	%W
Management												
SX/EX	3	777	0.4	21	1,186	1.8	52	1,309	4.0	98	1,968	5.0
SM	—	—	—	—	—	—	—	—	—	74	1,207	6.0
Total	3	777	0.4	21	1,186	1.8	52	1,309	4.0	172	3,175	5.4
Scientific & Professional	4,635	19,165	24.2	5,759	23,440	24.5	4,506	21,460	21.0	5,150	22,497	22.9
Admin. & Foreign Service	4,446	32,651	13.6	9,152	47,579	19.2	13,693	51,539	26.6	17,605	54,184	32.5
Technical	1,747	21,433	8.2	2,516	25,866	9.7	2,684	25,918	10.4	3,289	27,321	12.0
Total officers	10,831	74,026	14.6	17,448	98,071	17.8	20,935	100,226	20.9	26,216	107,177	24.5
Administrative Support	45,585	66,831	68.2	58,109	74,574	77.9	54,991	68,169	80.7	58,142	70,757	82.2
Operational	11,860	89,899	13.2	13,572	100,518	13.5	19,451	99,555	19.5	5,454	44,267	12.3
Total	68,276	230,756	29.6	89,129	273,167	32.6	95,487	268,139	35.6	89,922[a]	222,582[a]	40.4

Source: Public Service Commission, Annual Reports.
a. Exclude Canada Post Corporation employees.

TABLE C-3 **Participation of Women in the Public Service by Occupational Group: Statistics Canada Universe**

	1970	1975	1980	1982
Executive/scientific/professional	24.2	22.6	20.4	20.7
Administrative + foreign service	11.6	18.7	26.6	31.7
Technical	6.9	9.4	11.1	12.4
Total officers	13.8	17.2	21.1	24.2
Administrative support	67.0	77.3	80.4	82.2
Operational	14.5	13.3	22.3	23.5
Total	28.6	32.6	36.2	37.8

Source: Statistics Canada, Public Finance Division.

This echoes the D'Avignon Committee report of 1979 which called for "fair and equitable treatment for all, ensuring equal access of employment, training and development and career opportunities . . . creating an organizational climate that will prevent, eliminate or redress disadvantages that beset certain groups of employees."[5] The report suggested that new priorities necessitated a reinterpretation of merit — in other words, a change in the way the system was administered as distinct from the general principle of fairness and non-discrimination.

A few months later, in October 1983, Mr. Gray followed up the basic affirmative action policy formula with an announcement that a target had been set to more than double the number of women in the management category before 1987, from 217 to about 475. He emphasized that the target figure was not a quota: "The merit principle will still prevail in all Public Service appointments."[6]

According to a 1983 Public Service Commission planning document,[7] women had in 1975 made up less than 2 percent of all persons working above the Senior Executive 1 level, a proportion that had risen to about 5 percent in 1982. That year, a Senior Management level (with members promotable to the first rank of the executive category) was created by reclassifying all officers working at management jobs in other categories — the "senior executive minus one step" groups — into a group of general managers. Of this new category, women were just over 4 percent. They represented just over 7 percent of all the feeder groups for the new level. The PSC's planner claimed that ". . . it is reasonable to expect, that as a minimum, the Public Service could double the current number of women executives within the next four years," that is, if they were promoted only proportionately to their numbers who qualified. The authors thought that women could form more than 10 percent of the executive group by December 1986.

Comparison with the private sector's record for integrating women into the most elite ranks of executives is difficult, if not impossible, because of lack of reliable sector-wide statistics for the private sector, but available evidence suggests that the two sectors are not very different. Statistics Canada has found that women made up 30.5 percent of managers (middle levels and up) in the private sector as of December 1983, and that the proportion of women filling similar jobs in government (including the Crown corporations) was virtually identical at 30.6 percent. Eight years earlier, in December of 1976, women had made up 21 percent of all managers in private sector jobs, and 19.6 percent in government, again including the Crown corporations.[8]

The Public Service Commission's own four-year forecast of women's participation, given a more or less steady course, seems to suggest that Treasury Board's target is modest. There would appear to be enough strength in feeder groups inside the public service to meet demand for promotable women, without resorting to heavy outside recruiting or any other extraordinary measures. By December of 1986, PSC anticipates that 121 women at the Senior Management (SM) and SM Minus 1 levels will be promotable to the executive group. In December of 1982 there were 592 women at the SM Minus 1 level and 1,405 at the SM Minus 2 level, a pool of nearly 2,000 from which to draw to reach the 1986 and 1988 targets.[9]

In addition, there are some initiatives to strengthen women's representation at officer entry and middle levels. In the last decade, the PSC has taken steps to increase the recruitment of women university graduates, up to more than one-third of all university recruitments in 1982, from about one-quarter in 1975. However, this must be judged in the light of extreme restraint in hiring since 1978. In addition, the Career Assignment Program which, since its establishment in 1968, has groomed officers with the potential to work at management levels, has improved its recruitment of women: up to about one-third of participants in 1980, from about 20 percent in 1976. In 1981, almost two-thirds of new appointments to officer groups were women.[10]

REPRESENTATION OF FRANCOPHONES

The history of representation of francophones in the Canadian public service is far too broad a subject to treat in depth here. It is captured well in reports of the past two decades, most notably in the 1972 work for the Bilingualism and Biculturalism Commission by Christopher Beattie, Jacques Désy and Stephen Longstaff on the career patterns of anglophones and francophones in the Canadian Public Service.[11] At that time, the authors found that francophones were "generally absent" from the upper levels of the public service (with the exception of lawyers), having a much stronger presence at both the very highest positions and throughout all the lower levels. John Porter, nearly 20 years earlier, reported on the same tendency for the francophone presence to bulge at low levels, then decline through the middle to top ranks, reappearing only among the elite posts.[12]

The Bilingualism and Biculturalism Commission warned that francophones were seriously disadvantaged in their career progression through the middle and upper ranks by the extreme dominance of the English language in those realms. Hence, the career development of a francophone tended to be arrested at the entry to top management ranks. This, in turn, meant that there were no francophones to feed recruitment at highest levels, at which point the practice was to parachute prominent francophones in from outside. The Official Languages Act of 1968–69 addressed this problem by ensuring that French could be a language of work at all levels. It provides that: "The English and French languages are the official languages of Canada for all purposes of the Parliament and Government of Canada, and possess and enjoy equal rights and privileges as to their use in all the institutions of the Parliament and Government of Canada." (See Chapter 2 for a discussion of the organization that implements the act, the Official Languages Commission.)

Between 1974 and 1982, francophone participation has improved marginally, up from 24.6 percent to 26.8 percent of employees under the PSEA (see Table C-4). Since francophones represented about 26 percent of the total Canadian population in 1981,[13] some observers might be tempted to conclude that francophone participation is now fully satisfactory. But like women, although not so markedly, francophones are well represented in the support categories, and in administration and foreign service, but under-represented in the scientific and professional and management groups. They have a particularly low participation at the senior management level (17 percent).[14]

The PSC uses essentially the same mechanisms to try to redress the imbalances: appointments from outside, of which francophones formed 38 percent; improvements in career assignment program participation to develop more francophone middle-to-high level managers (this fluctuated between 40 and 28 percent between 1979 and 1982); and university recruitment, up to 39 percent of all recruits, from only 20 percent in 1967.[15]

SUMMARY

The overall effects of general affirmative action by government to improve its own record of employment of minorities appears to be modest at the higher levels. It would also seem that the Public Service Commission has had mechanisms (if only non "proactive" ones that pose no problems for the principle of appointing the single most meritorious candidate) in place for some time to try to improve the representation of women and francophones.

TABLE C-4 Francophone Participation: Employees Under the PSEA by Occupational Category

	1974			1976			1978			1980			1982		
	F	T	%F	F	T	%F	F	T	%F	F	T	%F	F	T	%F
Management															
SX/EX	208	1,123	18.5	259	1,268	20.4	281	1,356	20.7	281	1,309	21.5	414	1,968	21.0
SM	—	—	—	—	—	—	—	—	—	—	—	—	204	1,207	16.9
Total Management	208	1,123	18.5	259	1,268	20.4	281	1,356	20.7	281	1,309	21.5	618	3,175	19.5
Scientific + professional	3,857	19,115	20.2	4,539	22,205	20.4	3,881	21,291	19.3	3,881	19,981	19.4	4,652	22,164	21.0
Admin. + foreign service	8,813	36,796	24.0	12,040	46,307	26.0	12,799	48,035	26.6	13,550	49,326	27.5	15,300	53,882	28.4
Technical	3,317	21,146	15.7	4,393	24,287	18.1	4,421	24,476	18.1	4,675	24,881	18.8	5,384	27,176	19.8
Total officers	16,112	77,900	20.7	21,162	93,828	22.6	21,607	95,158	22.7	22,347	95,341	23.4	25,954	106,397	24.4
Administrative support	15,159	55,572	27.3	19,768	64,615	30.6	19,234	62,917	30.5	19,750	62,515	31.6	22,294	70,059	31.8
Operational	20,281	75,962	26.7	23,478	87,204	26.9	24,491	91,477	26.8	25,135	93,042	27.0	10,726	43,869	24.5
Total[b]	51,552	209,434	24.6	64,490	245,828	26.2	65,332	249,477	26.2	67,308	251,048	26.8	59,099[a]	220,649[a]	26.8

Source: Public Service Commission, Annual Reports.

a. Excludes Canada Post Corporation employees.

b. Totals exclude 49,156 people in 1974; 37,341 people in 1976; 29,730 people in 1978; 17,091 people in 1980; and 1,933 people in 1982 whose first official language was not specified on the pay document.

One is tempted to speculate that the latest initiatives have been considerably blunted by the effect of restraint in the public service since 1978. During the five years between 1977 and 1982, the rate of promotions dropped by 38 percent, the lateral transfer rate by almost 50 percent, and the separation rate declined by 30 percent.[16]

On the other hand, the fact that the merit system has seemingly not provided a framework for equity of participation through all groups and levels of the public service is not a new failing: it can be documented in administrative statistics through the century. Most popular diagnoses of the reasons for the failure do not go beyond the idea that unequal representation is a denial of the merit of certain groups, caused by prejudice from the social groups that enjoy power against interlopers. Normal administrative statistics with their categories of male/female, francophone/anglophone do not support a more complex analysis. In this regard, Treasury Board's new policy to assess the strength of feeder groups, and then to judge if departments have distributed opportunities fairly, is a gain for subtlety. Perhaps the board's analysts will discover the obstacles to realizing equal representation within the merit system by locating the points at which "ghettos" begin to form.

It may also be, however, that the causes of light female and francophone participation in higher level management jobs are not to be found in simple prejudice against them at point of entry to the government work force, and thus cannot be addressed by challenging workplace attitudes and by audits for compliance. Indeed, the causes of under-representation of females and francophones may be quite dissimilar, and therefore require to be addressed, if at all, by quite different methods. It may not be possible to meet the implicit normal target of 25 percent francophone and 50 percent women in all levels of work from among, to quote Mr. Gray, the "available, interested and qualified" applicants for federal public service jobs. Equally, the causes of under-representation of indigenous people, blacks and the handicapped may be diverse, and incapable of being covered by one policy. It may also be time to review the administration of policy for defining minorities (excepting women). Certainly there are moot questions about the "visible" minorities which turn out not to be so visible after all. If I apply for appointment or promotion in the public service, it is usually up to me whether or not I identify myself as a member of a minority group: so far, no one examines my pedigree or studies my skin before I am admitted to statistical membership in a minority group or in the presumed residual catch-all of pale male sound-bodied anglophone. In the spring of 1985, the most that had been done toward validation of current levels of various minorities was a voluntary questionnaire circulated by Treasury Board: all employees were asked to identify whether they were handicapped persons, indigenous people or members of visible minority groups. The information would be used to monitor their employment progress in terms of training, career mobility and occupational group and level. Self-identification, however, has a great deal to do with self-consciousness, a variable that can be importantly affected by any sensitizing initiative. Surely there are dangers in establishing powerful employment incentives for individuals to think of themselves and describe themselves as, in Diefenbaker's phrase, "hyphenated Canadians." Self-interest may create quite new groups, as persons without a current label perceive that they have been disadvantaged comparatively. As a result, it is possible that what once looked like a comfortably slumbering majority might fragment into still more special interest groups. In other words, at what point does a process stop?

Related, then, is the question of how to begin setting verifiable standards for membership in one or another group. A policy cannot be administered fairly and subjected to the continuous audits and reviews that are part of government unless its standards are objective and verifiable. What is a francophone? What is a native Canadian? What is a black Nova Scotian? What sorts of physical limitations qualify one as handicapped? Linguistic competence is fairly readily verified by use of objective written and spoken tests, but what of these racial and status visible minorities? The word "visible" is obviously meant to be an important modifier, but what is to stop an individual adding an element of visibility by adopting a costume or a bearing? Where membership is thought to convey any kind of advantage or disadvantage, one may well see a day when targets are experienced by group members as quotas, and they begin to challenge each other's bona fides.

Further, the operation of general social and economic forces may skew supplies of qualified and interested applicants for positions so profoundly that affirmative action in hiring becomes purely symbolic, meaning that the public service is not to be censured for failing to meet its targets. It is hard to imagine, for example, that the quality of the primary and secondary education systems available to native people will soon equal that of middle-class southern Canadians, and thus be adequate to prepare natives in the numbers required to represent them proportionately in our public service. Indeed, the invisible majority in all these schemes for sharing employment in government work forces is the group whose incomes and educational standards do not meet middle-class standards. The causes of under-representation of women are likely very different than for any other minority. For one thing, women are a majority except in higher-level employment. They are easily identified. Women are not disproportionately located in any one geographical location. Indeed, the only characteristic that women share is their gender. Many observers believe that factors such as the lack of better day-care facilities and after-school programs for their children inhibit female willingness (or perceptions of their capacity) to take on extraordinarily heavy management jobs during the years in which potential managers demonstrate their potential. In this regard, it is an open and bitter joke among federal public servants that many of the important training and development courses (the PSC's Developmental Career Assignment Program included) are residential, a simple factor that quite effectively prevents or postpones participation by women with young children. Likewise, many observers, women among them, are beginning to fear the emotional tension in the workplace that is ostensibly caused by affirmative action programs. The accomplishments of women are "explained away" by attributing them to the new mechanisms to assist women. Ironically, then, one of the results of the affirmative action approach can be that it justifies male workers in choosing to bypass and exclude female colleagues from the interesting and challenging aspects of work which are often collegial in nature.[17]

Overall, analysts of the outcome of the normal merit process should perhaps ask "who benefits?" rather than "who suffers?" The analysis of characteristics that seem to confer an advantage on individuals in their quest for occupational preference might illustrate the processes in society that systematically favour certain groups. In addition, the ways in which definitions can be used to systematically favour certain groups should be a constant subject of review.[18] In this way, the focus could be shifted to social development and change in society, as opposed to the manipulation of fragments of the public sector work force for symbolic purposes.

Appendix D
National and Provincial Wage Control Policy Initiatives and Legislation

Federal	Public Service Compensation Restraint Act, Bill C-124 (Royal Assent 4 August 1982)	"6 and 5" • Announced in 18 June 1982 MacEachen budget as a "two-year national effort to break inflation." • Break "vicious circle of inflationary expectations." • Act covers federal public servants, Crown corporations, RCMP, CAF, senators, MPs, their staffs, and federal judges. • Six percent for 1982/83 and 5 percent for 1983/84: no merit, increment, or performance payments are allowed for groups of employees with salary range above $49,000. • Compensation limits also apply to existing two- and three-year agreements, and for the first time government has required rollbacks of signed contracts and extended collective agreements for the length of the program (and because of labour legislation for federal employment, the right to strike and management's duty to bargain is effectively removed).
Newfoundland	May 1982	• Wage restraints on senior civil servants. • One hundred and seventy executives, DMs, and ADMs limited to 5 percent in 1982/83 (said wage restraint policy would not be extended to civil servants who are represented by the various unions).
	October 1982	• Announced a sliding scale on public sector salary increases: 4 to 7 percent over the next two years.

		• If employee was earning less than $13,000, increases would be limited to 7 percent in the first year and 6 percent in the second; up to $18,000, 6 and 5 percent; over $18,000, 5 and 4 percent.
		• Also announced that other contract clauses were open to collective bargaining, that "the right to strike was still there."
	December 1983	• Announced a two-year program limiting wage increases to one-half of inflation rate (3 percent) if earning less than $18,000 and 2 percent if earning more.
	April 1984	• Freeze on wage increases for two years.
Prince Edward Island	April 1984	• Introduced job sharing plus other part-time employment in order to reduce costs and minimize layoffs.
Nova Scotia	September 1982	• Six percent limit on wage and benefit increases.
		• Collective agreements which took place before 15 September are not affected.
		• New contracts must be for a one-year period and signed before 28 February 1983.
New Brunswick	May 1983 Budget	• One-year wage freeze on public sector employees.
		• No plans to legislate the wage freeze and it would not affect current contracts or those in advanced states of negotiations (it would apply to the next round of contracts).
Quebec	Bill C-70 — June 1982	• Rolls back public sector wages and imposes a three-year contract on more than 300,000 public sector workers.
		• Automatically outlaws strikes.
	Bill 105 — December 1982	• Wages of 145,000 civil servants cut by 19.45 percent for three months.
		• Cuts of 1.5 to 19.45 percent for

		160,500 workers (to soften the rollback on lower paid workers).
Ontario	Provincial Restraint Act September 1982	• Controls program to limit salary increases of more than 500,000 public servants. • Wage control year runs from 1 October 1982 to 30 September 1983; compensation plans and contracts expiring during that time are extended for 12 months with wage increases limited to 5 percent. • Contracts which expire after the control period are rolled back to 5 percent after the first year has expired. • Inflation Restraint Board established to administer the prices program (minimal control over publicly administered prices) and to monitor wage increases in the public sector.
	November 1983 — Public Sector Prices and Compensation Review Act (Bill 111) (Replaces Provincial Restraint Act)	• Returns the right to bargain collectively and for some, the right to strike, but places a 5 percent limit on public wage spending. • Doctors who were previously exempt have a 10 percent increase rolled back to 5 percent. • Removes the $35,000 limit beyond which employees got no wage increase (merit increases are now included within the 5 percent overall increase). • Inflation Restraint Board no longer has power to roll back wage increases but only to monitor them.
Manitoba	1983 Budget	• Limits hiring to the most essential positions.
Saskatchewan	October 1982	• Announced intention to limit wage increases to 1 percent below inflation.
Alberta	January 1983	• Guidelines of 5 percent on public service wage increases for fiscal year 1983/84.

	1984	• Reduce number of full-time positions in government and agencies by 2 percent.
British Columbia	1978	• Announced their intention that the rate of public service wage increases "should follow, not exceed appropriate private sector compensation patterns."
	1981	• Reasserted the 1978 statement.
	1982	• "Compensation stabilization plan," base inflation factor of 10 percent plus or minus 2 percent for special circumstances ("to adjust for serious distortions due to past compensationary experience"). • Increase of 11.9 percent for MPPs rolled back to 8 percent.
	October 1983 — Bill 3" Public Sector Restraint Act	• New way of thinking about government and about the expectations we have." • No provision for general compensation increases. • Another objective is to cut 10,000 jobs by September 1984.

Sources: Provincial Budget Speeches, 1982–84. Commercial Clearing House, *Provincial Pulse*, 1982–84.

Notes

INTRODUCTION

1. Richard Rose, *Understanding Big Government* (London: Sage, 1984).
2. Max Weber, *The Theory of Social and Economic Organization*, edited and with an introduction by T. Parsons (New York: Free Press, 1964), pp. 337–38.
3. Kenneth Thompson, "The Organizational Society," in *Control and Ideology in Organizations*, edited by Graeme Salaman and Kenneth Thompson (Cambridge, Mass: MIT Press, 1980), p. 11.
4. Frederick C. Mosher, *Democracy and the Public Service* (New York: Oxford University Press, 1968), p. 3.
5. R.K. Merton, "Bureaucratic Structure and Personality," in R.K.Merton, ed. *Social Theory and Social Structure* (New York: Free Press, 1968), pp. 249–60.
6. Weber, *Social and Economic Organization*, pp. 339 and 361. See also Thompson, "The Organizational Society."
7. J.E. Hodgetts, *The Canadian Public Service: A Physiology of Government 1867–1970* (Toronto: University of Toronto Press, 1973), p. 109. See also R. MacGregor Dawson, revised by Norman Ward, *The Government of Canada*, 5th ed. (Toronto: University of Toronto Press, 1970), on the principles of organization of administrative activity in Canada.

CHAPTER 1

1. J.A.R. Marriott, *English Political Institutions*, 4th ed., with Introductory chapters on the Constitution, 1910–38 (Oxford: Clarendon Press, 1938), p. 48.
2. Among the texts that we have found most useful are: Marriott, *English Political Institutions*; Sir Ivor Jennings, *Parliament*, 2d ed. (Cambridge: Cambridge University Press, 1961), and his *The British Constitution* (Cambridge: Cambridge University Press, 1941); R.H.S. Crossman, *The Myths of Cabinet Government* (Cambridge, Mass.: Harvard University Press, 1972); R. MacGregor Dawson, revised by Norman Ward, *The Government of Canada*, 5th ed. (Toronto: University of Toronto Press, 1970); Norman Ward, *The Public Purse* (Toronto: University of Toronto Press, 1951); J.R. Mallory, *The Structure of Canadian Government* (Toronto: Macmillan of Canada, 1971); and John B. Stewart, *The Canadian House of Commons* (Montreal: McGill-Queen's University Press, 1977).
3. For the regular forums that the House can make available for debate, see Dawson and Ward, *Government of Canada*, and Stewart, *Canadian House of Commons*.
4. Marriott, *English Political Institutions*, p. 104.
5. Dawson and Ward, *Government of Canada*, p. 251.
6. J.E. Hodgetts and O.P. Dwivedi, *Provincial Governments as Employers* (Montreal: McGill-Queen's University Press, 1974).
7. Ministers can be sued for even the highest acts of state, the courts deciding whether the acts were legal. See Marriott, *English Political Institutions*, p. 288.
8. Douglas Yates, *Bureaucratic Democracy: The Search for Democracy and Efficiency in American Government* (Cambridge, Mass.: Harvard University Press, 1982).
9. See V.S. Wilson, *Canadian Public Policy and Administration* (Toronto: McGraw-Hill Ryerson, 1981), chap. 4; Kenneth Kernaghan, "Politics, Policy and Public Servants: Political Neutrality Revisited," *Canadian Public Administration* 19 (Fall 1976): 432–56; Canada, Royal Commission on Financial Management and Accountability, *Final Report* (Ottawa: Minister of Supply and Services Canada, 1979), chaps. 9 and 10; and A.W. Johnson, "The Role of the Deputy Minister," *Canadian Public Administration* 4 (December 1961): 363–73.
10. Flora MacDonald, "The Minister and the Mandarins," *Policy Options* 1 (September/October 1980): 29–31. See also Mitchell Sharp's critique of the MacDonald article in

Paul W. Fox, ed., *Politics Canada*, 5th ed. (Toronto: McGraw-Hill Ryerson, 1982), pp. 476–79 and Andrew F. Johnson, "A Minister as an Agent of Policy Change: The Case of Unemployment Insurance in the Seventies," *Canadian Public Administration* 24 (Winter 1981): 612–33.

11. In 1981, Mrs. Thatcher had proposed the "Protection of Official Information Act," which would actually have increased secrecy, but it was allowed to die. See K.G. Robertson, *Public Secrets* (London: Macmillan, 1982), p.180. See also Jonathan Manthorpe, "Government Secrets Leakers Not Heroes in U.K., They're Criminals," *Citizen* (Ottawa), April 12, 1984, p. 21. In March 1984, a British judge jailed a 23-year-old Foreign Office clerk, Sarah Tisdall, for leaking two memos to a newspaper. These dealt with the minister's plans to avoid political responsibility/discussion of the arrival in Britain of cruise missiles from the United States. On the prosecution's own admission, the documents presented no threat to security. Miss Tisdall was prosecuted under section 2 of the Official Secrets Act. See "Judge Gaols Civil Servant for Leaking Policy Document," *Manchester Guardian Weekly*, April 1, 1984, p. 3; and Peter Jenkins, "Government Secrecy and the Individual Conscience," *Manchester Guardian Weekly*, April 8, 1984, p. 4. Tisdall appealed against sentence, not conviction, but was denied relief. More recently, in October 1984, Mr. Clive Ponting, a senior Ministry of Defence official, was sent for trial at the Old Bailey. He had sent papers to an MP which revealed government plans to withhold from Parliament information about the sinking of the Argentine ship, the *Belgrano*. See James Lewis, "The Week in Britain," *Manchester Guardian Weekly*, October 21, 1984, p. 14. The jury in this case returned to find Ponting guilty despite the judge's charge to it.

12. Section 91 enumerates federal responsibilities, section 92 specifies areas of exclusive provincial control and section 93 sets out authority over education. See Mallory, *Structure of Canadian Government*, and R.Van Loon and M. Whittington, *The Canadian Political System*, 3d ed. (Toronto: McGraw-Hill Ryerson, 1981), chaps. 6 and 7.

13. Marriott's other two tests of whether a constitution is really flexible are that there is no special machinery for constitutional amendment, and that there are no distinctions between ordinary and constitutional laws. For the definition of parliament, we defer to Erskine May, as quoted in M. Rush's, "Parliamentary Committees and Parliamentary Government: The British and Canadian Experience," *Journal of Commonwealth and Comparative Politics* 20 (July 1983), p. 139.

14. For a recent synopsis, see Peter Aucoin, "Parliamentary Government in Canadian Federalism," in *Party Government and Regional Representation in Canada*, volume 36 of the research studies prepared for the Royal Commission on the Economic Union and Development Prospects for Canada (Toronto: University of Toronto Press, 1985). See also Thomas D'Aquino, G. Bruce Doern and Cassandra Blair, *Parliamentary Democracy in Canada: Issues for Reform* (Toronto: Methuen, 1983); Donald Smiley, "Central Institutions," in *Canada and the New Constitution: The Unfinished Agenda*, edited by Stanley M. Beck and Ivan Bernier (Montreal: Institute for Research on Public Policy, 1983), pp. 19–91; D.V. Smiley, "The Structural Problem of Canadian Federalism," *Canadian Public Administration* 14 (Fall 1971): 326–43: J.R. Mallory, "Canadian Federalism in Transition," *Politics Quarterly* 48 (April 1977): 149–63; Allan Kornberg, Harold D. Clarke and Marianne C. Steward, "Federalism and Fragmentation: Political Support in Canada," *Journal of Politics* 41 (August 1979): 879–906; Alan C.Cairns, "The Governments and Societies of Canadian Federalism," *Canadian Journal of Political Science* 10 (December 1977): 695–725, and "The Other Crisis of Canadian Federalism," *Canadian Public Administration* 22 (Summer 1979): 175–95.

15. Donald Smiley, *Canada in Question: Federalism in the Seventies*, 2d ed. (Toronto: McGraw-Hill Ryerson, 1976).

16. See Robert Sheppard, "Ottawa's 'Envoy' to the Prairies," *Globe and Mail*, July 3, 1984, p. 8. For a broader analysis, see Peter Aucoin and Herman Bakvis, "Regional Responsiveness and Government Organization," in *Regional Responsiveness and the National Administrative State*, volume 37 of the research studies prepared for the Royal Commission on the Economic Union and Development Prospects for Canada (Toronto: University of Toronto Press, 1985).

17. See Michael Hicks, "The Treasury Board and Its Clients: Five Years of Change and Administrative Reform 1966–71," *Canadian Public Administration* 16 (Summer 1973): 182–205; and A.W. Johnson, "Management Theory and Cabinet Government," *Canadian Public Administration* 14 (Spring 1971): 73–81.

18. On this subject, see Ian D. Clark, "Recent Changes in the Cabinet Decision-making System in Ottawa," *Canadian Public Administration* 28 (Summer 1985): 185–201.

19. H.L. Laframboise, "Here Come the Program Benders," *Optimum* 7 (1976): 40–47.

20. Ian Clark, "Recent Changes," stresses that the minister remained in full control of the contents and timing of a memorandum to cabinet, but it is clear from the entire context that the detailed proposals for action went forward only as modified and elaborated by the interdepartmental consultation of officials.

21. See John Porter, "Higher Public Servants and the Bureaucratic Elite in Canada," *Canadian Journal of Economic and Political Science* 24 (November 1958): 483–501. On the British administrative class, see Peter Kellner and Lord Crowther-Hunt, *The Civil Servants: An Inquiry into Britain's Ruling Class* (London: Macdonald, 1980).

22. The print press, perhaps because of its own hunger for new information, vociferously champions anyone who contests with central institutions for information. In recent years, the Office of the Auditor General has been most active. In a recent editorial, "Holding out on Public Actives," (January 4, 1985, p. A8) the Ottawa *Citizen* repeatedly named a civil servant as the undoubted source of "faulty advice" to the prime minister. The writer had, and could have, no evidence of what advice went through what channels to the prime minister: under the cabinet system, policy advice is privileged, so that politicians will be free to follow it or ignore it as they judge fit. This in turn enables them to take responsibility for their judgments. There is no way the named civil servant could reply without breaking trust. The writer should have called for the prime minister's resignation. This editorial followed on an even more remarkable story in which the auditor general himself personally attacked the same civil servant for "stick-handling" the government's response to his unprecedented demands for documents. (See "Bad Advice," *Citizen*, December 3, 1984, p. 1.) In the same outspoken manner, despite the fact that there was a review coming up on the matter in the Federal Court, the auditor general said, "We cannot have the cabinet telling the auditor general what he can and cannot audit." It should be noted, also, that despite the use of the terms "audit" and "the books," the new powers that are at stake apparently have little to do with either, but concern access to strategic policy advice, which may or may not contain secondary financial analysis.

23. See Yates, *Bureaucratic Democracy*, especially pp. 32–61.

24. See the research emerging from the "institutions" research program of this Commission.

25. Two very accessible introductions to the non-departmental forms are found in J.E. Hodgetts, *The Canadian Public Service: A Physiology of Government 1867–1970* (Toronto: University of Toronto Press, 1973), and C.A. Ashley and R.G.H. Smails, *Canadian Crown Corporations* (Toronto: Macmillan of Canada, 1965). See also Privy Council Office, Submissions to the Royal Commission on Financial Management and Accountability, March 1979, for a clear exposition. On the policy significance of the non-departmental sector, see Allan Tupper and G. Bruce Doern, eds., *Public Corporations and Public Policy in Canada* (Montreal: Institute for Research on Public Policy, 1981); G. Bruce Doern and Richard W. Phidd, *Canadian Public Policy: Ideas, Structure, Process* (Toronto: Methuen, 1983); and W.T. Stanbury and F. Thompson, eds., *Managing Public Enterprises* (New York: Praeger, 1982).

26. Privy Council Office, "Crown Corporations: Direction, Control, Accountability — Government of Canada's Proposals" (Ottawa, 1977), p. 14.

27. For the financial significance of the Crown sector, see John L. Howard and W.T. Stanbury, "Measuring Leviathan: The Size, Scope and Growth of Governments in Canada," *Probing Leviathan*, edited by G. Lorimer (Vancouver: Fraser Institute, 1984), p. 87–112; and John W. Langford and Kenneth J. Hoffman, "The Uncharted Universe of Federal Crown Corporations," in *Crown Corporations in Canada: The Calculus of Instrument Choice*, edited by J.R.S. Pritchard (Toronto: Butterworth, 1983).

28. Statistics Canada, Public Finance Division, "The Public Sector — A Proposal" (Ottawa, January 1983).

29. On the origins of the major Crown corporations, see Tupper and Doern, *Public Corporations*, chap. 1, and Pritchard, *Crown Corporations*, chap. 1.

30. See the Privy Council Office submission, "Crown Corporations"; G. Bruce Doern, ed., *The Regulatory Process in Canada* (Toronto: Macmillan of Canada, 1978) and W.T. Stanbury, ed., *Government Regulation: Scope, Growth, Process* (Montreal: Institute for Research on Public Policy, 1980).

31. Privy Council Office submission, "Crown Corporations," p. 2-2.

32. Ibid., p. 2-10.

33. Ashley and Smails, *Canadian Crown Corporations*, p. 34.

34. See Economic Council of Canada, *Responsible Regulation* (Ottawa: Minister of Supply and Services Canada, 1979).

35. Jennings, *Parliament*, p. 36.

36. Ashley and Smails, *Canadian Crown Corporations*, p. 45.

37. Ibid., p. 60.

38. It will be recalled that the genus "planning – programming – budgeting systems" were being implemented continent-wide in the 1960s and that in 1971 the federal government actually began to present its Estimates to Parliament in a program format.

39. Ashby's law of requisite variety says that a "control" must reflect all the complexity of whatever is being controlled. Hence, political actors outside of cabinet have a choice of: 1) covering the full complexity of administration in its own terms; and 2) engaging in some credible sampling technique. Parliamentary systems do the second. Grievances make their way forward, and parliamentarians exact retrospective accountability for the "disasters" of administration. The disasters are a sample of all administration. See Stafford Beer, *The Heart of Enterprise* (Toronto: John Wiley, 1979), pp. 83–103.

40. See Sonia Sinclair, *Cordial But Not Cosy: A History of the Office of the Auditor General* (Toronto: McClelland and Stewart, 1979), and Sharon Sutherland, "The Office of the Auditor General of Canada; Watching the Watchdog," in *How Ottawa Spends Your Tax Dollars*, edited by G. Bruce Doern (Toronto: James Lorimer, 1981).

41. We discuss the federal bodies as typical of those which have been added to Canadian provincial and federal legislatures, although each province has its own group of such organizations. Perhaps most important, many provinces have had considerable positive experience with an ombudsman office. There is no equivalent at the national level. For a basic review of bodies in the provincial governments, see Appendix B on ombudsmen and rights commissions.

42. The OCG began with 98 people in 1978, increasing substantially to 160 in 1979. During the next three years, it added only 30 people, and then in 1983 dropped back to 164.

43. The phrase is Gordon Robertson's. He thought that the Privy Council Office should be careful to stay out of the field of political decision.

44. The Office of the Chief Electoral Officer is another watchdog of sorts, but it does not monitor the bureaucracy, so is not discussed here. All the bodies named in the text are listed as part of the legislature in the Government of Canada publication, *Organization of the Government of Canada 1980* (Ottawa: Minister of Supply and Services Canada, 1980).

45. For a discussion, see T.M. Denton, "Ministerial Responsibility: A Contemporary Perspective," in *The Canadian Political Process*, 3d ed., edited by Richard Schultz, Orest M. Kruhlak and John C. Terry (Toronto: Holt, Rinehart and Winston, 1979) pp. 344–63. In Britain, the prime minister is responsible for the civil service establishment. See also Brian C. Smith and J. Stanyes, *Administering Britain* (London: Martin Robertson, 1976), pp. 69–70.

46. Public Service Employment Act (PSEA), S.C. 1966–67, c. 71, s. 1, 3 (1) through (5).

47. Hodgetts, *Canadian Public Service*, p. 81.

48. For a discussion of the audit revolution that accompanied the surge in growth, see Sutherland, "Watching the Watchdog."

49. In July 1984, the auditor general filed a motion with the Federal Court of Canada asking that the finance minister and the energy minister be ordered to give the auditor general access to all government files on the purchase of Petrofina Canada by the Crown corporation Petro-Canada. Auditor General Dye wanted to assess whether the government (i.e., the political leadership), had taken into account the effect of the purchase on the country's "balance of payments, the value of the dollar, tax revenues and future capital spending requirements." See "Court Motion Seeks Records of Petrofina Buy," *Globe and Mail*, July 6, 1984, p. 5. It is noteworthy that the auditor general filed suit in his own right, with the express purpose of independently evaluating the wisdom of government policy. In court, his lawyers summed up on March 20, 1985, by saying that the auditor general needed cabinet's papers so that he could establish whether the cabinet "had done its homework" before the decision to acquire Petrofina was taken.

50. For example, The *Globe and Mail*, in an editorial, "To Audit the Books," May 9, 1984, p. 6, states that Mr. Dye "reports to Parliament, not the government," without speculating about what that can mean in a parliamentary system where the government controls a majority of seats in the lower house. The closing sentence is "Yes, indeed, Canadians would like their man to look the deal over." However, the auditor general, being appointed, is less clearly a representative of the popular will than are members of the government and opposition. And, in fact, the auditor general's lawyers argue that he is better placed to keep secrets from the press and the public than is the government because the OAG is not subject to access provisions.

51. See the useful paper by John J. Kelly and Hugh R. Hanson, *Improving Accountability: Canadian Public Accounts Committees and Legislative Auditors* (Ottawa: Canadian Comprehensive Auditing Foundation, 1981). Appendix B of this study provides comparative data on the powers and functions of the auditors for all the Canadian legislatures. Prince Edward Island, Quebec, Ontario, Alberta and (in part) British Columbia have given their auditors some version of a "value for money" mandate. Since Kelly and Hanson published their charts, Quebec introduced its Bill 90, the Auditor General Act (first reading was June 20, 1984); New Brunswick's Auditor General Act received assent (July 17, 1981); and Saskatchewan's Provincial Auditor Act received assent (May 18, 1983).

52. See the Official Languages Act, R.S.C. 1970, c. 0-2, and also *Organization of the Government of Canada*, pp. 49–51.

53. See the Commissioner of Official Languages, *Annual Report 1981* (Ottawa: Minister of Supply and Services Canada, 1981), p. 1.

54. See Canada, *Minutes of Proceedings and Evidence of the Joint Committee on Official Language Policy and Programs*, Issue No. 1 (May 15, 1984), p. 1:21.

55. *Minutes (Language Policy)*, Issue No. 2 (October 10, 1980), p. 2:7.

56. *Annual Report 1981*, p. 8.

57. Canada, *Minutes of Proceedings and Evidence of the Standing Committee on Justice and Legal Affairs*, Issue No. 1 (December 14, 1983), p. 1:28.

58. Ibid., Issue No. 4 (July 11, 1979), p. 4:13.

CHAPTER 2

1. J.E. Hodgetts, *The Canadian Public Service: A Physiology of Government 1867–1970* (Toronto: University of Toronto Press, 1973), p. 68.

2. Frederick C. Mosher, *Democracy and the Public Service* (New York: Oxford University Press, 1968), p. 189.

3. As noted earlier, the name change of the federal civil service to a "public" service was effected at this point, apparently because one of the commissioners thought that the term "civil" was too obscure for comprehension by Canadians. However, as it references all non-military branches of state administration, it carries more meaning than the term "public."

4. Financial Administration Act, R.S.C. 1970, c. F-10, s. 7(1).

5. The development of schemes for personnel classification in Canada captures part of

the Canadian vacillation between British and American models. See Hodgetts on this, e.g., his *Canadian Public Service*, pp. 33–34.

6. Richard M. Bird, in collaboration with Meyer W. Bucovetsky and David K.Foot, *The Growth of Public Employment in Canada* (Toronto: Butterworth for Institute for Research on Public Policy, 1979), p. 41.

7. Hodgetts, *Canadian Public Service*, p. 283.

8. Ibid.

9. Financial Administration Act, s. 26.

10. Public Service Commission, *Annual Report 1983* (Ottawa: Minister of Supply and Services Canada, 1984), p. 14.

11. Canada, Royal Commission on Financial Management and Accountability, *Final Report* (Ottawa: Minister of Supply and Services Canada, 1979).

12. The authoritative expression of this view is in the d'Avignon Report. See Canada, Special Committee on the Review of Personnel Management and the Merit Principle, *Report* (Ottawa: Minister of Supply and Services Canada, 1979).

13. Rosemary Speirs, in a long article, "Tory Network Helps Ontario Fill 3,500 Posts," *Globe and Mail*, January 10, 1984, p. 1, arrived at that figure by adding all of Ontario's order-in-council appointments, paid and unpaid, although one might properly be reluctant to class as a sinecure a position with unpaid voluntary service. "Patronage appointees," she says, "run 370 different agencies, boards and commissions across the province ranging from ombudsman at $87,225 and Ontario Hydro chairman at $74,635 to non-paying but prestigious positions on the boards of art galleries, universities and hospitals." She noted that a *Globe* survey found that about half of the appointees could be regarded as Conservative partisans. John Cruickshank, in an article in the *Globe* on December 28, 1983, p. 1, "Queen's Park: Where the Sun Never Sets," presented a figure of 600 separate agencies, boards and commissions. He reported that the province's sunset legislation to terminate useless agencies actually presided in the five years of its operation over a net gain in the number of bodies headed by patronage appointments.

14. Significant presidential appointments have always, under an article of the constitution, required the advice and consent of the Senate. In 1983, there were more than 1,600 full-time patronage appointments requiring Senate confirmation, and approximately 2,200 part-time appointments, some of which require Senate approval. See John Macey, Bruce Adams and J. Jackson Walter, *America's Unelected Government: Appointment of the President's Team* (Washington, D.C.: National Academy of Public Administration, 1983). The full-time appointments are largely personnel for cabinet offices, heads of independent agencies, members of regulatory commissions, directors of government corporations, ambassadors, and federal judges. In the Canadian federal government, patronage appointments are generally of the same kinds, although one cannot directly compare the kind and incidence of appointments because the system of government is so different. The senior personnel secretariat of the Privy Council Office maintains a listing of governor-in-council appointments that enumerates full-time appointments as 111 deputy minister level jobs and 359 others (such as members of agencies, boards and commissions, but not the 104 senators), for a total of 470. Part-time appointments total 1,750. The *Globe and Mail* added up all full-time and part-time order-in-council appointments made in Pierre Trudeau's last month in office for a total of 225 appointments.

In Great Britain, the Cabinet Office's own count of full-time appointments to public bodies for which ministers have a degree of accountability comes to 491. There are also almost 34,000 part-time appointments for which there is either no remuneration or a per-meeting fee. The Cabinet Office's listing excludes appointments to the criminal and civil court system, agricultural marketing boards and to local authorities and bodies controlled by them. Comparability between the three systems is therefore extremely tenuous, but it does appear that Canadian politicians dispense a good many full-time appointments considering the comparatively small size of the Canadian federal bureaucracy. For more information, see Great Britain, Cabinet Office (Management and Personnel Office), *Public Bodies 1983* (London: HMSO, April 1983).

15. The Royal Commission on Conditions of Foreign Service alludes to a view among foreign service officers that the ordinary officer is left to toil without reward in third world postings while those with connections and pull flit between the grand cities of the world. Abuse is the more galling because promotions are normally very hard to obtain in the career diplomatic service. See Canada, Royal Commission on Conditions of Foreign Service, *Report* (Ottawa: Minister of Supply and Services Canada, 1981), pp. 247–52 and passim. Using the service, as the *Globe* says, as "a gold watch for political hacks" (Jeffrey Simpson, *Globe and Mail* editorial, July 5, 1984), is a fairly serious affront to the prestige and morale of the Department of External Affairs. Just who is judged to be a political hack pure and simple depends, of course, on one's perspective.

16. See the 1983 Estimates for the department. For a discussion, see Sharon Sutherland, "The Justice Portfolio: Social Policy Through Regulation," in *How Ottawa Spends 1983*, edited by G. Bruce Doern (Toronto: James Lorimer, 1983), pp. 173–208. The new Conservative government was reported to have sent 600 letters to Liberal-appointed federal prosecutors and lawyers to tell them that their services were "under review." Jack Walker and John Kessel, "600 Grit-hired Lawyers to Lose Government Jobs," *Citizen*, October 4, 1984, p. 1. Subsequently, the government appointed its own supporters to many of these positions. For details, see the counts by the *Kitchener-Waterloo Record*, reported in the *Citizen*, March 21, 1985, p. A5.

17. See Peter H. Russell, "Constitutional Reform of the Judicial Branch: Symbolic vs. Operational Considerations," *Canadian Journal of Political Science* 17 (June 1984): 227–53. The judicial appointments process is likely to lead reforms, if only because the June-July patronage appointments to the judiciary flouted a fairly well established convention. The appointment to the bar of Mr. Pinard was the first in more than a decade to proceed without being screened and rated by the Canadian Bar Association (CBA). The convention of assessment by the CBA's Committee on Judicial Appointments was agreed to in principle by Pierre Trudeau when justice minister in 1967, and implemented by John Turner in that portfolio. The form of the consultation is that the cabinet suggests its nominees to the CBA Committee, which returns its confidential rating of: 1) highly qualified, 2) qualified, 3) qualified with reservations, or 4) not qualified. Since 1967, no candidate rated as "not qualified" has been appointed, according to the CBA. Even though the consultation is not required by any law, it is clear that flouting it will almost inevitably lead to a more formal process.

18. As of April 1984, there were 15 organizations in the federal government that had separate employer status. These included eight advisory/research/granting/cultural organizations; four regulatory or quasi-regulatory bodies; and two miscellaneous organizations, a communications security establishment and the managers for private funds of members of the Canadian Armed Forces. None of these play a service-wide role like that of the Office of the Auditor General. All the bodies whose functions are in some ways similar to those of the Office of the Auditor General (i.e., the PSC, Official Languages, the information and privacy commissioners, the Canadian Human Rights Commission, Status of Women), have Treasury Board as the employer. Nor are there other precedents for the OAG's special status. Even the staff of the Supreme Court and the Federal Investment Review Agency have Treasury Board as the employer. See Treasury Board's 1984 *Personnel Management Manual*, chap.16.

19. On March 29, 1974, Alexander Peter Treu's home was raided by the RCMP. They seized quantities of "confidential and secret" documents, and charged him with possession of classified documents without security clearance, and with failure to safeguard them. It was the first case to be tried under the Official Secrets Act in more than a decade. Proceedings were held in camera and Treu was found guilty and sentenced to two years in a penitentiary (the maximum sentence for the offence is 14 years). The lower court decision was overturned in February of 1979 and the Crown did not appeal. The provision under which Treu was charged is in section 4 of the act, and is called the "leakage" provision: it is far broader than "communication" of secret information. It imposes liability for recipients of official information, for "unlawful retention" and for "failure to take reasonable care" of retained documents. Treu had, in fact, obtained what he thought was adequate clearance for the files in his possession as a consultant. For an interesting discussion of this affair and of the subsequent case

involving the Toronto *Sun*, see Stanley A. Cohen, "Freedom of Information and the Official Secrets Act," *McGill Law Journal* 25 (1979): 99–110.

20. Cabinet Directive no. 35, "Security in the Public Service of Canada," December 18, 1963, declassified in 1978. There was a royal commission on security in 1969.

21. Edgar Gallant, Jennifer McQueen and Trefflé Lacombe, "Message from the Commissioners of the Public Service of Canada to Federal Employees," *Dialogue Express* (February 1984).

22. Bert Hill, "NDP's Cassidy Urges Pullback of Guidelines on PS Political Action," *Citizen*, July 20, 1984, p. 4. See also Michael Cassidy, "Brief on the Fundamental Rights of Federal Public Employees," July 19, 1984, unpublished paper, available through NDP headquarters.

23. "Notes for an Address by Commissioner Jennifer R. McQueen to Public Administration Students," Carleton University, September 18, 1984.

24. J.L. Manion, letter of July 23, 1984, to all deputy heads. See also John Hay, "Federal Contract System Abused: Study," *Citizen* January 19, 1985.

25. See, for examples, the Public Service Commission of Canada, *Rights and Responsibilities of Public Servants* (Ottawa: Minister of Supply and Services Canada, 1979).

26. For a review of the issues and the literature, see V. Seymour Wilson, "Mandarins and Kibitzers: Men in and Around the Trenches of Political Power in Ottawa," *Canadian Public Administration* 26 (Fall 1983): 447–61.

27. As in many other areas of study of Canadian society, no one has matched John Porter's early piece, "Higher Public Servants and the Bureaucratic Elite in Canada," *Canadian Journal of Economics and Political Science* 24 (November 1958): 483–501. Another good study is that by Christopher Beattie, Jacques Desy and Stephen Longstaff, *Bureaucratic Careers: Anglophones and Francophones in the Canadian Public Service*, Documents of the Royal Commission on Bilingualism and Biculturalism, No. 11 (Ottawa: Information Canada, 1972). Less comprehensive, but still interesting, is P.J. Chartrand and K.L. Pond, "A Study of Executive Career Paths in the Public Service of Canada," (Chicago, 1970, mimeo). Colin Campbell's recent book, *Governments Under Stress: Political Executives and Key Bureaucrats in Washington, London, and Ottawa* (Toronto: University of Toronto Press, 1983), makes dramatic claims that Canadian central agency officers are less often motivated by public service ideals than are their counterparts in London and Washington. But Campbell's samples of officials in the three countries are not comparable: he has a virtual census of central agency managers in Canada, and availability samples (as opposed to scientifically chosen representative samples) of high officials in the United States and Britain. His empirical work does not therefore add legitimate support to many of his conclusions on this point.

28. A recent such episode took place in the miscellaneous estimates committee when members requested that the PSC table a legal opinion that the Department of Justice had provided supporting the commissioners in their request that public servants refrain from campaign activity for candidates in the federal election. Legal counsel refused, on the grounds that the opinion had been provided to the government, while committee members objected that the PSC was not the government, but an agent of Parliament. See Canada, *Minutes of Proceedings and Evidence of the Standing Committee on Miscellaneous Estimates*, Issue No. 6, Thursday, April 5, 1984, p. 6:32.

29. "Crown princing" is the PSC's disapproving term for a departmental fait accompli. A person is moved (redeployed) into a position one level above his or her own, ostensibly for "development." After some months, the PSC is asked to promote the acting incumbent to the full level. The acting incumbent is obviously in a preferred position, and can often win the subsequent competition from a standpoint of knowing most about the job.

CHAPTER 3

1. D.A.L. Auld, "Fiscal Knowledge and Preferences in Ontario," Working Paper No. 2 (Toronto: Ontario Economic Council, March 1977), Introduction and p. 59.

2. Canada, Royal Commission on the Economic Union and Development Prospects for Canada, *Major Findings from Briefs and Transcripts*, Fall 1983 (Ottawa: Commission Secretariat, 1973), p. 122. A selection of comments expressed at the hearings illustrates typical viewpoints:

> We are . . . very concerned with the bureaucratic growth — not just here but throughout Canada. Bureaucracy is becoming the main employer in Canada. Certainly in the Yukon it is the main employer. This leads to problems where government sets the pace. We feel that it should be the private sector who sets the pace. *Yukon Visitors' Association, Whitehorse,* Day 2, p. 1,007.

> . . . growth in government bureaucracy may not be possible in the future because first, unemployment will be a result not only of labour force growth, but also of labour displacement through information technology — in both private enterprise and government bureaucracy; and, second, we may be near the "political limits" of growth of government — the public may not want to see further concentration of economic power. *Canadian Council on Social Development*, Brief No. 109, p. 15.

> We do not want to suggest a centrally planned economy but rather one that recognizes and allows for the area where private enterprise can function more efficiently in a lasting long-term safe environment. *Northern Development Council*, Brief No. 148, p. 3.

> The private sector creates wealth. The government does not. *Calgary Chamber of Commerce*, Brief No. 558, p. 71.

> . . . we very much resent government in direct competition with the private sector and . . . inexorable inflationary growth of the public service sector. *Prairie Implement Manufacturers' Association*, Brief No. 808, p. 7.

3. The seminal comparative study on the growth of the public economy is D.R. Cameron's survey of eighteen capitalist countries between 1960 and 1975. He notes that while the political complexion of a government is a sufficient condition to bring about growth of the public sector, it is not necessary. Instead, the relative openness of the economy is the determinant. See D.R. Cameron, "The Expansion of the Public Economy: A Comparative Analysis," *American Political Science Review* 72 (1978): 1,243–61. In Manfred Schmidt's article, "The Growth of the Tax State: The Industrial Democracies, 1950–1978," in *Why Governments Grow: Measuring Public Sector Size*, edited by C.L. Taylor (Beverly Hills: Sage, 1983), p. 265, he states: "A sequence of economic, sociological, and political characteristics that derived from the openness of the economy, such as high industrial concentration, high unionization, and strong labor confederations, and the domestic requirements produced by a strong integration in the world market result in large increases in spending supplements and an expansion of the public sector." Partisan control is therefore by no means conclusive. See also F. Gould, "The Growth of Public Expenditures: Theory and Evidence from Six Advanced Democracies," in Taylor, *Why Governments Grow*, pp. 217–39, and the collection of articles in F.G. Castles, ed., *The Impact of Political Parties* (London: Sage, 1982).

Further sources for information on comparative jurisdictions are: Charles T. Goodsall, *The Case for Bureaucracy* (Chatham, N.J.: Chatham House Publications, 1984); James B. Kau and Paul H. Rubin, "The Size of Government," *Public Choice* 37 (1981): 261–74; Patrick D. Larkey, Chandler Stolp and Mark Winer, "Theorizing about the Growth of Government: A Research Assessment," *Journal of Public Policy* 1 (1981): 157–220; John P. Martin, "Public Sector Employment Trends in Western Industrialized Economies," in *Public Finance and Public Employment*, edited by Robert H. Haveman (Detroit: Wayne State University Press, 1982); Richard A. Musgrave, "Why Public Employment," in ibid., pp. 9–19; Richard Parry, "Territory and Public Employment: A General Model and British Evidence," *Journal of Public Policy* 1 (1981): 221–50; Richard Parry, *United Kingdom Public Employment: Patterns of Change 1951–1976*, Study No. 62 (Glasgow: University of Strathclyde, Centre for the Study of Public Policy, 1980); B. Guy Peters, *Public Employment in the United States: Growth and Change*, Study No. 63 (Glasgow: University of Strathclyde, Centre for the Study of Public Policy, 1980); Richard Rose, "What If Anything Is Wrong with Big Government?" *Journal of Public Policy* 1 (1981): 5–36; and Bjorn Wittrock, "Governance in Crisis and Withering of the Welfare State: The Legacy of the Policy Sciences," *Policy Sciences* 15 (1983): 195–203.

4. It is not possible to reconstruct these two tables to reconcile satisfactorily the discrepancies for Canada's tax revenue in 1975 and 1978. The only apparent reason is that Schmidt's table includes revenue from social security contributions while Table 3.2 does not appear to include them.

   A recent OECD study identifies Canada's per capita public sector employment at sixth lowest out of the 21 OECD developed countries. Interestingly, a further breakdown shows federal employment ranking at third lowest while provincial/local is 13th lowest. (P.S. Heller and A.A. Tait, *Government Employment and Pay: Some International Comparisons*, Occasional Paper 24, Washington, D.C.: International Monetary Fund, October 1983, Table 21, p. 41.)

5. As described in David Stager, *Economic Analysis and Canadian Policy* (Toronto: Butterworth, 1976), GNP includes the incomes of Canadian citizens working abroad as well as residents of Canada. GDP includes "only the factors of production located in Canada. GDP is equal to GNP minus indirect taxes less subsidies, minus income received from non-residents, plus income paid to non-residents," p. 79.

6. Walter Eltis, "The Growth and Influence of Expenditure: The United Kingdom, 1961–1979," in Taylor, *Why Governments Grow*, pp. 73–96.

7. Karl W. Deutsch, "The Public Sector: Some Concepts and Indicators," in Taylor, *Why Governments Grow*, pp. 25–32.

8. See ibid., p. 30. If the military-industrial complex were added to the public sector component in the United States, the United States would likely lose its comparability to Japan or Switzerland as a bastion of free enterprise.

9. Richard Rose, "Disaggregating the Concept of Government," in Taylor, *Why Governments Grow*, p. 161.

10. Statistics Canada, *Provincial Government Employment*, cat. no.72–007 (January–March 1983), pp. 6–7.

11. Sid Tafler, "B.C. Job Cuts Partly Fake, Workers Say," *Globe and Mail* March 19, 1984, p. 1.

12. See especially Richard M. Bird, in collaboration with Meyer W. Bucovetsky and David K. Foot, *The Growth of Public Employment in Canada* (Toronto: Butterworth for Institute for Research on Public Policy, 1979).

13. The population statistics in Figure 1 do not agree exactly with Table 3.3 because of the exclusion of military personnel and post office seasonal help.

14. A study completed at the end of May 1984, by the Treasury Board secretariat, reported that, as of that date, 4,400 full-time jobs and 5,500 part-time jobs had been decentralized. The projects began in the 1970s. A further 2,700 full- and part-time jobs were to be relocated in the near future.

15. Statistics Canada, *Federal Government Employment*, cat. no.72–004 (January – March 1983), pp. 55–63.

16. Frederick Mosher defines a profession as a clear-cut field of work which requires higher education to at least a bachelor's level and offers a lifetime career to its members. He divides public service professionals into two groups: one where the only employer is government, and another where government competes with the private sector for their labour. Monopoly professionals include types like the military, where all work for the central government, and school teachers, whose employment is spread in several levels of government. Competitive professions include law, medicine, engineering and architecture. Mosher notes as the common denominators of professions: 1) the drive to elevate the profession's status; 2) a concentration on the work substance of the field as opposed to general administrative tasks; and 3) an emphasis on autonomy along with a kind of antipathy of government. Many professions are indeed used to dealing with government as an outside force or opponent, and even when under the government umbrella will choose to organize in opposition, as professionals, to government's policies. See Mosher's *Democracy and the Public Service* (New York: Oxford University Press, 1968), pp. 106–30 for a useful discussion.

17. Statistics Canada, *Local Government Employment*, cat. no.72–009 (January–March 1983), pp. 5–7.

18. Perhaps the most commonly cited total for government employment is 24 percent. This is the statistic developed for 1975 in the IRPP study, *Growth of Public Employment*, by Bird in collaboration with Bucovetsky and Foot. The Bird statistic is readily reconciled with the figures developed in this study. The discrepancy in the final ratio arises from two sources. First, in arriving at total government employment, we exclude the Canadian armed forces, Christmas post office staff, and part-time hospital workers and education sector employees (because there is no way to tell how many part-time workers would form the equivalent to a full-time employee). Secondly, Bird's larger total is not normed against the total labour force but rather against the employed labour force, a number which moves with the unemployment rate. If we include the armed forces and part-time employees, and take the total as a percent of employed labour force for 1975, our 1975 figure is very close to Bird's. This is comforting for all of us, particularly as the present study has been able to report sub-totals for the various levels of enterprise employment and for other categories that were not available at the time of the IRPP research. Our choice of total labour force, instead of currently employed workers as a denominator, came about, first, because employment since 1975 is fairly volatile, whereas stability is essential for a norming figure; and secondly, because it seemed fair to both government and the people not currently in work but still desiring to work. The unemployed worker creates pressures and expenses for a government well beyond those generated by the non-working citizens: manpower centres and retraining, unemployment insurance, job creation programs, incentive programs to potential employers, and so forth. As well, it is in the potential workers' interest that we have governments that remember that more work is needed, and do not simply choose to have the size and kind of government that is based on the numbers, and perhaps needs, of those who have steady jobs.

CHAPTER 4

1. See Canada, *Ethical Conduct in the Public Sector: Report of the Task Force on Conflict of Interests* (Ottawa: Minister of Supply and Services Canada, 1984), for current proposals for the federal domain. See also K. Kernaghan, *Ethical Conduct: Guidelines for Government Employees* (Toronto: Institute of Public Administration of Canada, 1975).

2. See Gérard Hébert, "Public Sector Bargaining in Quebec," in *Conflict or Compromise: The Future of Public Sector Industrial Relations*, edited by M. Thompson and G. Swimmer (Montreal: Institute for Research on Public Policy, 1984), chap. 7.

3. See Thompson and Swimmer, *Conflict or Compromise*, chap. 1, and J.Finkelman and S.B. Goldenberg, *Collective Bargaining in the Public Service: The Federal Experience*, Vols. 1 and 2 (Montreal: Institute for Research on Public Policy, 1983).

4. See V. Seymour Wilson, "Language Policy," in *Issues in Canadian Public Policy*, edited by G. Bruce Doern and V. Seymour Wilson (Toronto: Macmillan of Canada, 1974), chap. 10. See also the annual reports of the Commissioner of Official Languages. For related Quebec developments, see William D. Coleman, "A Comparative Study of Language Policy in Quebec," in *The Politics of Canadian Public Policy*, edited by M. Atkinson and Marsha A. Chandler (Toronto: University of Toronto Press, 1983), chap. 2.

5. "Agreement Pleases McKenzie: Rights Body to Hear Language Discrimination Complaint," *Winnipeg Free Press*, October 26, 1984, p. 5. The CHRC rejected McKenzie's complaint when it was first brought in 1982, on the grounds that giving preference to francophones is not ethnic discrimination.

6. See Willard A. Mullins and V. Seymour Wilson, "Representative Bureaucracy: Linguistic/Ethnic Aspects in Canadian Public Policy" *Canadian Public Administration* 21 (Winter 1978): 513–38, and Kenneth Kernaghan, "Representative Bureaucracy: The Canadian Perspective," *Canadian Public Administration* 21 (Winter 1978): 489–512.

7. See Canada, House of Commons, *Equality Now: Report of the Special Committee on Visible Minorities in Canadian Society* (Ottawa: Queen's Printer, 1984). The report is interesting as a product of the experiment in special investigations by House committees: it graphically illustrates that MPs naturally develop constituencies and thereby expand public demands and expectations.

8. See also Conrad Winn, "Affirmative Action for Women: More Than a Case of Simple Justice," *Canadian Public Administration* 28 (Spring 1985): 24–46.

9. Peter H. Russell, "The Effect of a Charter of Rights on the Policy-Making Role of Canadian Courts," *Canadian Public Administration* (1982): 1–33. On the evolution of a rights-oriented society in Canada, see C. Williams, "The Changing Nature of Citizen Rights," in *Constitutionalism, Citizenship and Society in Canada*, volume 33 of the research studies prepared for the Royal Commission on the Economic Union and Development Prospects for Canada (Toronto: University of Toronto Press, 1985).

10. In reality, there is always conflict in these two roles. See Richard W. Phidd and G. Bruce Doern, *The Politics and Management of Canadian Economic Policy* (Toronto: Macmillan, 1978), chap. 1.

11. See A. Maslove and Gene Swimmer, *Wage Controls in Canada 1975–1978* (Montreal: Institute for Research in Public Policy, 1980), and D.A. Wilton, "An Evaluation of Wage and Price Controls in Canada," *Canadian Public Policy* 10 (June 1984): 167–76.

12. See G. Swimmer, "Six and Five" in *How Ottawa Spends* 1984, edited by Allan Maslove (Toronto: Methuen, 1984): 240–81.

13. See M. Gunderson, "The Public-Private Sector Compensation Controversy," in Thompson and Swimmer, *Conflict or Compromise*.

14. Swimmer, "Six and Five."

15. Treasury Board secretariat (TBS) in the 1970s adopted a strategy of "over-designa-tion." Unions could challenge TBS's designation, but a Public Service Staff Relations Board hearing to resolve a challenge could delay the entire process, putting off a legal strike by as much as two months. More recently, TBS in 1981 designated nearly all air traffic controllers as essential to the public's safety and security. In 1982 the Supreme Court ruled that the employer has the right to determine the level of service: without that constraint, the PSSRB now determines the number of designated employees necessary to maintain that level. See A.V. Subbarao, "Settlement of Interest Disputes in Essential Services: Public Policy Before and After the Supreme Court Decision," working paper (Ottawa: University of Ottawa), pp. 83–86.

16. See Leo Panitch and Donald Swartz, "From Free Collective Bargaining to Permanent Exceptionalism," in Thompson and Swimmer, *Conflict or Compromise*, chap. 12.

17. See A. Maslove, M. Prince and B. Doern, *Federal and Provincial Budgeting: Goal Setting, Co-ordination, Restraint and Reform*, volume 41 of the research studies prepared for the Royal Commission on the Economic Union and Development Prospects for Canada (Toronto: University of Toronto Press, 1985), chap. 9.

18. See Public Service Commission, *1984 Annual Report*. In 1977, term appointments were 31 percent of all appointments. By 1983, they were at 55 percent. Absolute numbers of term appointments, however, have remained almost stable since 1977.

19. See Allan Tupper and G. Bruce Doern, eds., *Public Corporations and Public Policy in Canada* (Montreal: Institute for Research in Public Policy, 1981), chap. 1; J.R.S. Prit-chard, ed., *Crown Corporations in Canada: The Calculus of Instrument Choice* (Toronto: Butterworth, 1983). See also John Langford, "The Question of Quangos: Quasi-Public Service Agencies in British Columbia," *Canadian Public Administra-tion* 26, (Winter 1983): 563–76.

20. See Economic Council of Canada, *Responsible Regulation* (Ottawa: Minister of Supply and Services Canada, 1979); and W.T. Stanbury and F. Thompson, *Regulatory Reform in Canada* (Montreal: Institute for Research on Public Policy, 1982).

21. See G. Bruce Doern and Glen Toner, *The NEP and the Politics of Energy* (Toronto: Methuen, 1984), chap. 2.

22. See *Financial Times*, October 3, 1983, pp. 26–27.

23. For views of the central agency growth, see Colin Campbell, *Governments Under Stress: Political Executives and Key Bureaucrats in Washington, London, and Ottawa* (Toronto: University of Toronto Press, 1983), chaps. 4, 11 and 12; V.S. Wilson, *Cana-dian Public Policy and Administration* (Toronto: McGraw-Hill Ryerson, 1981), pp. 274–87; and G. Bruce Doern and Richard W. Phidd, *Canadian Public Policy: Ideas, Structure, Process* (Toronto: Methuen, 1983), chaps. 7, 8, 9 and 19.

24. See C. Campbell and G. Szablowski, *The Superbureaucrats* (Toronto: Macmillan of Canada, 1979).

25. For provincial developments tied to budgetary accountability see, Maslove, Prince and Doern, *Federal and Provincial Budgeting*, chaps.6 and 8.

26. See Sharon Sutherland, "On the Audit Trail of the Auditor General: Parliament's Servant, 1973–1980," *Canadian Public Administration* 23, (Winter 1980): 616–44.

27. See Doern and Phidd, *Canadian Public Policy*, chaps. 13 and 18.

28. Measuring this element is extremely difficult. At the time of the assumption of power by the Mulroney government, it was reported that 600 contract Liberal lawyers would lose their work to be replaced presumably by Tory lawyers. (See *Citizen*, October 4, 1984, p. 1.) Analysis suggests that advertising expenditures have increased greatly over the past decade (See W. Stanbury, G. Gorn and C. Weinberg, "Federal Advertising Expenditures" in *How Ottawa Spends 1983*, edited by G. Bruce Doern (Toronto: James Lorimer, 1983), pp. 133–72. Another partial measure could be used by referring to professional and special services, as a proxy. One sees it at a total of $443 million (in the Public Accounts) for 1970–71 and at $2,289 million for 1982–83. In real terms, the 1982–83 figure decreases to about $760 million. The increase overall is 60 percent or roughly 5 percent per annum. This may well reflect some element of more pay for less work, as it is likely that the cost of these services has increased more quickly than the general index for government goods and services.

29. See Dale M. Andreas, "The Provincial Ombudsmen: Supervisors of Bureaucracies," in *Provincial Government and Politics*, edited by Donald Rowat (Ottawa: Carleton University, Department of Political Science, 1972), pp. 251–76; and also Wilson, *Canadian Public Policy and Administration*, pp. 248–55.

30. The legislation took a long time to get through. Finally proclaimed in the spring of 1983, it came into force in July 1983. Two commissioners were put into place, a privacy commissioner and an information commissioner. See also John D. McCamus, ed., *Freedom of Information: Canadian Perspectives* (Toronto: Butterworth, 1981).

31. See Peter Aucoin and H. Bakvis, "Regional Responsiveness Government Organization," in *Regional Responsiveness and the National Administrative State*, volume 37 of the research studies prepared for the Royal Commission on the Economic Union and Development Prospects for Canada (Toronto: University of Toronto Press, 1985).

32. On the concurrent impacts of several of the kinds of reforms discussed here, see H.L. Laframboise, "The Future of Public Administration in Canada," *Canadian Public Administration* 25 (Winter 1982): 507–19 and "Conscience and Conformity: The Uncomfortable Bedfellows of Accountability," *Canadian Public Administration* 26 (Fall 1983): 325–43.

CHAPTER 5

1. See J.E. Hodgetts, *The Canadian Public Service: The Physiology of Government 1967–1970* (Toronto: University of Toronto Press, 1973).

2. S.M. Lipset, *Agrarian Socialism*, updated ed. (New York: Doubleday, 1968), chap. 12. For comparative analysis of these early concerns, see Donald Kingsley, *Representative Bureaucracy* (Yellow Springs, Ohio: Antioch Press, 1944).

3. See R.Whitaker, *The Government Party* (Toronto: University of Toronto Press, 1977).

4. See J.L. Granatstein, *The Ottawa Men: The Civil Service Mandarins 1935–1957* (Toronto: Oxford University Press, 1983), and V.S.Wilson, "Mandarins and Kibitzers: Men in and Around the Trenches of Political Power in Canada," *Canadian Public Administration* 26 (Fall 1983): 446–61.

5. While the party/bureaucracy connection is central, basic published analyses of Canada's political parties rarely make the connection, let alone discuss it. These basic sources include Hugh G.Thorburn, ed., *Party Politics in Canada*, 4th ed. (Toronto: Prentice-Hall, 1979); J. Brodie and J. Jenson, *Crisis Challenge and Change: Party and Class in Canada* (Toronto: Methuen, 1980); W. Christian and C. Campbell, *Political Parties and Ideologies in Canada*, 2d ed. (Toronto: McGraw-Hill Ryerson, 1983); and

C. Winn and J. McMenemy, *Political Parties in Canada* (Toronto: McGraw-Hill Ryerson, 1976). The same can be said until very recently about most of the literature on public administration and public policy cited in earlier chapters.

6. See Harold D. Clarke, Jane Jenson, L. LeDuc and J. Pammett, *Absent Mandate* (Toronto: Gage, 1984).

7. See the sources cited in note 5 above for discussions of the regionalizing phenomenon.

8. This was both a general view and one applied to specific policy sectors such as energy policy. See Jeffrey Simpson, *The Discipline of Power* (Toronto: Personal Library, 1981), and G. Bruce Doern and Glen Toner, *The Politics of Energy* (Toronto: Methuen, 1984).

9. There is a sense in which it may have suited the other parties to charge the Liberals with extreme and tasteless politicization of the public service. It may well be that a perception of politicization was created by a relatively modest number of appointments that were disliked by one or another constituency, for whatever reasons. In any event, one finds the same handful of names cropping up in discussions of excessive politicization, although very few of these were actually appointments under the Public Service Employment Act (see chap. 2). For example, Michael Pitfield's appointment as Clerk of the Privy Council was often reviled as unjust politicization, but in fact this post is an order-in-council appointment, and therefore justly a political appointment. The one high-level person who was released when the Conservatives came to power who did hold an appointment under the PSEA was Ed Clark. Mr. Clark was prominently associated with the National Energy Program, a fact that effectively politicized his job but not in a partisan sense. See G. Bruce Doern and Richard W.Phidd, *Canadian Public Policy: Ideas, Structure, Process* (Toronto: Methuen, 1983), pp. 220–24.

10. See Marsha A. Chandler and W.M.Chandler, *Public Policy and Provincial Politics* (Toronto: McGraw-Hill Ryerson, 1979), chap. 3.

11. On the general role of caucuses (albeit not focussed on the caucus connection to the issue of bureaucratic control), see Paul G.Thomas, "The Role of National Party Caucuses," in *Party Government and Regional Representation in Canada*, volume 36 of the research studies prepared for the Royal Commission on the Economic Union and Development Prospects for Canada (Toronto: University of Toronto Press, 1985).

12. See G.Perlin, *The Tory Syndrome* (Montreal: McGill-Queen's University Press, 1980).

13. See William A. Niskanen, Jr., *Bureaucracy and Representative Government* (Chicago: Aldine-Atherton, 1971). For an overall survey and critique of the basic ideas behind the public choice approach, see Doern and Phidd, *Canadian Public Policy*, chap. 6, and M.Sproule-Jones, "Institutions, Constitutions, and Public Policies: A Public-Choice Overview," in *The Politics of Canadian Public Policy*, edited by M.Atkinson and M.Chandler (Toronto: University of Toronto Press, 1983), pp. 127–50.

14. See, e.g., S. Dupré, D. Cameron et al., *Federalism and Policy Development* (Toronto: University of Toronto Press, 1973); Keith Banting, *The Welfare State and Canadian Federalism* (Montreal: McGill-Queen's University Press, 1982); Malcolm Taylor, *Health Insurance and Canadian Public Policy* (Montreal: McGill Queen's University Press, 1978); and R. Simeon, *Federal-Provincial Diplomacy* (Toronto: University of Toronto Press, 1972).

15. See Simpson, *Discipline of Power*, chap. 5.

16. Brian Mulroney, M.P., "Notes for an Address to the Progressive Conservative Canada Fund," Congress Hall, Ottawa, April 11, 1984.

17. Report of the Progressive Conservative party's Task Force on Revenue Canada, April 1984, available through party headquarters.

18. See Donald C. MacDonald, ed., *The Government and Politics of Ontario* (Toronto: Macmillan of Canada, 1975), chaps. 1 and 9.

19. See C. Hindle, "Practical Problems in the Evaluation of Crown Corporation Performance," paper presented to Symposium on Crown Corporations, Royal Commission on the Economic Union and Development Prospects for Canada, June 1, 1984.

20. See Allan Maslove, Michael J. Prince and G. Bruce Doern, *Federal and Provincial*

Budgeting: Goal Setting, Co-ordination, Restraint and Reform, volume 41 of the research studies prepared for the Royal Commission on the Economic Union and Development Prospects for Canada (Toronto: University of Toronto Press, 1985), chap. 9.

21. The Conservative campaign managers explicitly borrowed the polling techniques and methods of analysis that had been developed in the Republican campaign in the United States. For an insight into those srategies, see Richard B.Winthlin, "The Republicans Take To DP (Data Processing) in the Campaign Battle," *The Economist*, August 16, 1984, pp. 14–15.

APPENDIX C

1. J.E.Hodgetts, "Special Problems in the Administration of the Merit System," in J.E.Hodgetts, William McCloskey, Reginald Whitaker and V. Seymour Wilson, *The Biography of an Institution: The Civil Service Commission of Canada 1908–1967* (Montreal: McGill-Queen's University Press, 1972) pp. 461–497. The PSEA charges the Public Service Commission with the responsibility of interpreting the principle of merit so that it can be administered. Currently, this involves a balancing of organizational and "public" interest with the more classical ideas of equality of access and equity of treatment of the individual applicant. See Public Service Commission, *1982 Annual Report* (Ottawa: Minister of Supply and Services Canada, 1983), pp. 10–13.

2. In 1971, following the recommendation of the Royal Commission on the Status of Women in Canada, the Office of Equal Opportunities for Women (EOW) was established as a separate unit inside the Public Service Commission. Its mandate was to promote equality of women in federal hiring. The office was disbanded in May 1984, its main activities being relocated in the Women's Programs Centre within the operations directorate, staffing programs branch. Commissioner Jennifer McQueen said that the purpose was to permit greater influence on operational processes such as recruitment, referral, counselling and training. These changes were announced in press releases of March 26 and May 1, 1984, by the PSC's Public Affairs Directorate. One of the more useful initiatives of this office was to publish statistics on the availability of qualified women in the labour market and in the public service's own ranks. This effort greatly facilitates the establishment of reasonable targets for departments in their promotions. EOW should not be confused with the Advisory Council on the Status of Women and the Office of the Coordinator, Status of Women. The Office of the Coordinator, Status of Women, is the central contact point for responsibility centres in federal government departments that deal with status of women concerns. It monitors progress of departmental policies, and co-ordinates policies affecting women, enjoying a virtual central agency status. It reports to a minister, and Treasury Board is designated as the employer for its small staff. The Advisory Council, on the other hand, is more like a research organization, helping to formulate policy by compiling background research. It is run by a board of order-in-council appointees, and has separate employer status.

3. See Chapter 3 for an explanation of the various universes for enumerating public service employees.

4. Treasury Board of Canada, "Affirmative Action in Federal Public Service," June 27, 1983, news release from the Communications Division. It should also be noted that the Public Service Commission in general prefers to administer the merit principle on traditional lines, and has not been an enthusiastic partner in "proactive" exercises that complicate the application of the merit system.

5. Canada, *Report of the Special Committee on the Review of Personnel Management and the Merit Principle* (Ottawa, September 1979), p. 7.

6. Treasury Board of Canada, "Numerical Target Set for Women in the Management Category," October 13, 1984, news release from the Communications Division.

7. This document, "Women Executives in the Public Service of Canada," February 1983, was prepared by the Human Resources Planning and Analysis Program, Management Category Programs Branch, Public Service Commission. It was released to the Royal Commission by the commissioners' secretariat. Another important document on the progress of women is the Human Resources Planning Division's *Women in the Canadian Public Service 1980*.

8. Telephone interview, Statistics Canada, Labour Force Survey. The data cited have not been published. See also Karen Benzing, "Male Bosses Look Out! Women Execs Are Gaining Turf," *Citizen*, July 24, 1984, pp. 45 and 52. Benzing also took her statistics from Statistics Canada's Labour Force Survey unpublished data. The definition of management work by Statistics Canada would include jobs well below the federal government's Senior Management level. For an interesting review of affirmative action, see also Frank Musten, "Affirmative Action: A Token of the Times," and L.D.Cross, "Women in the Public Service: Nowhere to Go," *Ottawa Business Life* (September/October 1984), pp. 8–31.

9. Public Service Commission, "Women Executives," p. 8.

10. Ibid. As of September 1984, more recent figures were not available.

11. Christopher Beattie, Jacques Désy, and Stephen Longstaff, *Bureaucratic Careers: Anglophones and Francophones in the Canadian Public Service*, Documents of the Royal Commission on Bilingualism and Biculturalism, Number 11 (Ottawa: Information Canada, 1972.)

12. John Porter, "Higher Public Servants and the Bureaucratic Elite in Canada," *Canadian Journal of Economics and Political Science* 24 (November 1958): 483–501.

13. Statistics Canada, 1981 Census.

14. Using a preliminary definition of senior manager that is slightly different from that in use since the establishment of the Senior Manager level, the Public Service Commission closely documented the extent of francophone concentration in certain groupings for the years 1975 to 1979. Basically, francophones were concentrated in program administration, administrative services and personnel administration. More than one-half of the total francophones employed were in these three groups. There are no recent analyses of the ideal background for development of a senior executive, but the Porter and Beattie et al. studies, cited above, all suggest that it does not depend heavily on these groups. One suspects that while they are attractive to entry-level persons because the salaries are high and conditions of work can be made attractive, jobs that are defined by linguistic skills are dead ends, if only because they develop few other capacities.

15. Public Service Commission, *Annual Reports*.

16. Ibid. It must be remembered that since 1981, about 60,000 post office employees are no longer part of the PSEA universe. This loss also removed some of the promotion and transfer activity from that universe; hence any comparisons over time should take this factor into account. Our estimates which use rates instead of absolute numbers do so. See also Nicole Morgan and Charles Moubarek, *Nowhere to Go?* (Montreal: Institute for Research on Public Policy, 1981).

17. See Musten, "Affirmative Action."

18. The Beattie et al. study cited above investigated the regional origins of federal public servants. The authors found that 50 percent of the francophone middle level was from Quebec and 40 percent from Ontario. Given that less than 10 percent of the total francophone population resides in Ontario, from the perspective of "representational bureaucracy," this is a decided over-representation of a regional group. From the perspectives of the requirements of the Official Languages Act, however, region is not relevant. In our Conclusions, we suggest that this is the sort of question that a parliamentary committee on the public service ought to wrestle with.

THE COLLECTED RESEARCH STUDIES

Royal Commission on the Economic Union and Development Prospects for Canada

ECONOMICS

Income Distribution and Economic Security in Canada (Vol.1), *François Vaillancourt, Research Coordinator*

Vol. 1   Income Distribution and Economic Security in Canada, *F. Vaillancourt* (C)*

Industrial Structure (Vols. 2-8), *Donald G. McFetridge, Research Coordinator*

Vol. 2   Canadian Industry in Transition, *D.G. McFetridge* (C)
Vol. 3   Technological Change in Canadian Industry, *D.G. McFetridge* (C)
Vol. 4   Canadian Industrial Policy in Action, *D.G. McFetridge* (C)
Vol. 5   Economics of Industrial Policy and Strategy, *D.G. McFetridge* (C)
Vol. 6   The Role of Scale in Canada–US Productivity Differences, *J.R. Baldwin and P.K. Gorecki* (M)
Vol. 7   Competition Policy and Vertical Exchange, *F. Mathewson and R. Winter* (M)
Vol. 8   The Political Economy of Economic Adjustment, *M. Trebilcock* (M)

International Trade (Vols. 9-14), *John Whalley, Research Coordinator*

Vol. 9   Canadian Trade Policies and the World Economy, *J. Whalley with C. Hamilton and R. Hill* (M)
Vol. 10 Canada and the Multilateral Trading System, *J. Whalley* (M)
Vol. 11 Canada–United States Free Trade, *J. Whalley* (C)
Vol. 12 Domestic Policies and the International Economic Environment, *J. Whalley* (C)
Vol. 13 Trade, Industrial Policy and International Competition, *R. Harris* (M)
Vol. 14 Canada's Resource Industries and Water Export Policy, *J. Whalley* (C)

Labour Markets and Labour Relations (Vols. 15-18), *Craig Riddell, Research Coordinator*

Vol. 15 Labour-Management Cooperation in Canada, *C. Riddell* (C)
Vol. 16 Canadian Labour Relations, *C. Riddell* (C)
Vol. 17 Work and Pay: The Canadian Labour Market, *C. Riddell* (C)
Vol. 18 Adapting to Change: Labour Market Adjustment in Canada, *C. Riddell* (C)

Macroeconomics (Vols. 19-25), *John Sargent, Research Coordinator*

Vol. 19 Macroeconomic Performance and Policy Issues: Overviews, *J. Sargent* (M)
Vol. 20 Post-War Macroeconomic Developments, *J. Sargent* (C)
Vol. 21 Fiscal and Monetary Policy, *J. Sargent* (C)
Vol. 22 Economic Growth: Prospects and Determinants, *J. Sargent* (C)
Vol. 23 Long-Term Economic Prospects for Canada: A Symposium, *J. Sargent* (C)
Vol. 24 Foreign Macroeconomic Experience: A Symposium, *J. Sargent* (C)
Vol. 25 Dealing with Inflation and Unemployment in Canada, *C. Riddell* (M)

Economic Ideas and Social Issues (Vols. 26 and 27), *David Laidler, Research Coordinator*

Vol. 26 Approaches to Economic Well-Being, *D. Laidler* (C)
Vol. 27 Responses to Economic Change, *D. Laidler* (C)

* (C) denotes a Collection of studies by various authors coordinated by the person named.
   (M) denotes a Monograph.

POLITICS AND INSTITUTIONS OF GOVERNMENT

Canada and the International Political Economy (Vols. 28-30), *Denis Stairs and Gilbert R. Winham, Research Coordinators*

Vol. 28 Canada and the International Political/Economic Environment, *D. Stairs and G.R. Winham* (C)
Vol. 29 The Politics of Canada's Economic Relationship with the United States, *D. Stairs and G.R. Winham* (C)
Vol. 30 Selected Problems in Formulating Foreign Economic Policy, *D. Stairs and G.R. Winham* (C)

State and Society in the Modern Era (Vols. 31 and 32), *Keith Banting, Research Coordinator*

Vol. 31 State and Society: Canada in Comparative Perspective, *K. Banting* (C)
Vol. 32 The State and Economic Interests, *K. Banting* (C)

Constitutionalism, Citizenship and Society (Vols. 33-35), *Alan Cairns and Cynthia Williams, Research Coordinators*

Vol. 33 Constitutionalism, Citizenship and Society in Canada, *A. Cairns and C. Williams* (C)
Vol. 34 The Politics of Gender, Ethnicity and Language in Canada, *A. Cairns and C. Williams* (C)
Vol. 35 Public Opinion and Public Policy in Canada, *R. Johnston* (M)

Representative Institutions (Vols. 36-39), *Peter Aucoin, Research Coordinator*

Vol. 36 Party Government and Regional Representation in Canada, *P. Aucoin* (C)
Vol. 37 Regional Responsiveness and the National Administrative State, *P. Aucoin* (C)
Vol. 38 Institutional Reforms for Representative Government, *P. Aucoin* (C)
Vol. 39 Intrastate Federalism in Canada, *D.V. Smiley and R.L. Watts* (M)

The Politics of Economic Policy (Vols. 40-43), *G. Bruce Doern, Research Coordinator*

Vol. 40 The Politics of Economic Policy, *G.B. Doern* (C)
Vol. 41 Federal and Provincial Budgeting, *A.M. Maslove, M.J. Prince and G.B. Doern* (M)
Vol. 42 Economic Regulation and the Federal System, *R. Schultz and A. Alexandroff* (M)
Vol. 43 Bureaucracy in Canada: Control and Reform, *S.L. Sutherland and G.B. Doern* (M)

Industrial Policy (Vols. 44 and 45), *André Blais, Research Coordinator*

Vol. 44 Canadian Industrial Policy, *A. Blais* (C)
Vol. 45 The Political Sociology of Industrial Policy, *A. Blais* (M)

LAW AND CONSTITUTIONAL ISSUES

Law, Society and the Economy (Vols. 46-51), *Ivan Bernier and Andrée Lajoie, Research Coordinators*

Vol. 46 Law, Society and the Economy, *I. Bernier and A. Lajoie* (C)
Vol. 47 The Supreme Court of Canada as an Instrument of Political Change, *I. Bernier and A. Lajoie* (C)
Vol. 48 Regulations, Crown Corporations and Administrative Tribunals, *I. Bernier and A. Lajoie* (C)
Vol. 49 Family Law and Social Welfare Legislation in Canada, *I. Bernier and A. Lajoie* (C)
Vol. 50 Consumer Protection, Environmental Law and Corporate Power, *I. Bernier and A. Lajoie* (C)
Vol. 51 Labour Law and Urban Law in Canada, *I. Bernier and A. Lajoie* (C)

The International Legal Environment (Vols. 52-54), *John Quinn, Research Coordinator*

Vol. 52 The International Legal Environment, *J. Quinn* (C)
Vol. 53 Canadian Economic Development and the International Trading System, *M.M. Hart* (M)
Vol. 54 Canada and the New International Law of the Sea, *D.M. Johnston* (M)

Harmonization of Laws in Canada (Vols. 55 and 56), *Ronald C.C. Cuming, Research Coordinator*

Vol. 55 Perspectives on the Harmonization of Law in Canada, *R. Cuming* (C)
Vol. 56 Harmonization of Business Law in Canada, *R. Cuming* (C)

Institutional and Constitutional Arrangements (Vols. 57 and 58), *Clare F. Beckton and A. Wayne MacKay, Research Coordinators*

Vol. 57 Recurring Issues in Canadian Federalism, *C.F. Beckton and A.W. MacKay* (C)
Vol. 58 The Courts and The Charter, *C.F. Beckton and A.W. MacKay* (C)

FEDERALISM AND THE ECONOMIC UNION

Federalism and The Economic Union (Vols. 58-72), *Mark Krasnick, Kenneth Norrie and Richard Simeon, Research Coordinators*

Vol. 59 Federalism and Economic Union in Canada, *K. Norrie, R. Simeon and M. Krasnick* (M)
Vol. 60 Perspectives on the Canadian Economic Union, *M. Krasnick* (C)
Vol. 61 Division of Powers and Public Policy, *R. Simeon* (C)
Vol. 62 Case Studies in the Division of Powers, *M. Krasnick* (C)
Vol. 63 Intergovernmental Relations, *R. Simeon* (C)
Vol. 64 Disparities and Interregional Adjustment, *K. Norrie* (C)
Vol. 65 Fiscal Federalism, *M. Krasnick* (C)
Vol. 66 Mobility of Capital in the Canadian Economic Union, *N. Roy* (M)
Vol. 67 Economic Management and the Division of Powers, *T.J. Courchene* (M)
Vol. 68 Regional Aspects of Confederation, *J. Whalley* (M)
Vol. 69 Interest Groups in the Canadian Federal System, *H.G. Thorburn* (M)
Vol. 70 Canada and Quebec, Past and Future: An Essay, *D. Latouche* (M)
Vol. 71 The Political Economy of Canadian Federalism: 1940-1984, *R. Simeon and I. Robinson* (M)

THE NORTH

Vol. 72 The North, *Michael S. Whittington, Coordinator* (C)

COMMISSION ORGANIZATION

Chairman
Donald S. Macdonald

Commissioners

Clarence L. Barber	William M. Hamilton	Daryl K. Seaman
Albert Breton	John R. Messer	Thomas K. Shoyama
M. Angela Cantwell Peters	Laurent Picard	Jean Casselman-Wadds
E. Gérard Docquier	Michel Robert	Catherine T. Wallace

Senior Officers

Executive Director
J. Gerald Godsoe

Director of Policy	*Senior Advisors*	*Directors of Research*
Alan Nymark	David Ablett	Ivan Bernier
	Victor Clarke	Alan Cairns
Secretary	Carl Goldenberg	David C. Smith
Michel Rochon	Harry Stewart	
Director of Administration	*Director of Publishing*	*Co-Directors of Research*
Sheila-Marie Cook	Ed Matheson	Kenneth Norrie
		John Sargent

Research Program Organization

Economics	**Politics and the Institutions of Government**	**Law and Constitutional Issues**
Research Director	*Research Director*	*Research Director*
David C. Smith	Alan Cairns	Ivan Bernier
Executive Assistant & Assistant Director (Research Services)	*Executive Assistant*	*Executive Assistant & Research Program Administrator*
I. Lilla Connidis	Karen Jackson	Jacques J.M. Shore
Coordinators	*Coordinators*	*Coordinators*
David Laidler	Peter Aucoin	Clare F. Beckton
Donald G. McFetridge	Keith Banting	Ronald C.C. Cuming
Kenneth Norrie*	André Blais	Mark Krasnick
Craig Riddell	Bruce Doern	Andrée Lajoie
John Sargent*	Richard Simeon	A. Wayne MacKay
François Vaillancourt	Denis Stairs	John J. Quinn
John Whalley	Cynthia Williams	
	Gilbert R. Winham	
Research Analysts	*Research Analysts*	*Administrative and Research Assistant*
Caroline Digby	Claude Desranleau	Nicolas Roy
Mireille Ethier	Ian Robinson	
Judith Gold		
Douglas S. Green	*Office Administration*	*Research Analyst*
Colleen Hamilton	Donna Stebbing	Nola Silzer
Roderick Hill		
Joyce Martin		

*Kenneth Norrie and John Sargent co-directed the final phase of Economics Research with David Smith